Stairway to Heaven

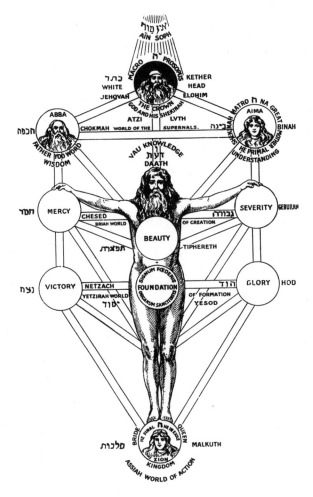

The Sephirotic Tree of Life showing Adam Kadmon and the "missing" *sephira* of *Da'ath*. From Golden Dawn initiate A. E. Waite's *The Holy Kabbalah*.

Stairway to Heaven

Chinese Alchemists, Jewish Kabbalists, and the Art of Spiritual Transformation

PETER LEVENDA

continuum

NEW YORK • LONDON

2008

The Continuum International Publishing Group Inc
80 Maiden Lane, New York, NY 10038

The Continuum International Publishing Group Ltd
The Tower Building, 11 York Road, London SE1 7NX

www.continuumbooks.com

Printed in the United States of America

Library of Congress Cataloging-in-Publication Data

Levenda, Peter.
    Stairway to heaven : Chinese alchemists, Jewish kabbalists, and the art of
spiritual transformation / Peter Levenda.
        p. cm.
    Includes bibliographical references (p.) and index.
    ISBN-13: 978-0-8264-2850-9 (pbk. : alk. paper)
    ISBN-10: 0-8264-2850-9 (pbk. : alk. paper)   1. Mysticism – Miscellanea.
2. Cabala. 3. Occultism. 4. Alchemy. I. Title.

BF1999.L3395 2008
204'.2 – dc22
                                                            2008016128

To Norman Mailer

A stairway to heaven shall be laid down for him,
that he may ascend to heaven thereon.

— The Pyramid Texts

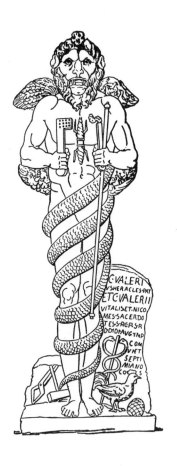

One of the Mithraic statues of Chronos, or Time. Note the four wings and the Lion's head, which are identical to Ezekiel's Vision. The figure holds two "keys," reminiscent of the tools used in the Egyptian Opening of the Mouth ceremony, which represent the seven stars of the Dipper. Also note the "thunderbolt" in the center of the figure's chest, which is virtually identical to the *dorje,* or "thunderbolt," of Tibetan Buddhism and Indian religion (see p. 137 below).

Contents

Part Four
ASCENT AND THE DIPPER
IN MODERN ESOTERICISM
Page 133

Acknowledgments

The inspiration for this book came from a course in Jewish mysticism taken at Florida International University in the spring of 2006. It had the impact of ordering my thinking on a number of issues concerning initiation, spiritual transformation, and mysticism, enabling me to look back over research undertaken over the last thirty years or so and to see it in a different — albeit more coherent — light. So for this I have to acknowledge the very great influence of Dr. Oren Baruch Stier.

Additional input came from a wide variety of individuals, most of them professors of religion and religious history, and this book is the result of their combined efforts to educate a hopeless autodidact. In this context I would like to acknowledge Dr. Erik Larson, Dr. Steven Heine, Dr. Nathan Katz, Dr. Albert Wuaku, and Dr. Aiysha Musa; their influence can be seen in these pages, although any mistakes or errors of judgment herein are entirely mine and do not represent their attitudes toward the subject matter at hand.

In another context, that of the social responsibility of churches and their religious personnel, I would like to acknowledge Dr. Anamaria Bidegain. ¡Venceremos! Most especially, I have to note the uncommon support of Dr. Christine Gudorf, who took a chance on this opinionated and wayward soul. Many thanks.

And, of course, to Prof. Daniel Alvarez. As always.

In addition, I have to acknowledge the many conversations and collective brain-storming that took place over the past few years with many individuals. You know who you are, but in case you don't: Alexander Conroy, for talk about the Golden Dawn and Christian Kabbalah; Wilis Endahekowati, for insight into Theravada Buddhism; Sitia Hidayah, for our long conversations on philosophical anthropology and postmodernism (*semangat!*); and to Karyna do Monte (Qumran and one, two, many Temples!), Sarah Muwahida (religion and social responsibility), Erin Weston (collaborator on Asian issues) . . . and Harriet, Moises, Juan, Bhante, and so many others.

To Russ Shulkes, the only rabbi I know with his own pair of bowling shoes.

To Noel Dowling and Norris Church, just because.

To Ellen Randolph, for our lengthy conversations on the nature of initiation.

I am also grateful to the Luce Foundation for a Fellowship to Indonesia in the summer of 2007, and to the Center for Religious and Cross-Cultural Studies (CRCS) at the Universitas Gadjah Mada in Yogyakarta for their kind hospitality and stimulating educational environment.

To Rose and Vivica, of course!

Finally, to the wonderful people at Continuum, foremost among them Gabriella Page-Fort, and especially to the recently retired Frank Oveis, my editor for several years, a gentleman and a scholar whose keen eye and sense of humor made for many inspirational exchanges. He's the kind of editor you want to impress. I'm still trying!

Preface

As mentioned above, this book is the result of a class I took at Florida International University in the spring of 2006. It was provocatively entitled "Jewish Mystical Texts" and was given by Dr. Oren Baruch Stier, a noted specialist in Holocaust studies with numerous books to his credit on the subject, particularly with respect to memory and its uses and manifestations. As memory and identity are special areas of my own interest, and have been for the past thirty years, I was naturally drawn to this course and imagined it would be a discussion of the Zohar and other Kabbalistic sources.

Prior to my academic work, I had studied and written extensively on the western esoteric tradition, beginning with *Unholy Alliance: A History of Nazi Involvement with the Occult* in 1994 and continuing with my *Sinister Forces* trilogy. At the same time, I was heavily involved in international trade and was based for many years in Asia, enabling me to travel throughout Asia, Europe, and South America, where I availed myself of access to churches, temples, mosques, shrines, and ancient ruins and monuments to broaden my knowledge of how religious sentiments, criticized by many in the twentieth and twenty-first centuries as irrational, influence our political and social lives. As someone who came of age in the era known as the Sixties, I was always torn between an inclination toward spirituality on the one hand and a feeling that social responsibility was more important on the other.

Studying the core texts of the Rosicrucian furor of the seventeenth century, *Fama Fraternitatis* and the *Confessio,* I was impressed by the balance between social consciousness and spiritual illumination they represented. Although the Rosicrucians as such did not really exist, the legend of this fraternity dedicated to spiritual transformation through the study of Kabbalah and alchemy — but which nonetheless operated in the world as a source of healing and medical ability — seemed to be an indication that a life dedicated to the sacred quest need not be aloof from the concerns of everyday living and that, indeed, others shared my feelings on this matter. The writings of the Sufi masters who spoke of "living in the world but not of the world" also seemed to show that others were as conscious of this dichotomy between the individual and society as was I.

But it was during the course on Jewish mystical texts that pieces of a gigantic puzzle began to fall into place. Expecting talk of the Sephirotic Tree and *gematria*, a form of numerology employed by Jewish scholars on biblical texts, to my amazement it was all that and much more. I was introduced to an area of Jewish mystical practice and belief that I thought had all but disappeared in the world, aside from the odd reference in Christian Kabbalistic texts that state, quite clearly, that the tradition had died out. The tradition to which I refer is *hekhalot* and *merkavah* mysticism.

Like many Americans interested in the subject, my exposure to Jewish mysticism was confined to the general works on Kabbalah and the ubiquitous Tree of Life: a glyph composed of twenty-two paths linking ten spheres that is said to represent the entire created universe. This diagram can be found used by esoteric orders and secret societies throughout Europe and the Americas, particularly those that came of age in the last 150 years or so. It is used as an emblem of spiritual attainment, a veritable "ladder of lights" indicating the path of spiritual progress beginning with *Malkuth*, the World, at the bottom and extending upward to reach *Kether*, the Crown, at the very top, after crossing a dangerous area between spheres four and three known as the Abyss. This diagram is familiar to most students of western occultism and can be found in its various forms in virtually every book published in the last thirty years on the subject of the Kabbalah.

However, in Dr. Stier's class I was introduced to another, earlier form of Jewish mysticism that entailed a different "ladder of lights" altogether, one that traces its origin to the vision of Ezekiel in the Bible. In this vision, in the first chapter of the Book of Ezekiel, the prophet is standing by the banks of a river in Babylon and beholds a wondrous sight. It is so wondrous, in fact, that attempts to duplicate it accurately as a drawing or illustration are usually doomed to failure. The language is confusing and seems to defy rational understanding. Yet an entire class of Jewish mystics used it as their template for a genre of mystic text known as "ascent literature." This literature represents a practice or technique of raising oneself — spiritually, we assume — on a series of seven stages until one is face to face with the Divine. These stages are referred to sometimes as seven palaces (or *hekhalot*) or seven chariots (or *merkavot*). Hence, this literature is more specifically referred to as *hekhalot* or *merkavah* mysticism.

It was during this class, which involved readings from Scholem, Dan, and many other important scholars of the Kabbalah and of Jewish mysticism generally, that I began to realize that this practice was mirrored in other mystical and occult techniques in different parts of the world, down to the very specific numbering system. It made me ask the question: Where did this practice originate, and what is the basic understanding that forms its bedrock?

I may not have been able to answer the first part of the question, but the second part was soon revealed to me when I remembered my studies of more than thirty years ago in an area of Chinese mysticism known as Shang Qing Daoism. This technique also involves a spiritual ascent upon seven planes or stages. It incorporates many of the ideas that I would find in *hekhalot* and *merkavah* texts and perhaps holds the key to an understanding of the world that was held by the ancient people of more than one culture, from the Middle East to the Far East. It is an area of archaeological and anthropological study that has largely been ignored because it requires a specialist's knowledge of phenomena outside the training of most archaeologists and anthropologists: the area of celestial mechanics.

There have been a number of books in recent years that have attempted to show that astronomy played a much more important role in the life and culture of ancient civilizations than we had previously given them credit for. These books have been popular studies that purported to show, for instance, that the Pyramids of Gizeh were arranged to imitate the constellation Orion, a controversial position that has been attacked by Egyptologists as without foundation. So I decided to give this type of research a much closer look and found that there is a small but growing field of paleoastronomy that has much to offer the serious investigator into ancient "mysteries."

By examining the religious and mystical texts of Sumer, Babylon, Egypt, India, and China with the added instrument of astronomical data, I was forced to consider that a certain basic level of understanding of the important role astronomical navigation and timekeeping had in the earliest recorded histories of the world was necessary for a full appreciation of the nature of religious myth and ritual and most particularly of mystical and shamanistic practices. While much attention is usually given to environmental factors in the development of the world's great civilizations, scant attention is paid to the vital place astronomy enjoyed in shaping culture. This influence is characterized as a prescientific and largely superstitious cult of star-worshipers, primitive humans in awe of astral phenomena such as eclipses and comets. Evidence to hand demonstrates that this characterization of the ancient mind-set may be far from the truth.

Peter Levenda
Miami, 2008

Introduction

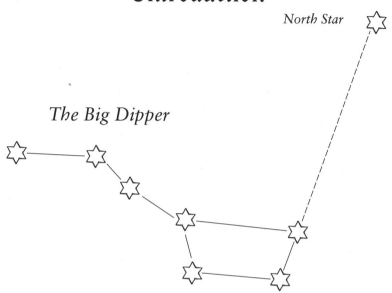

North Star

The Big Dipper

This is a study of ascent literature, that corpus of texts and liturgies that propose to enable a human being to ascend from the earth to the heavens and to come before the Throne of God. While it is the intention of the author to demonstrate that ascent literature has existed since the time of ancient Egypt and Babylon, and that versions of it appear as far away as Africa, India, and China, ascent literature per se came to the attention of academics in the last sixty years or so since the publication of Gershom Scholem's *Major Trends in Jewish Mysticism* only as a peculiarly Jewish phenomenon. Although there had been other commentators and researchers who were aware of the genre,[1] it safely can be said that it was Scholem who put ascent literature on the map, along with the more familiar subjects of Kabbalah studies such as the *Sepher ha-Zohar*, the *Sepher Yetzirah*, and similar documents. Ascent literature, typified by such texts as the *Ma'aseh Merkavah*, the *Heikhalot Rabbati* and *Heikhalot Zutarti*, and the *Re'iyyot Yehezkel*, are usually interpreted within the narrow framework of Jewish studies although — with claims that elements of this literature can be found in the Epistles of Paul as well as in the Dead Sea Scrolls — the field has widened considerably. There have been attempts to connect the Jewish ascent

1

literature with similar practices in Babylon[2] and Egypt,[3] but so far there has been no comprehensive look at the "connective tissue" that binds these, and many other, practices to each other.

That connection is to be found in the one place to which all ascent texts invariably refer: the heavens. The neglect of this particular and somewhat peculiar area of study may be due to the increasing specialization of Bible scholars who cannot be expected to have a background in astronomy or the other hard sciences and thus may not notice astronomical allusions or be prepared to interpret them literally.

Further, it is assumed, in the twentieth century, at least, that references to the "heavens" in these texts are metaphorical, since that is how we use the term today. However, to view these references in this manner is to ignore the reality experienced by the ancients for whom the heavens were an important factor in religion and science. In fact, the heavens were integral to an understanding of agriculture, climate, hunting, and navigation. At night, the heavens provided a vast pallet of countless stars and planets — as well as comets, meteors, and other phenomena — on which the handwriting of the gods could be perceived and against which cosmic dramas were believed to be enacted. Thus, allusions to the "heavens" or to the "seven heavens" were references to a place understood to be as real as the earth, and as immediately relevant.

The phenomenon of celestial ascent is one that has captured the imagination of a generation of scholars since the post–World War II era. It could be said to have begun with the publication of Gershom Scholem's *Major Trends in Jewish Mysticism* in 1941 with its examination of the *merkavah* and *hekhalot* literature and received another boost in 1951 with Mircea Eliade's *Shamanism: Archaic Techniques of Ecstasy.* (Eliade and Scholem were both members of the highly influential Eranos circle, which met annually in Ascona, Switzerland, a group chaired by the psychiatrist Carl G. Jung.)

Since then, the theme of celestial ascent has been the subject of many books, papers, articles, theses, and dissertations spanning cultures as diverse as Siberian shamanism, Chinese alchemical practices, Jewish mysticism, et alia. That this is a theme encountered in various forms throughout the ancient world is demonstrated by the published work of Eliade's student Ioan Couliano, including *Psychanodia* and his posthumously published *Out of This World: Otherworldly Journeys from Gilgamesh to Albert Einstein.*

There is an element that is missing from many studies of celestial ascent, however, and that is the nature of the heavens themselves: the very goal of the mystic and adept. Most approaches to this theme either ignore or minimize this aspect, yet a closer examination of the available texts — from those of ancient Egypt and Babylon to Han dynasty China — will reveal a surprising consistency among the various cultural and religious approaches to celestial ascent, a consistency that transcends indigenous doctrinal differences.

In order to understand this approach, one has to re-create the physical context of the culture under discussion. Most analyses of the ancient Egyptian religion, for instance, take into consideration the importance of the Nile and its periodic flooding as an essential aspect of Egyptian religious ideas and themes. Analyses of Babylonian religion include references to the Tigris and Euphrates where appropriate, etc. However, beyond these regional differences between cultures and cults there exists a transcendent aspect of the environment that is often marginalized in the scholarly literature.

Of course, it has not helped that popularizers like Erich von Danniken have "jumped the couch" in an attempt to show that human civilization is the result of assistance from space aliens. The difficulty in disentangling the science from the speculation in modern attempts at understanding religion, magic, and mysticism is sometimes profound. We don't have a useful vocabulary for the purpose, and the nature of academia today resists all efforts at forming multidisciplinary investigations of the same phenomena. Specialization is normative in religious studies as it is in virtually every other discipline (gone are the days of the Renaissance man!), and while various scholars may be aware of other developments in their respective fields, developments taking place outside their normal area of study, they appropriate that information at their peril.

Therefore, it is with some trepidation that I present evidence for the existence of a "universal" cult of celestial ascent, a cult based on a phenomenon that may be observed by anyone living in the northern latitudes. It has been specifically mentioned, described, and encoded in the literature of the technology of ecstatic flight in many cultures and even plays a part in the structure of present-day secret societies in the West even though its members may be unaware of its implications. Quite simply, this phenomenon consists of the Pole Star and those circumpolar stars that revolve around it; and all of the myths, legends, and interpretations that have grown up around ideas of immortality and eternity that are linked to them. In order to support my thesis, I am obliged to offer two basic concepts that may be useful as this discussion progresses.

The first is the "map." By this I mean the cosmological systems of the various cultures under investigation. Cosmology is the "surround" in game theory terminology: the matrix in which the actions (the rituals, the liturgical and mystical praxis) of the cult take place. While different cultures have vastly different interpretations of cosmology, they do refer to the same observable phenomena as everyone else: the rising and setting of the sun, for instance, or the phases of the moon. Knowing the cosmological system of a culture will enable us to more deeply comprehend its mystical technologies.

The second is the "vehicle." By this I mean the method by which the mystic or priest is able to navigate the cosmology, the "map." In the case of celestial ascent it is not unusual to see references to chariots, for instance, and we come across celestial chariots in India, China, Egypt, Babylon, and elsewhere, including in the famous vision of the biblical prophet Ezekiel.

My interest is entirely focused on the technology of celestial ascent, stripped of its doctrinal interpretations for the various religions within which this technology is expressed. The implications of this technology where spiritual transformation is concerned constitute part 2 of this study. Everywhere this technology is described, it is accompanied by details of a transformative nature. What we have before us may be more profitably characterized as something out of the cognitive sciences, some locus where psychology, psycho-biology, biochemistry, and physics meet. The history of religion may very well be, as de Santillana suggested, the history of science, for within both we find the dream of celestial ascent.

The ascent literature of the ancient Jewish mystics was not written in a vacuum. The very opening chapters of Genesis depict a God operating in space, creating stars and planets, organizing the cosmos. Some of the stories we find in Genesis are now understood to be related to Babylonian texts, such as the story of Noah and the Flood. Indeed, Abraham visits Babylon and witnesses the building of one of its famous ziggurats: the Tower of Babel. Later, after Solomon's Temple has been built, the Babylonians once again occupy center stage by destroying the Temple and enslaving the children of Israel. It is within this context that we read the first chapter of Ezekiel, the text believed to be the inspiration for the Jewish ascent texts that will begin to appear as early as the third century CE or as late as the sixth century CE.

But the children of Israel had also been in captivity in Egypt, and it is in Egypt where we will begin our discussion of ascent practices and beliefs. We will notice early on that the Pyramid Texts of the ancient Egyptians offer many clues as to the meaning and purpose of the later Jewish ascent texts.

The thread that connects all of these seemingly disparate cultural ideas and practices is a simple one, but one that we moderns tend to ignore: the heavens and most particularly the fixed stars. When the ancient Egyptians looked up, they saw pretty much the same astronomical features seen by the ancient Babylonians; in turn, this was the same sky seen by the Indo-Europeans throughout Central Asia and India, across Russia and all the way to China, Japan, and North America. The night sky in the northern latitudes provides several important features that came to the notice of our ancient astronomers, wherever they were located geographically above the equator: the Pole Star, and its attendant circumpolar stars.

The stars were a source of constant wonder and inspiration to ancient humanity. Like a giant Rorschach test, random splatterings of stars were identified as constellations and asterisms, given names and identities and characteristics, and even used as indicators of circumstances on earth. On a more utilitarian level, they were also used as a means of calculating the passage of time — in the creation of calendars, the world over — and as determining directions in space: the stars as navigational tools. In ancient times, astronomy and astrology were one (as were chemistry and alchemy). If a science had no meaning attached to it, then it was not worthy of study. Astronomy/astrology had meaning, not only in its ability to predict future events but in the very patterns of the stars themselves that hinted at mythological and religious events and persons.

Even today, it is common to speak of "heaven" as the abode of God, to pray while looking up, to depict God and angels as floating on clouds in the sky. Yet very little research has been done in this potentially explosive field. There has been very little critical analysis of sacred texts from the point of view of astronomical mysticism. Some popular works of the past ten years or so have attempted, with varying degrees of success, to reevaluate the ancient Egyptian Pyramid and Coffin Texts from this point of view. The problem with these efforts, no matter how lucidly drawn or carefully demonstrated, is that they lack the imprimatur of academia. Their authors are usually not academics or, if they are, they have degrees in other fields.

That is about to change. The field of paleoastronomy has been widening in the last decade. Attempts at demonstrating the astronomical knowledge and concern of neolithic hunters, for instance, have born fruit and compel us to ask the question: If neolithic humans were able to observe the stars and reverence them, how much more so later civilizations, such as the Sumerian, Babylonian, ancient Egyptian, ancient Indian, ancient Chinese, etc.? Ideas about the stars and the relevance of the stars to human affairs were integrated into religious and occult (i.e., exoteric and esoteric) practice from the very beginning of recorded history. The Sumerian cuneiform texts are clear evidence of this. These ideas were not abandoned by later movements and cultures, as I intend to show. The Torah is replete with astronomical references, and the works of the *hekhalot* and *merkavah* mystics in later centuries merely reflect this preoccupation.

Ancient astronomy provided a structure for what would later be called the "descent to the Chariot" of the *merkavah* mystics; it would also provide the template for the initiation rituals of the secret societies of the West. There is a continuum of thought and practice that links seemingly unrelated groups, ideologies, religions, cults, and magical orders across space and across time. We have all looked up. What is amazing is that we have all seen the same thing.

The Pole Star (or North Star) is the point in the heavens around which the rest of the visible universe seems to revolve. It is found due north, and is the king of all it surveys. The circumpolar stars revolve around it endlessly, like courtiers before the king's throne. For a navigator at sea, knowing where the North Star is located is of vital importance, for it is the direction from which all other directions — east, south, and west — are derived. Once located, even on the featureless ocean and with no other landmarks, one can plot an accurate course of direction. One is never lost.

Although the sun "rises" in the east and "sets" in the West, the precise point on the horizon at which it does so varies from day to day and season to season, thus contributing a significant error factor without the use of precise tables erected for the time and place the calculation is made. The North Star, however, always can be relied upon to signify true north.

The status of "North Star" or "Pole Star" has changed with the millennia, due to an astronomical phenomenon known as the precession of the equinoxes. While too complex to describe in detail here, suffice it to say that there is a shift that takes place over thousands of years from one candidate for North Star to another. Today, the North Star is Polaris; in ancient times it was Thuban, and a number of others depending on the historical epoch we study. This gradual shift from one "North Star" to another may have given rise to some of our ancient myths and legends, as authors such as David Ulansey[4] and de Santillana and von Dechend[5] have proposed. However, it is the nature of the North Star in general that will occupy our attention in the pages that follow, and a particular emphasis will also be placed on the circumpolar stars: these are stars that revolve around the North Star and are never seen to rise and set like the stars of the zodiac, for instance. They are always visible, and can be used as accurate timekeepers and direction-finders.

This constancy, this ultimate reliability, is what inspired millennia of priests and mystics. If there truly was a Creator God, then the closest one could come to knowing such a Being would be through the very center of God's universe, the point around which everything in that creation revolved. It became the direction of immortality, of resurrection, of spiritual power. And to arrive there, one had to use a vehicle. As we shall see, this was often described as a chariot.

In the Jewish ascent texts, the heavens are precisely numbered. While some texts differ, the majority of the *merkavah* ("chariot") documents discuss a heaven of seven levels. While we do not know precisely what practice was employed to reach these seven heavens, later Kabbalists, such as Abraham Abulafia, would discuss various means for inducing a kind of trance state in which the seven heavens would be visualized, each in turn. This was considered a dangerous practice, and generally was frowned upon by the Jewish religious leaders, the rabbis.

As spiritual consciousness became more sophisticated and detailed in its projections and its technologies, the Pole Star and its circumpolar "attendants" became, in a sense, internalized, or, rather, an analogue was discovered between the actual, visible stars and something quite like them on earth and eventually within the human body itself. We shall explore these ideas in the chapters that follow, and watch how this very basic concept became further and further refined until we witness the phenomenon of New Age–type spiritual organizations, esoteric orders, and secret societies. Without being consciously aware of their consistency with ancient belief systems, these orders unerringly invoke quite similar ideas and employ virtually identical practices.

So in order to follow this line of reasoning we will begin chronologically with the earliest known written scriptures, those of the Egyptians and Babylonians, before examining the Jewish ascent texts themselves. We will also look at African, Indian, and Chinese systems before moving on to the more modern western esoteric movements and their more famous, or infamous, proponents. An excursus on alchemy is also necessary, for it will help us understand the relationship between ascent literature and some of the more arcane and cryptic systems eventually reflected in the rituals of groups like the Hermetic Order of the Golden Dawn: groups that have exerted tremendous influence over the so-called New Age movement of the present day. It will also help us understand how a technology that was originally employed to animate corpses and statues eventually became a technology for individual, human spiritual transformation.

Part One

Ancient Modes
of Ascent

The Opening of the Mouth ceremony being performed on the mummy of
Hunefer, about 1350 BCE. Note the bull at the bottom of the diagram. The
Thigh of the Bull was the Egyptian name for the Big Dipper asterism. From
the *Papyrus of Hunefer,* sheet 5.

THE PURPOSE IN THE FOLLOWING two chapters is to make a case that ideas of celestial ascent were current at the time of the ancient Egyptian and Babylonian empires, that they shared several important characteristics in common, and that they both had as their inspiration the seven stars of the Dipper and the *axis mundi* represented by the Pole Star. This is relevant to the argument that the Jewish ascent techniques known as *merkavah* or *hekhalot* mysticism were based on previous ideas of immortality that were connected to astronomical phenomena and observation. Under discussion is the Egyptian burial practices and specifically the "Opening of the Mouth" ceremony, the Sumero-Babylonian myths and practices concerning the Descent of Inanna/Ishtar to the Underworld, as well as the "Washing of the Mouth" ceremony used for consecrating statues of the gods.

Chapter 1

Ascent Myth and Ritual in Ancient Egypt

*A stairway to heaven shall be laid down for him, that he may ascend
to heaven thereon.* — The Pyramid Texts[1]

Egypt is considered by many to be the spiritual home of western esotericism.
It was the discovery of the *Corpus Hermeticum* during the Renaissance that
led European intellectuals to the conclusion that the Greek god Hermes
and the Egyptian god Thoth were one and the same:[2] representations of
Wisdom and particularly of divine secrets and occultism, a rich store of
learning that had just come to light in fifteenth-century Italy. Later, Egyptian themes would be incorporated into a wide variety of secret societies
and occult orders, and Cagliostro would famously add the Egyptian "mysteries" to the craft of Freemasonry. A famous occult grimoire (or manual of
practical magic) called the *Black Pullet*[3] takes as its setting the pyramids of
Egypt at the time of Napoleon's invasion. In the nineteenth and twentieth
centuries, Egyptian gods and goddesses were inextricable parts of the rituals
and initiation ceremonies of the Hermetic Order of the Golden Dawn and
of many of that venerable organization's offshoots and sister associations.
Even the infamous British occultist Aleister Crowley used Egyptian concepts
and iconography to characterize the New Age, calling it the Aeon of Horus; he received the scripture of his movement in Cairo in 1904 after seeing
what he called the Stele of Revealing in the Egyptian Museum there. Thus,
Egyptology has exerted a tremendous influence over twentieth-century occultism and continues to do so today. It is the contention of this study that
a connecting link between Egyptian religion, Jewish mysticism, Babylonian
magic, and even Chinese alchemy is to be found in the "ascent literature"
of their respective schools.

When we speak of "ascent literature," the reference is usually to the
merkavah texts of Jewish mysticism with some scholars seeing influences
from or to Gnosticism, Zoroastrianism, Manichaeanism, Mithraism, early
Christianity (notably the letters of Paul), and the Qumran community. Other
scholars have boldly asserted influences from Babylon, and we will consider

this in the following chapter. For now, though, we will look at what I am calling the "ascent literature" of ancient Egypt: the Coffin Texts, the Pyramid Texts, and what is popularly known as the Book of the Dead. In the texts we will discover themes that are reminiscent of the *merkavah* literature and, even more importantly, we will begin to uncover the secrets not only of the mummification and resurrection rituals of the Egyptians but also the systematized ascent of the Jewish mystics.

The Pyramid Texts

One of the oldest sacred scriptures in the world,[4] the Pyramid Texts are hieroglyphic texts that were found in a fifth dynasty pyramid, a tomb for a dead pharaoh, Unas. While they lack the elaborate illustrations of what would later be called the Egyptian Book of the Dead, their spells ensuring the peaceful afterlife of the deceased are remarkably similar to the much later ascent literature of the Jewish mystics, so much so, in fact, that we can begin to discern the outline of a pattern of religious thought that has so many details consistent with the *merkavah* texts that we are forced to look at both from a fresh perspective.

The Pyramid Texts evidently were intended to guide the soul of the pharaoh through the various stages of death and astral resurrection, so that he could take his place among the gods — and the stars. The date of the pyramid where the texts were found can reliably be assigned to the reign of Unas, who ruled circa 2375–2345 BCE. That would make the Pyramid Texts almost eighteen hundred years older than the vision of Ezekiel, which took place in Babylon in 593 BCE and upon which the various documents of the *merkavah* mystics are based.

It should be noted that this pyramid was not excavated until the late nineteenth century, which gives us two important pieces of data. In the first place, its age and the condition of the hieroglyphic text found there ensures that the Pyramid Text itself is an unadulterated scripture, i.e., it is perhaps the most ancient written scripture in existence. The later Coffin Texts and the Papyrus of Ani (a recension of which is known as the Book of the Dead) were composed centuries later, but they contain numerous elements that are virtually identical to the Pyramid Texts, indicating that they represent a continuum of religious ideas and ideology that flowed unperturbed for more than two thousand years, still operative in Egypt during the time of Christ.[5]

In the second place, the Pyramid Texts give us the first ever account of a celestial ascent. The importance of this cannot be overestimated, for what we are looking at is (1) arguably the oldest written scripture in existence, which is simultaneously (2) the first ever ascent document. In other words, *celestial ascent is represented in the oldest known form of scripture.*

We are on dangerous ground from an academic perspective, perilously close to the universalism of an Eliade or a Frazer, so we must tread softly. Mircea Eliade has been criticized for projecting cases of Siberian shamanism onto many other world cultures, seeing in the practices of indigenous religions in countries other than northern Russia similar if not identical practices and beliefs. The trend in postmodern anthropological circles is to view each culture and its religious and mystical material as independent and heavily contextual. Thus, it would be impolitic to compare the visionary and ecstatic practices of the Siberian shamans with those of, for instance, Haitian vodouisants or Australian aborigines, particularly if the intent was to show that they represent identical themes or perspectives. That approach was considered racist and colonialist, a projection of old white men's fear of, or prurient fascination with, the Other onto "native" (i.e., nonwhite hence "uncivilized" or "unlettered") peoples. While birth, puberty, and death are pretty much universals for all human beings, to suggest that there is a commonality of approach to these universals, particularly in the details, is considered anathema: it does not do justice to the richness of individual cultures or sells them short by implying that they contributed nothing new to the discussion.

From that point of view, then, it would be quite a risk to suggest that the beliefs expressed in the Pyramid Texts were somehow common currency throughout the Middle East simply because they express a few ideas in common with those of Babylon and the children of Israel or, indeed, that all of these beliefs sprang from a common source or were somehow identical to each other. We will simply follow the evidence and see where it leads us. It is to be admitted that it's a kind of "hermetic hermeneutics" we are practicing here, a glass bead game of symbols and symbol-systems, a literary analysis of themes and contexts, but it is consistent with the epigraphic and archaeological data and *quantitatively* the argument will be compelling; if it is also *qualitatively* impressive, then we have done our job.

The Pyramid Texts were discovered and first presented to the world by that indefatigable Egyptologist Gustave Maspero. Later, translations would appear in German and English. The most recent academically acceptable version is the one by Faulkner, published in 1969, to which most still refer.

What immediately calls our attention is the set of hieroglyphics on the north wall of the tomb's antechamber. (Wherever we look during this study, something as basic and mundane as the four directions — north, south, east, and west — will be seen to have consistent relevance for our case, in particular the north and the north-south axis.) These spells can be thought of as the Ur-*merkavah* texts, for they prefigure, by some three millennia, what the Jewish mystics would write in their own spells and prescriptions for ascent. Many of the basic elements will be found there, and in addition some new information that may help shed some light on the later, Kabbalistic practices.

The Pyramid Texts are broken down into "Utterances," and these in turn have line numbers. If we begin at the beginning on the North Wall, we read the following:

Utterance 302:

458: To say the words: "Serene is the sky, Soped lives, for it is Unas indeed who is the living son of Sothis. The Two Enneads have purified (themselves) for him as Mesekhtiu and the Imperishable Stars. The House of Unas which is in the sky will not perish, the throne of Unas which is on earth will not be destroyed.

This immediately brings our attention to a number of factors. First, Unas, the dead pharaoh, is thought of as claiming his place in the sky. Thus, the idea that the soul (in this case, what the Egyptians called the *akh,* sometimes spelled *ax:* the imperishable part of the spirit) goes to the heavens after death is shown to be more than four thousand years old. Second, we note the identification of Mesekhtiu, which is the Great Bear constellation, also known as Ursa Major, and the important reference to the "Imperishable Stars." These stars are those that do not descend below the horizon and hence do not "perish" but revolve endlessly in the night sky. The only stars that do this are those that revolve around the Pole Star, the significator of true north. Of course, this inscription is found on the North Wall of the antechamber and this is not by accident, as the other three walls contain inscriptions proper to their cardinal directions.

Utterance 302 goes on as follows:

"...The throne of Unas is with you, Re. He will not give it to any other. 461: Unas ascends (on it?) toward heaven near you, Re, while his face is like that of hawks, his wings are those of apd-geese, his talons like the fangs of He-of-the-Dju-ef-nome. 462: There is no word against Unas on earth among men, there is no crime of him in heaven among gods. Unas has done away with the word against him, Unas has annihilated it in order to rise toward heaven. 463: Upuaut has let Unas fly to heaven amongst the gods. Unas has moved his arms like a smn-goose, he has beaten his wing like a kite. He flies up, O men! Unas flies up away from you!"

In this paragraph, we come across a motif of Unas flying upward toward the heavens, birdlike, flapping his arms. Unas is joining his brothers the gods and ascending on his throne. This is a very interesting line, because it suggests that somehow the throne is also flying. Also intrinsic to this and to most of the Pyramid Texts is the understanding that Unas is blameless:

"there is no word against Unas on earth among men, there is no crime of him in heaven among gods." The importance placed on ethical or moral purity in regards to the ascent to heaven is one that will influence millennia of mystical teachings and seekers.[6]

This Utterance is followed by a number of other spells, until finally we reach numbers 305 and 306, which speak of a ladder to heaven:

> 472: To say the words: "The ladder is tied together by Re before Osiris. The ladder is tied together by Horus before his father Osiris, when he goes to his soul [*ax*], one of them is on this side, one of them is on that side while Unas is between them. 473: Are you then a god whose places are pure? I come from a pure [place]! Stand [here] Unas, says Horus. Sit [here] Unas, says Seth. Take this arm, says Re. 474: The spirit [*ax*] belongs to heaven, the body [*Sa.t*] to earth...."

Utterance 306

> 476: To say the words: "How beautiful is indeed the sight, how good indeed to see, so say the gods, when this god ascends to heaven, [when] Unas ascends to heaven 477: while his power is over him, the fear on both his sides, his magical power in front of his legs... 479: and you ascend, Unas, to the sky, you climb on it in this, its name of ladder. Heaven be given to Unas, earth be given to Unas, so said Atum.... Lo, you come into being against him as the Bull of the wild bulls, who remained (after the fight), he remains, he remains, the bull who remained and you will also remain, Unas, at their head, at the head of the spirits forever!"

And then the enigmatic phrase in Utterance 312:

> 501: To say the words: "May the bread fly up! May the bread continue to fly up to the 7 Houses of the Red Crown!"

The Red Crown refers to Lower Egypt, which is northern Egypt, as opposed to the White Crown, which refers to Upper Egypt, the southern part of the country. Thus, the Red Crown is emblematic of the "north" and the seven houses, to which the bread flies up, are therefore in the northern sky, which is how these Utterances began. It would not take a leap of imagination to propose that these seven houses refer to the seven stars of the *Mesekhtiu*, the Great Bear constellation. Further, it is obvious by a close reading of these Utterances that Unas is to reside in the northern sky as a star among the other Imperishable Stars that revolve around the Pole Star. Since these texts are quite possibly our oldest scriptures, it is virtually impossible to tell where this concept originated or why. We can conjecture that since these particular stars are circumpolar and never set below the horizon that they became symbols of immortality. That still does not explain why the ancient Egyptians believed that an immortal soul or *ax* inhabited the physical body or *sa.t*, and that this immortal soul would survive death to reside in the heavens.

It is a mystery that may never be solved, unless eventually we discover even more ancient writings that can provide us with some answers. In fact, the mystery deepens as more information becomes available, for the Pyramid Texts also give us our first glance at a bizarre ceremony designed to "animate" — i.e., in the sense of invoking an *anima* or spirit into him — the dead king, the famous Opening of the Mouth ritual, which was part of ancient Egypt's funerary practices, a technique that was employed for more than two thousand years and that appears in greater detail in the Papyrus of Ani, one recension of the famous Book of the Dead.

The Opening of the Mouth

The Opening of the Mouth was a ritual originally used to invoke the spirit of a god into a statue of that god. Its full title is "The Opening of the Mouth and Eyes" and may be an enactment of human birth events such that by mimicking human birth one was able to duplicate that process in giving life to an inanimate statue. The sacred instruments in use during the ritual include those that might have also been used to cut the umbilical cord of a human baby, and the actual opening of the mouth and eyes may be a reference to cleaning the baby's mouth and eyes of birth fluids and helping it to breathe independently.[7] This is speculation, of course, and there does not seem to be a step in the ritual specific to the statue's nose, which would be logical if this were a reenactment of a human birth and its concomitant requirement to clear the baby's nasal passages so that it can breathe ambient air rather than obtaining oxygen from its mother through the umbilicus. Instead, the statue's eyes are "opened" so that it may see, and its mouth is "opened" so that it may speak ... but its nose is not "opened" so it may breathe. According to E. A. Wallis Budge, one of the early experts on Egyptology and specifically on the Book of the Dead:

> The ceremony of "Opening the Mouth" is very ancient, and probably dates from the end of the Neolithic Period in Egypt. It was performed on the gods after they were created, and was ever after performed on all dead men whose relatives could afford to pay for the ceremony. The Egyptians foresaw that when a man had been made into a mummy, if life were restored to him by magical means, it would be impossible for him to move his members because of the bandages with which they

were swathed, and he could not breathe because his mouth would be closed by swathings also. The priests therefore invented a series of ceremonies, and composed a liturgy to be recited whilst the ceremonies were being performed, the effect of which would be to remove the swathings from the body and permit it to open the nostrils, and to breathe, eat, drink, think, and walk.[8]

The instruments used in this ritual are indicative of an astronomical purpose as well. One of the most familiar of these to Egyptologists is the adze, a length of meteoric iron fashioned into a strange but very specific shape. This is the instrument used to "open the mouth" of the statue and, in later usage, that of the pharaoh's mummy. It appears in many papyri depicting this ritual, and the odd shape of the instrument is intriguing for it resembles almost perfectly the shape of the constellation we know in America as the "Big Dipper": the seven stars that make up the most clearly visible asterism of the larger constellation known as Ursa Major, or the Great Bear — what in ancient Egypt was called *Mesekhtiu,* mentioned in Utterance 302 above along with the Imperishable Stars.

This instrument is referred to as the Thigh of Set, and at times in other hieroglyphic panels we can see that the thigh of a bull is also presented during the Opening of the Mouth ceremony. These are all cognate symbols, referencing a common motif. The Bull is the Bull of Heaven, what we call the Great Bear but which the ancient Egyptians referred to as the Bull. The thigh of the Bull is the Big Dipper asterism, which is also called the Thigh of Set since Set was identified with this constellation. This may be a euphemism, for one of the other instruments of the Opening of the Mouth ceremony is a wand or staff in the shape of a serpent, according to some Egyptologists, but which on observation can be seen to resemble a phallus much more than a serpent. The word "thigh" has often been used as a euphemism for phallus, such as in the term "wounded in the thigh" when used of Amfortas in the Grail legend as recounted by Chretien de Troyes; of Adonis, "wounded in the thigh" by a boar's tusk; and of some pertinent Babylonian myths concerning Gilgamesh and the Bull of Heaven that we will examine in the next chapter. These "thighs" are all euphemisms for the phallus, and the wound is symbolic of castration, for in each of these myths there is a clear link with fertility and birth. When the Egyptian god Osiris is slain and dismembered by Set, according to the myth, it is the phallus that is most especially sought by his wife and sister, Isis, so that she may become impregnated by it and give birth to Horus, the avenging son of Osiris and Isis. This phallus has been referred to by some cults as the Talisman of Set,[9] for it was believed that Set had hidden the phallus knowing of its magical potency; also, in the legend of the battle between Set and the avenging son of Osiris, Horus, Set's member is torn off, which could also be the reason for calling Ursa Major the "Talisman of Set" or the "Thigh of Set."

The relevance for us is that there is a thread of data that connects fertility, birth, animation of the dead or lifeless (pharaoh and statue, respectively), and celestial ascent with the cardinal direction north and with the seven stars of the Big Dipper. Before we go further, let's look at what Budge tells us about this important doctrine.

The Egyptian Afterlife

The Other World was a complicated place for the ancient Egyptians. Besides being the abode of the gods, it was distant enough from the abode of humans that terrible dangers lurked in the places between human and divine lands. According to Budge, the only beings who could traverse these vast and forbidding distances were the gods themselves; the newly mummified pharaoh could also successfully navigate the passage but only if he was provided with the right tools and weapons. That meant that the pharaoh, upon whom the Opening of the Mouth ceremony had been performed, could return to this world from the Other.

The Other World was envisioned as a metal plate or dome that covered the earth and was supported by four pillars, one for each of the cardinal directions. One could cover the distance between the earth and the heavens by means of a "ladder," as mentioned in the Pyramid Texts above, or by the pharaoh's throne, which seemed to be able to rise up or fly. These motifs of ladder and throne are recurrent in many Middle Eastern religions — one only has to think of Jacob's Ladder, for instance — but it is probably in Egypt that we find the first recorded instance of using a ladder to climb to heaven.

Access to the Other World was by means of gates. As the Egyptian religion underwent changes and modifications throughout the millennia, the number of these gates would fluctuate. One would find ten, fourteen, sixteen, or twenty-one such gates.[10] These are all suggestive numbers, indicating a struggle to perfect a kind of mystic numerology that would satisfy various cosmological conceptions. In the Jewish Kabbalah, for instance, there is the attempt to equate the seven *merkavah* with the ten *sefiroth,* an approach we will discuss later. In the Pyramid Texts, however, there seem to be seven gates, and they represent a specific idea. In later recensions of the Book of the Dead these seven gates are referred to as the seven *arit:* a word that translates as "mansions" or "halls" according to Budge.[11] This term will come up again in our study of Jewish mysticism, where heaven is understood to be divided into seven *hekhalot* or "palaces," a term that is sometimes used interchangeably with *merkavah,* or "chariot."

The seven *arit,* or gates of the Other World, are what Budge refers to as the "Mansions of Osiris" and are analogous to the African practice of forts or strongholds that stretch in chains across the desert, places where travelers would find security from wandering brigands, and food, water, and shelter, before setting off on their next day's journey. The deceased pharaoh would be given the requisite passwords and amulets that would enable him to pass safely through the gates of these "mansions," a concept that arises once again in the *merkavah* literature, where the mystic is provided with the correct *nomina sacra* and the appropriate seals or sigils to permit him safe passage through the *hekhalot.*

> In the case of the Seven Arits no soul could hope to gain admission to any one of them unless it was able to state the names of the doorkeeper and watcher and herald, and to repeat a formula which would convince them of its good faith. The writer of the Book of the Dead composed a Chapter in which the names of all the officials of the Arits were given, as well as the seven formulae that secured for those who knew them admission into the Arits.[12]

Compare this to the practices of the Jewish mystics of the first and second centuries CE as recounted by Ariel:

> They practiced an ecstatic and visionary form of mystical experience in which each rabbi prepared himself for his ascent to the celestial world through asceticism and rituals of purification. He visualized himself ascending through seven heavens and through the seven palaces in the highest heaven, the aravot. Along the way, he gained admission to each heaven and palace by presenting the correct password to the angelic gatekeeper. These passwords consisted of magical formulae and secret names of God or His angels.[13]

This basic structure is attested by Scholem,[14] Arbel,[15] and many other experts on Jewish mysticism and Kabbalah. While there is general agreement that some of these concepts may have been borrowed from Babylonian and/or Assyrian culture, there is virtually no recognition of the Egyptian contribution to this idea unless it is first-century BCE–first century-CE Egypt, then a hotbed of Hellenistic and Roman influences. I submit that the idea of passing through seven mansions or palaces, using secret names and formulae at each stage, in order to reach a celestial throne is at least as old as the Pyramid Texts and was widely understood in Egypt for more than two thousand years continuously. The implication of this data is that Moses, and at least some of the other Jews who fled with him from Egypt, would have been aware of it too.

Other Considerations

The Egyptian afterlife was seen to be vulnerable to human influence. If the right ceremonies were performed, and if his life had been blameless and lived in accordance with the laws and traditions of his culture, a deceased king could be assured of immortality and take his place among the gods and the stars. For the first time in recorded human history we see a kind of mutuality between the living and the dead, between the earth and the Other World (seen as located in the heavens). We see the dependence of the dead king on his still-living subjects to perform the right ceremonies. We see the dependence of the living upon the gods, among whom the king would take his place. We see, in other words, a kind of permeability between the two Worlds.

While the Other World was believed to be approachable by an individual human being only upon death in the context of the Pyramid Texts and the Papyrus of Ani, a transformation of this perspective would occur slowly over time. Eventually the same rites performed only for dead kings, the pharaohs, would be performed for other people, men and women, who had the financial ability to pay for them. The mummification procedures that ensured the immortality of the soul would be performed for nonroyals, and their tombs dot the Egyptian landscape. Heaven became accessible to everyone in theory; so the question has to be asked: Could one approach heaven while still alive? Could the ladder to heaven be found by mere mortals, and could the ascent take place as long as the right formulae were known?

I am not the first to suggest that the Pyramid Texts and the other Books of the Dead of ancient Egypt represent a kind of ascent literature. Thirty years ago, Whitney M. Davis, in an article published in the *Journal of Near Eastern Studies* suggested the same thing.[16] He also provided some guidance to the Books of the Dead in an attempt to analyze the basic themes that he identified as nine in all: from the basic idea of the mortuary ritual, the characteristics of what he calls the "pure soul" and its preparation for the afterlife, and other concepts including the idea of the celestial gate. The "pure soul" is the *ka* of the pharaoh, and this is the fulcrum on which the idea of heavenly ascent is balanced.

To the ancient Egyptians, the soul of the pharaoh was divine; the pharaoh's role in Egypt was similar to that of the "son of heaven" in Japan. There was the sacred bloodline that was the physical conduit for the divine essence, but the *ka* in Egypt was more important and was believed to "descend" into the pharaoh officially only at the time of his coronation. Thus, when the pharaoh died, his *ka* actually returned to the celestial regions from whence it had come.

What we witness in Egypt with the passing of time, however, is that the mummification rites — and the corresponding Opening of the Mouth ritual — came to be performed for ordinary citizens. The implication was that the *ka* itself was immortal and that every human being was in possession of it. If everyone had a *ka,* then everyone's *ka* could theoretically ascend into the celestial realms. This "democratization" of heaven was an important development in the history of religion and one that has been but rarely commented upon, for even though the world was divided into social classes from the royalty to the nobility to the wealthy and eventually down to the lowliest economic and social stratum, heaven was open to anyone who could afford to have the correct rituals performed. That was still not total democratization, of course, but eventually the concept of the immortality of the human soul became normative in the religions of the Middle East.

Often this soul was depicted as a bird with a human face. In some illustrations in the pyramids, it can be seen flying over the head of the deceased as it leaves the tomb. (Winged humans, or birds with human features, are a common motif in Middle Eastern religion, and the symbol will surface again in some unlikely places, as we shall see in the following chapters.) The idea that the soul has wings is consistent with the concept of celestial ascent. While the Books of the Dead speak of a ladder to heaven, an ascent to heaven by throne, and other forms, in the end the *ka* of the deceased is what enters the celestial realm and the depiction of the *ka* is always as a winged being and usually as a bird with a human face.

While the funeral rites would be performed for every pharaoh, it was not automatically assumed that the *ka* of the pharaoh would be able to rejoin the celestial realm from which it had originated. A "negative confession" had to be recited on behalf of the *ka,* stating that the deceased had not violated any laws of heaven or earth. Thus, even at this relatively early stage in the development of written scripture, the moral and ethical imperative was a fundamental unit of the ascent and its successful outcome. In the later texts, those from the Papyrus of Ani, for example, we can see illustrations of the soul of the deceased being weighed on a set of scales. The lighter the soul, the greater its chance for attaining immortality and becoming an "Osiris": a resurrected one, taking its place among the stars.

R. O. Faulkner, the author of the standard translation of the Pyramid Texts, wrote an article exploring the celestial elements of this form of Egyptian ascent literature.[17] He admits — as of 1966 when the article was published — that this aspect of the Pyramid Texts and even of Egyptian religion in general had not been examined very much, and he hoped to trigger some interest by presenting a short paper in which some elements of celestial doctrine were identified.

In the article he discusses the identification of the king with the stars and even with specific constellations. In the first place, the stars are characterized as gods; the king, as a divine emissary himself, takes his place among these stars, that is, he becomes deified upon his death and with the performance of the appropriate funerary rites, such as the Opening of the Mouth. The theme of the circumpolar stars, the Imperishable Stars of the Pyramid Texts, is examined, from their initial assistance to the dead king to the point where the king takes his place among them, becoming one of them and even assuming a degree of authority over them.

In a much older source, an article published in 1932 by G. A. Wainright in the *Journal of Egyptian Archaeology,* we read of the history of iron in Egypt. This may seem like an irrelevant excursus, but iron is fundamental to the understanding of the Opening of the Mouth ceremony since the adze that was used to "open the mouth" of the deceased was made of meteoric iron and fashioned in the shape of the "Big Dipper" asterism as we have seen above.

Meteoric iron was identified with the ritual for many reasons, according to Wainright.[18] For one thing, it was known as iron that fell from the sky, and meteors were believed to be "thunderbolts." The Egyptians were aware of its heavenly source, and associated it with thunder (probably due to the exciting phenomena that accompany the crash of a meteor to earth). This "celestial iron" was prized as an artifact and, indeed, for centuries the Egyptians believed that *all* iron came from the heavens. There were several sites in ancient Egypt where meteors had crashed and were a source of meteoric iron for years for the manufacture of special implements. One of these was Letopolis, which Wainright describes as "thunderbolt city" due to the large quantity of meteoric iron found there and the fact that the high priest of Letopolis was the chief "Opener of the Mouth."[19] The "Four Children of Horus" who are mentioned in the Pyramid Texts as participating in the Opening of the Mouth ceremony are identified by Wainright with the city of Letopolis and, just as importantly, with four of the seven stars of the Dipper.[20] What is not explained by Wainright is precisely why meteoric iron is associated with the Dipper.

There is one possibility, and it is one that has yet to be established. Had the iron been magnetized, then it would have pointed north (or, to be more precise, north-south). This is a problematic area, for we do not know if the Egyptians knew or understood magnetism as the earliest records we have on magnetism are of a much later date. However, if there was any ferrous oxide present in the meteoric iron that fell into Egypt and if its north-south pointing properties were known, it would go a long way toward explaining the identification of iron with the north. The magnetic properties would have appeared miraculous or supernatural and would have provided an obvious reason for the Egyptians to develop this complex mythologem of north-iron-Dipper-immortality.

To make this issue complicated even further, iron is identified with the Egyptian god of chaos, Set. According to Plutarch in *Isis and Osiris,* iron is referred to as the "bone of Typhon" (Typhon being another name for Set). According to the legend, when Horus defeated Set in battle he claimed authority over Set's dominion and used his instruments of power as his own. This would seem to be consistent with the identification of the Dipper as the "Thigh of Set" even though it is used in the Opening of the Mouth ceremony to make the deceased pharaoh into an Osiris, assisted by the "Children of Horus." Therefore, we have Set identified both with iron and with the Dipper, and the ceremonial adze made out of (meteoric) iron in the shape of the Dipper, and the foreleg of the ox offered as sacrifice at the Opening of the Mouth ceremony and also identified with Set and the Dipper.

This is, of course, the direction in which we have been headed. The stars are identified as the Other World, the land of immortality. The dead king, prepared by the appropriate rites and ceremonies, ascends to join them, specifically to the stars in the north, the circumpolar or imperishable stars, and in the process becomes a star himself. It is a process of transformation, except that the king is already believed to possess a divine spark, a *ka,* whose origin is in the stars. This apotheosis — and its association with the north and the circumpolar stars and most specifically with the constellation Ursa Major — is the key to this particular mystery.

Of course, other stars and planets had special characteristics for the ancient Egyptians and were important in other ways. The sun, moon, and planets were all important for various specific functions; the stars and constellations Sothis (Sirius) and Osiris (Orion) were just as important in the funeral rites and in Egyptian ritual generally. However, in the specific formulae of the Opening of the Mouth ritual that would guarantee the dead pharaoh's immortality, it is the constellation of Ursa Major and all the myths and rites associated with it that take center stage. Ursa Major is the key to understanding the Egyptian ritual of ascent.

Is it also key to understanding other forms of celestial ascent?

Chapter 2

Ascent Myth and Ritual in Ancient Babylon

Arguably the oldest civilization with a recorded history and a recorded religion is that of ancient Sumer. Our best estimates give us a date somewhere in the fourth millennium BCE for the appearance of the Sumerian city-states in what is now Iraq.[1] There are votive inscriptions on cuneiform clay tablets that date to the third millennium BCE, which is the same era as that of the oldest Egyptian Books of the Dead. It is generally accepted that Sumer is the oldest known civilization of the Middle East, if not the oldest in the world, so its scriptures and rituals are an important area of study for historians of religion. This area of research is still quite problematic, however, in part due to the large volume of cuneiform tablets that have not yet been translated and others that are fragmentary and incomplete. We have access to some of the Sumerian liturgical literature and some of their religious documents, and noted Sumerologist Samuel Noah Kramer has written that "history begins at Sumer";[2] the same could be said of religion with Sumer giving us the first story of the Flood, the first resurrection story, the first creation epic, etc.

When it comes to the Other World, however, we have a fully articulated myth cycle that duplicates in several aspects ideas of the Other World we encounter in the Pyramid Texts and the other Books of the Dead. In addition, we also have some clues in the very architecture of the Sumerian temples themselves and in the rituals associated with them. It should be pointed out that there are two schools of thought when it comes to describing the religion of ancient Sumer and Babylon. The first, represented by the opinion of A. Leo Oppenheimer — most especially in his *Ancient Mesopotamia: Portrait of a Dead Civilization*[3] — is that we can know next to nothing about Sumerian religion, that much of what we say we know is based on conjecture and speculation. There is strength to his argument, certainly; we are constantly filling in lacunae in our script where Sumer is concerned and are nowhere near finished understanding that remote culture.

The other school of thought can be represented by Samuel Noah Kramer, Sir Leonard Woolley,[4] and more recently Thorkild Jacobsen.[5] The consistency of Sumerian myth, liturgies, and spells is such that we can make some

24

comfortable assumptions about what the Sumerians believed and how they ordered their cosmos. Their scriptures were preserved by the Semitic cultures that invaded Sumer, and the Sumerian language was maintained as a kind of priestly or sacred tongue — similar to the way in which Latin was preserved as the sacred language of the Catholic Church. For that reason, we have been provided with enough material to draw some interesting conclusions.

The Ziggurat

The single most famous example of Sumerian — and later Akkadian and Babylonian — architecture is the ziggurat. This is a stepped pyramid; in other words, rather than the smooth-sided pyramids of the Egyptians, this type has several pronounced levels, one atop the other. It was the prototype for the Tower of Babel in the Bible (Gen. 11:4–5), an enormous edifice that rose to the heavens. The ziggurat served as the sacred precincts of the Sumerian city. Each city had its own god, considered as its guardian and ruler, and the ziggurat is where the god lived. There were several buildings associated with the ziggurat, some of them chapels for lesser gods, and the ziggurat itself was often surrounded by a double-walled perimeter. On certain sacred days, the high priest of the city, who was also its secular ruler, would ascend to the top of the ziggurat to commune with its god.

Some of the ziggurats had three levels, some more. In Babylon, as at Borsippa, the ziggurat of Marduk had seven levels and a temple in blue-glazed brick at the top where the *hieros gamos,* or sacred marriage, would be performed. This was probably the ziggurat mentioned as the Tower of Babel, for "Babel" is Babylon, a word that means "Gate of the Gods." The ziggurat of Babylon itself was known as *E-temen-an-ki,* the "foundation of heaven and earth." According to Herodotus, who was writing in the fifth century BCE, a priestess would spend the night at the top of the ziggurat of Babylon to await the sexual advances of Marduk.[6] From other sources, we know that a sacred marriage would take place between the statues of the gods — statues that had been "charged" or "animated" by a ritual strikingly similar to the Egyptian Opening of the Mouth — on certain days of the year, and in other cases the king himself would ascend to the top of the ziggurat on specific days and mate with the goddess Inanna (Ishtar).[7]

The number seven has importance in Sumerian and Babylonian culture as much as it does in the Egyptian,[8] and consistent with the Egyptian version "seven" is related to astronomical phenomena and to the gods. While the Sumerian number system is a sixty-base system, from which we derive our 360-degree circle, seven has special significance for Sumerian ascent and descent myths and rituals. This might be seen as odd, since seven is the one number between one and ten that cannot divide a circle of 360 degrees

evenly. Thus, it does not "fit" into the sixty-base system but is still the structure of the Underworld and of the astral gods, seven seeming to represent
transcendence: i.e., a number that stands outside the created world of 360
degrees. The Tower of Babel itself had seven levels as the Sumerians reached
for the heavens. And the goddess Inanna herself, who mated with the king
of Babylon, would descend seven levels into the Underworld.

The Descent of Inanna

This text may be thought of as another of the world's oldest scriptures and as
the account of a descent into the Underworld by one of its most cherished
and important goddesses: Inanna, the goddess of love and the "Queen of
Heaven." As a story, it is compelling in the details of its plot: Inanna goes
to the Underworld to visit her sister Queen Ereshkigal, the Queen of Death,
who lives below the earth in a palace reached by passing through seven
gates and seven gatekeepers. We are not certain why she is going there, as
accounts differ. Nonetheless, a "dance of the seven veils" takes place in
which Inanna must remove an item of her clothing and jewelry at each level
until she arrives before Ereshkigal completely naked. Ereshkigal, enraged
at this invasion of her domain by a living goddess, kills her with a look
(the first recorded "evil eye") and hangs her on a nail as a corpse (the first
crucifixion?). The Queen of Heaven stays in this state for three days and
three nights. Inanna, however, anticipating danger, has left an attendant at
the entrance to the Underworld with probably the first instance in history
of the hoary instruction "If I'm not back in three days, call the cops." The
attendant sounds the alarm, and one of the other gods, Enki, eventually
comes to the rescue by fashioning two sexless creatures (the world's first
robots) and charging them to enter the Underworld with the food of life
and the water of life to revive Inanna and bring her back to the World. This
they do, and Inanna returns triumphant through the seven gates — collecting
her clothing as she proceeds — and exits the Underworld, but accompanied
by demons.

There is another section of this story that may have an agricultural or
astronomical parallel, and that is the fate of Dumuzi, the shepherd god who
is Inanna's lover. According to the laws of the Underworld, a living being
may not ascend from death unless someone else has taken his or her place
below. Thus, Inanna sends Dumuzi — who she finds hanging out and relax-
ing even though the love of his life has been dead for three days — to stand
in for her in Ereshkigal's "kingdom." The demons that have accompanied
Inanna in her return to life then seize Dumuzi, who tries various means of
escaping his fate, but to no avail. Dumuzi then dies and is brought to the
Underworld and becomes a god of the Underworld. The death of Dumuzi

was observed throughout the Middle East with much wailing and mourning every year for centuries; today the month of July still is called *Tammuz* in Iraq after the Sumerian god, and the Shi'ite mourning festival for the death of Ali, the Prophet's cousin, at the Battle of Karbala is reminiscent of the way Dumuzi's death was observed in ancient times.

Another scriptural reference to Inanna and seven gates is the story of the way she brought the gifts of civilization to her people, after tricking the god Enki to give them to her when he was drunk. She obtains his promise and the hundred gifts after a night of feasting and drinking in Enki's palace, the Abzu ("Abyss") of Eridu. She sets off on her boat to travel through the seven gates that separate Eridu from her city of Uruk. Enki awakens, realizes what has happened, and sends demons and sea monsters after her to stop the boat and retrieve the gifts. After much drama, however, Inanna manages to reach the shore with her bounty, and there is much celebration in Uruk.

This theme of seven gates and a perilous passage between one world and the next will be expanded upon by cultures as different as the Israelites and adherents to the cult of Mithra; we have already seen the Egyptian version of this passage and its association with celestial phenomena. As we proceed, this theme becomes clearer and the implications of it profound as well as its consistent emphasis on a few, very specific, details. It is perhaps worth while to mention here that the planetary body associated with Inanna is Venus, but that she is also associated with the seven stars of the Big Dipper in Ursa Major.[9] Later Hermetic societies, such as the Golden Dawn of the nineteenth century CE, would identify themselves with this "mythologem" in a very precise manner.[10]

Gilgamesh

While the goddess Inanna made at least two perilous voyages through seven gates — the first to and from the Underworld of Queen Ereshkigal, the second to and from the "Abyss" of the god Enki — this heroic quest was not limited to the gods alone. One of ancient Mesopotamia's most cherished human figures, Gilgamesh, does the same thing as recorded in the *Epic of Gilgamesh*.

Gilgamesh is a human lord of the city of Uruk (Erech), the same city that is sacred to Inanna. Gilgamesh, realizing he is mortal and eventually will die, decides that he needs a way to ensure his immortality, at least in name. To that end, he determines he will voyage to a mysterious place called the "Land of the Living" and from there bring back the highly prized cedar wood for his palace in Uruk. In order to do this, he must cross seven mountains and defeat seven demons he will encounter on the way. Although he is able to do this, the last demon, the dreaded Humwawa, guards the mighty cedars and threatens Gilgamesh with death.

In a strange interlude, fragmentary in the Sumerian version, Gilgamesh falls into a deep sleep from which it is almost impossible to awaken him. When he does awake, he is thoroughly determined to defeat Humwawa, come what may. One wonders if this "deep sleep" was a kind of trance or dream state, for if it was we may have before us a prototype of the Jewish "descent to the Chariot," which seemed to entail entering into a trance; this, however, is pure conjecture at this point for there is no evidence to determine one way or another if the "deep sleep" of Gilgamesh was a trance or simply an exhausted sleep after his traversing of the seven mountains.

That day, he cuts down seven cedar trees and finds himself in Humwawa's chamber in the forest. A struggle ensues, Humwawa pleads for his life, but in the end he is slain by Gilgamesh, and the story abruptly ends.

In later Babylonian recensions there are many additional details and more complex characterizations. One of the important features is the attempt by Inanna to seduce Gilgamesh, an attempt that fails. Inanna, enraged, asks the other gods to help her punish the human. She threatens to raise the dead from the Underworld unless they assist her. In the end, she manages to send the Bull of Heaven to attack Uruk. This beast does tremendous damage to the city before Gilgamesh and his colleague Enkidu destroy it.

The identity of the Bull of Heaven is rather unclear. From available translations, we can see that it is a celestial figure (as its name implies) for the God of the Sky, An, tells Inanna that "its pasture is on the horizon" and "it can only graze where the sun rises."[11] Once Gilgamesh has slaughtered the Bull, he butchers it and then slaps Inanna with its haunch.[12] Again, we see some themes conflated here that are reminiscent of, but so far not conclusively linked to, the Egyptian motif of the haunch of the Bull and its connection with the stars of the Dipper. Inanna — goddess of Venus but also, as we have mentioned, of the Dipper — asks the God of the Sky for the Bull to destroy Gilgamesh, but Gilgamesh slays the Bull and hits Inanna with its haunch, the haunch that is used to perform the ceremony of the Opening of the Mouth in Egypt.

What is even more unusual is what is reported in a version of the text from Me-Turan (present day Tell-Haddad). After Gilgamesh has slaughtered and butchered the Bull, he distributes its carcass among his people, the people of Uruk, Inanna's sacred city, and then:

> He consigned its carcass to the knacker's, and turned its two horns into flasks for pouring fine oil to Inana in E-ana. For the death of the Bull of Heaven: holy Inana, it is sweet to praise you![13]

E-ana ("House of Heaven") is the Temple of Inanna in Uruk. Thus, the horns of the Bull of Heaven become flasks for Inanna's temple and her sacred service. It is interesting to note that the title "Bull of Heaven" was that given to Set in ancient Egypt; as we have seen, the Bull's Thigh is also the Thigh of Set and refers to the Ursa Major constellation and specifically the seven stars of the Dipper. Both Set and the Sumerian "Bull" were enemies that had to be destroyed; once defeated, their remains were used in various ways by the conquerors. We may be looking at a myth that has its origins in astronomical phenomena, except that the motif of slaying the Bull reappears in the cult of Mithras which makes its appearance at least two thousand years after the earliest "slaying of the Bull" myth in Egypt or Babylon; this would seem to preclude the speculation current in some circles that the slaying of the Bull refers to the precession of the equinoxes.

That the Bull of Heaven grazes where the sun rises implies that it is a constellation that is to be found in the east, which would not correspond with the Dipper, which is found in the north. It could be a reference to Taurus, which would seem obvious, except that Taurus only rises in the east at specific times of the day and night throughout the year and is not permanently in the east. According to the Babylonian star catalogue, the MUL.APIN, the Bull of Heaven *is* Taurus and furthermore is to be found on the Path of Anu, followed by the constellation of Orion, which is identified in Babylon with Gilgamesh. Orion is called "the Loyal Shepherd of Heaven" in the MUL.APIN, which is interesting since Dumuzi, the lover of Inanna, is the Shepherd God. Both Dumuzi and Gilgamesh had problematic relationships with Inanna, however, which might have led to their being identified with each other on some level. For now, though, let us proceed to an investigation of the MUL.APIN and the astronomical/astrological beliefs of the ancient Sumerians and Babylonians.

The MUL.APIN

The date of the earliest composition of the MUL.APIN is believed to be about 1000 BCE with the earliest known versions dating to the seventh century BCE. The positions of the stars in the MUL.APIN are considered correct for about 1300 BCE.

The statement that the Bull of Heaven grazes where the sun rises might be an allusion to the fact that Taurus is on the ecliptic, i.e., is one of the signs of the zodiac which is represented by the Path of Anu. According to the ancient Mesopotamians, there were three important celestial paths: that of Anu (An), of Enlil, and of Ea (Enki). The Path of Enlil is the symmetrical, circular path made by the stars that revolve around the north celestial pole, at a declination from about 12 degrees to 33 degrees above the celestial equator. The other two paths intersect the ecliptic at various points and to various extents. Taken together, these three paths are representative of what the ancient Mesopotamians knew of the organization of the fixed stars.

An, Enlil, and Enki were the supreme gods of the Sumerians. Anu or An was the god of the sky, Enlil of the earth, and Ea or Enki of the waters. They are routinely invoked in charms and spells as well as in more formal incantations and prayers. As we see from the MUL.APIN, they were also associated with the paths of the stars. Like the Egyptians, the Sumerians and Babylonians connected their gods with celestial phenomena. Inanna — also known as Ishtar and later Ashtoreth to the Semites (who becomes the fearsome Astaroth of the medieval grimoires, a male demon and evidence of the demonification of all the pagan Gods by the Jewish and Christian faiths) — is identified with the planet Venus and with the Dipper as well as with the "Bull of Heaven" that she sends against Gilgamesh; Nergal, the god of war, is identified with Mars; Marduk, the defeater of the sea creature Tiamat, who later becomes the biblical *tehom*, is associated with Jupiter, and so on.

Just as the heavens were dangerous for the Egyptians, so too the Sumerian heavens are a dangerous place. There is a conflation of the idea of the Underworld with the skies above the world. At times the Underworld is perceived as being located geographically below the earth; at other times it is visualized as a place between the earth and the very outermost part of the sky where reside the gods. Indeed, if the Underworld is at once below the earth and in the heavens it may demonstrate that the ancients had a better grasp of geography than our more recent ancestors, for it could be said that the Underworld, i.e., that region "below the earth," is certainly the same as the heavens, since the earth is suspended in space and is surrounded by the heavens. More quaintly, it could be argued that there were two aspects to the Underworld: that those who merited it ascended to the heavens, while those who did not remained below the earth to lead a dreary existence in the afterlife. Both destinations could be thought of as the Underworld or, at the very least, the Other World.

Observation of the sky was thus tantamount to listening to what the gods had to say. It was the place where omens were born, for celestial phenomena could be interpreted as the speech of the gods and indicators of future events. Astronomy was the handmaiden to astrology for much of recorded human history; it was the skeletal structure on which the nerves and muscles of astrological interpretation were layered. Therefore we find the ancients paying close attention to the stars and planets, laboriously recording their every movement as close as they were able without instruments, telescopes, or computers. The MUL.APIN text is evidence of this meticulous care and the ingenuity with which the ancient astronomers tried to understand the motions of the celestial bodies; and it was through observations such as these that the circumpolar stars were identified and an all-important position at the very "top" of the heavens around which these stars rotated was discovered.

This is the Pole Star, and it changes due to the precession of the equinoxes. At the time the Pyramid Texts were being written and the first Sumerian cuneiform scriptures composed, about 3000 BCE, the Pole Star or North Star was not our present-day Polaris but the star Thuban in the constellation Draco. Many authors, both academic and popular,[14] have written about the precession and the shift from one "Pole Star" to another as the reason for many of the world's myths. It is believed by some that the shift of a Pole Star from one point in space to another caused panic or anxiety in world civilizations as it seemed the linchpin holding the universe together had come unstuck or disappeared altogether. Some of this speculation is based on faulty science or even wishful (or "wistful") thinking; in other cases, the evidence seems a bit more compelling. However, is it reasonable to assume that this precession was even noticed? After all, it takes thousands of years for true north to move from one star to another. It is a gradual process that only those who possessed a written record of its movement over centuries would recognize.

In any event, we have to ask ourselves why a civilization that fought for survival against droughts, famines, floods, pestilence, and wars would have spent so much time, decades leading to centuries, in compiling detailed observations of the stars, creating star lists, and developing mechanisms for explaining such complicated ideas as the ecliptic and the zodiacal belt. Either it was believed that one could predict *something* using this data — world events, natural disasters, the birth and death of kings — or it was felt that the stars really were gods in control of human destiny. Possibly the real reason was some combination of these factors; for while observing the sun and moon in their courses was useful for making calendars, which are themselves useful for knowing when to plant and when to harvest, knowing the details of every fixed star visible to the naked eye had to be of only limited practical value. Yet time and expense were devoted to this effort by societies advanced enough that they could afford to employ persons to watch the stars who were otherwise not directly involved in agriculture or defense. And just as the idea of heavenly ascent after death moved, with the passage of time, from the sole privilege of kings and royals to that of the average citizen, so too did the computation of astrological data move from the erection of horoscopes for kings and nations to that of the common man and woman keen on knowing their personal, individual destinies: to read the handwriting of the gods.[15] The "democratization" of the concept of the soul was reflected in the democratization of the concept of the stars and their influence.

This democratization did not extend to the complex calculations under-lying its practice, however. Just as kings turned to their court astrologers and other specialists in astral observations for advice on the dictates of the Divine, so did the average citizen have to consult experts: not just for the computations of the positions of the planets and the stars, but also for their interpretation. In the last several hundred years, these two disciplines began to move apart so that the computations belonged properly to the science of astronomy and their interpretations to the "pseudo-science" of astrology.

It is a loaded concept, "pseudo-science," for it makes several assumptions that are not necessarily based on fact. To call something a "pseudo-science" is to devalue it; but it also assumes that the practice being devalued masquerades as "science."

Until the seventeenth century, the Roman Catholic Church arrogated to itself the right to decide how the world was created and how the cosmo-logical scheme worked. The world was created in six days by God, and the earth was at the center of the universe. Good deeds were rewarded after death, and bad deeds were punished. Christ rose from the dead on Sunday after his execution on Friday afternoon. Bread and wine are transformed into his flesh and blood, respectively, during the Mass. All of this could be considered "pseudo-science." So could Moses receiving the Commandments from God on Mount Sinai, or the Prophet Mohammed speaking with the archangel Gabriel. Science, in the person of its scientists, has refrained from calling religion a "pseudo-science" even as it disagrees heartily with many of its positions on issues that are clearly "scientific," the emotional controversy over evolution being a case in point.

Astrology, however, is a pseudo-science only inasmuch as it is not an element of the doctrine or practices of an organized — western, European — religion. Astrology is still used today in many Asian communities to calculate the best days for a wedding, buying a house, holding a specific religious ceremony, etc., all within a religious framework, whether it be Buddhism, Daoism, Hinduism, etc. What is at stake is not the "correct" or even the "most useful" way of understanding the world and how it works; what is at stake is the meaning we attribute to worldly function. Science cannot offer us a meaning or an interpretation of events; scientific reductionism can only explain the mechanics but not the "ghost in the machine." From that point of view, we could call science a "pseudo-religion" in that it insists on its own definitions of cosmos, creation, life, etc.

Neither of these pejoratives, pseudo-science or pseudo-religion, is very useful. They do not carry information beyond that of a polemical nature. We are no further ahead in our understanding of the world — and our pur-pose for being here — than before. Human knowledge and experience have become Balkanized by this inability to understand each other's theoretical language and by the insistence of each faction on elevating its own special-ized field of knowledge or interpretation above all others in importance or relevance. There is no cohesive, inclusive argument. No place in the world where we can stand and regard the whole of creation, of reality. Thus, we have to look elsewhere.

To the ancients, and to the creators of the MUL.APIN, that meant looking "up."

The gods of the Sumerians, Akkadians, and Babylonians live in the heav-ens. Their three most important divinities — Anu, Enlil, and Ea — describe huge arcs or "paths" in the sky. This concept of immense "astronomical" distance was reflected in the later *merkavah* texts in every discussion of the seven celestial palaces and the distances between them. As the sun, moon, and planets were observed to move in relation to the paths of the fixed stars, two separate categories of celestial personalities were determined: the plan-ets or "wanderers," who moved endlessly across the heavens, and the stars, who formed the backdrop against which the planets danced. Of course, the so-called fixed stars were also seen to move, to rise and set like the planets, but they maintained a fixed relationship to each other. One constellation did not morph and become another or merge with another. The planets, however, could be seen to rise against the backdrop of one constellation one month and the next constellation the following month. The planets moved swiftly when measured against the stately rotation of the constellations and at times they even seemed to move backward or retrograde, something the stars never did.

Among all the stars and their constellations, a few stand out as being of more importance. We have already mentioned the circumpolar stars and in particular the constellation known as the Great Bear or Ursa Major, known to the Mesopotamians as the Great Wagon or MAR.GID.DA. This is a con-cept that is shared by so many peoples around the world as to be virtually universal, the difference being those who refer to the same constellation as the Bear or *arktos,* a term that is suggestive of other meanings, other reso-nances as we will see later. The ancient Greeks also referred to Ursa Major as *amaxa,* or "chariot," a name they borrowed from the Babylonians, who actually broke down the constellation into the constituent parts of a chariot including "the yoke, the pole, and the side pieces" which are "equated with divine beings."[16]

Other stars and constellations had other significance for the ancient Mesopotamians as well, and these deserve some examination.

On the Path of Enlil we find MAR.GID.DA and the planet Jupiter along with many other constellations and individual stars; altogether there are thirty-three "stars" identified with this Path. On the Path of Anu, we find our modern constellation of Perseus, which is identified here with Dumuzi, the Shepherd God. On the same Path we find the constellation Orion, which is called SIPA.ZI.AN.NA and specifically identified with Gilgamesh. We also find another cluster of seven stars, which is of importance: the constellation of the Pleiades, also known as the Seven Sisters. At times, it is difficult to determine from cylinder seals and other texts whether the seven stars of the Dipper or those of the Pleiades are intended. Also on the Path of Anu we find the planets Venus, Mars, Saturn, and Mercury. There are a total of twenty-three stars on this Path.

On the Path of Ea, which contains fifteen stars, we find a star, Regulus, identified with Ea himself. There is also an intriguing reference to the first star of our present-day constellation Libra, which is associated with the AB.ZU, the Abyss of Ea/Enki, and therefore signifies the entry to the Underworld. This is a theme that deserves more attention than we can give it here, but we should mention that the star NU.MUSH.DA on this Path marks the date of the Vernal Equinox just as Libra marks the date of the Autumn Equinox at the opposite point on the circle. We may say that, just as the first star of Libra marks the beginning of autumn and the descent into the Underworld, the star NU.MUSH.DA marks the beginning of spring and possibly the escape from the Underworld. The translation of the term NU.MUSH.DA is "the Swarm" and may be a reference to the escape of Inanna from the Abyss of Ea/Enki, or it may be a reference to Inanna's *other* escape from the Underworld, that of Queen Ereshkigal, when she was accompanied by a horde of demons. Thus, the religious texts of the ancient Mesopotamians were linked in many ways to the appearance, motions, and positions of the stars. This is an association that is of tremendous importance as we proceed, for it is a system of religious correspondences that we in the West have almost completely lost and that survives only in the most cherished of our "pseudo-sciences," astrology, thus making it difficult for us to understand the coded information that is buried in our own scriptures and the mystical practices that have been taking place in secret for more than two thousand years. What the scriptures encode in text, the practices encode in deed.

Mis Pi and *Pit Pi*

The Mesopotamians had a ritual virtually identical in concept to the Egyptian Opening of the Mouth ceremony; like the Egyptian version, it was designed to instill a divine force into an inanimate object. The discovery of tablets describing this ritual and the way it was performed in Nineveh and Babylon have generated some excitement among scholars for the window it provides onto the religious and mystical beliefs of these ancient people, among whom the people of Israel would eventually find themselves either as neighbors or as combatants and slaves.

What is astonishing to an observer is the fact that both of these rituals, the Egyptian and the Mesopotamian, which have so much in common with each other, are so unusual and unique in the literature. Both rituals involve the statue of a god (the original Egyptian version, we remember, was used on statues before it was used on the mummies of kings); both involve "charging" or "consecrating" the statue; both involve "opening the mouth" of the statue in elaborate ceremonies that are linked to celestial forces and astronomical motifs. In fact, it is here that we come across an astonishing piece of data: one of the earliest mentions of a lodestone.

This comes from a Babylonian tablet describing the ritual,[17] and dates from roughly the sixth century BCE. It is known that the Greeks were probably the first to record the existence of this magnetic ore about 500 BCE (the word "magnet" comes from the name of the area in present-day Turkey where this ore was mined, Magnesia). Finding it on a sixth century BCE tablet is certainly intriguing, but it does not advance our study very much further except to suggest that if the lodestone was known to the ancient Babylonians of that period, it might have been known to other peoples even earlier. However, it is not revealed if the Babylonians knew that the lodestone "pointed" north; they were probably mystified by the strange attractive properties of the ore but had not identified it as a possible tool in navigation. However, it does show up here in a list of dozens of other minerals and organic material to be thrown into a basin of holy water for the Washing of the Mouth ceremony.

To the Egyptians, the most important element of this ritual was the Opening of the Mouth, what is known in the Babylonian texts by the Akkadian term *pit pi*. While this ritual formed part of the overall ceremony in Babylon, it would seem that the *mis pi* or Washing of the Mouth was more central to the rite. Washing the mouth of the temple priests was also required before they could approach the gods, and this seems to be a method of ensuring the purity of the sacred vessel for receiving the divine essence, a practice that is still required today by Muslim worshipers who must wash their feet, hands, face, and mouth before entering the mosque to pray.

While washing the statue's mouth was the core part of the ritual, the mouth still had to be "opened." This seems to be the "charging" or "animating" part of the ritual, the aspect of the ceremony that gives the statue life. In fact, the mouth-opening concept was used not only for statues of the gods but also in spells and divination. When an image was made of a targeted victim in a spell of "black magic," for instance, its mouth would be "opened" ritually in order to render it animate so that the spell would be effective. In divination, the bag containing the diviner's tools would also be ritually "opened" in this manner.

In the previous chapter, we discussed the possibility that the Opening of the Mouth ceremony referred to childbirth, a concept championed by Ann Macy Roth.[18] In the Babylonian context, however, there is some dissension with Peggy Jean Boden[19] arguing for, and Angelika Berlejung[20] against, the idea that the Washing of the Mouth ceremony is similarly referred. However, the entire procedure of preparing a statue of a god in this fashion and consecrating it, giving it life and invoking the divine presence into it, seems reminiscent of the process of human (or at least mammalian) birth since such is the only "life-giving" event with which most humans are familiar.

Another feature in common with the Egyptian version is its reliance upon the celestial forces to cooperate in the ritual. The planetary and stellar gods and goddesses are invoked at various stages in the ceremony, which, for the statue of a god, takes at least three days and involves a procession of the god from the temple to an orchard and a body of water and then the procession back. The god would be transported in a chariot in both directions, the way it is still done in many cultures.[21] First, the statue was taken in procession from the "House of the Craftsmen," which is self-explanatory, to the river-bank, where certain ablutions were performed: acts of ritual purity. Then the god is transported to "the Garden." It is here, in the Garden, that the principal rituals lasting more than a day were performed. At the completion of the Garden rituals, the statue was then moved to the Temple Gate and then to the Cella: the inner area of the Temple reserved for the god, the Sanctuary. The final mouth-washing ceremony takes place here, a final incantation is recited (seven times), and the accoutrements of the god are placed on the statue at night. After this, the priest returns to the riverbank for a final ablution and purification. The rite is over.[22] We should remember a detail of this ritual for later comparison, which is the central locus of the rite. This takes place in a garden and not in the temple; the relevance of this will become clear in chapter 5.

Gods were moveable, transportable, and something of the divine essence was contained within their statues if these statues were properly prepared — charged, consecrated, their mouths washed and "opened" — this essence coming from the abode of the gods, that is, from the stars.

This essence is called *me* (pronounced "may") in the Sumerian literature and refers to those hundred gifts Inanna swindled out of her father, Enki. These are qualities considered necessary for civilization and human life and they proceed from the gods. The Washing of the Mouth and Opening of the Mouth ceremonies were designed to imbue the otherwise lifeless statues with *me* and thus render them animate and powerful. In the Babylonian version of this ritual, offerings are made to a variety of celestial personalities, from An, Enlil, Enki, the Moon God Sin, the Sun God Shamash, Adad,

Marduk, Gula, Ishtar, and including Jupiter, Venus, and the other planets, as well as the Wagon (Ursa Major), the Plough (Andromeda), Pisces, Virgo, etc. Separate offerings are made to the Paths of An, Enlil, and Enki. There are fourteen separate mouth-washings in total in the Babylonian ritual; each of them involves multiple astronomical quanta, usually a mixture of individual stars, planets, and entire constellations. Associated with these fourteen washings are different offerings that must be made, one for each quantum being invoked. Thus, for the third Washing nine gods are invoked so there are nine offerings, etc.

When it comes to attracting the powers of the stars, the *me*, for magical purposes, the one constellation that stands out is the Wagon, Ursa Major.[23] In a set of incantation texts known as the *Sultantepe* and dating from 619 BCE we read of special invocations of the Wagon constellation in order to receive prophetic dreams. In these invocations, the Wagon is described in this way:

> Without you the dying man does not die and the healthy man cannot go on his journey.[24]

This is a characterization that is consistent with the idea of the Wagon as a vehicle, even insofar as to help a dying man to die, i.e., obtain his place among the stars. The association of the Wagon with death and travel is a theme that will recur, even in other cultural contexts, as we will see in chapter 6.

This consistency of the ritual pattern should be viewed in relation to the idea of the *me*. Somehow, the sacrifices that are made to the celestial bodies ensure that the *me*, the divine force or attribute, is drawn into the statue. While the statue may be thought of as a particular deity — Inanna, for instance, or Marduk — a multiplicity of celestial bodies are invoked and sacrifices are made to them in order to charge the statue with *me*. Is the god, then, an entire cosmological system? Or is it merely necessary to obtain the good graces of all the important celestial bodies in order that the consecration ritual proceeds normally and is successful?

It may alternatively be proposed that this complicated ritual was designed around a third purpose: that of following a mathematical pattern necessary for a human agent — in this case, the priest performing the ceremonies — to attain a level of power great enough to attract the *me* from the heavens. It is entirely possible that the priest himself was being prepared by all of these various sacrifices so that he would be able to take his place among the heavenly court and thereby assure the success of his ritual.

This concept was raised, albeit in a different context, by Tzvi Abusch, a noted Sumerologist who examined the *Maqlu* text of ancient Babylon (a manual of exorcism) with an eye toward discerning the spiritual transformation undergone by the exorcist who was interested in counteracting the evil effects of "witches," particularly on a specific day in the year when it was believed that the dead came back to haunt the living (in the fifth month, or *Abu,* of the Mesopotamian calendar, roughly equivalent to our August or zodiacal sign Leo).[25] According to Abusch, the exorcist — although not a priest like those involved in the Opening and Washing of the Mouth ceremonies but a lay practitioner — undergoes a ritual ascent to the heavens in order to identify himself with the stars[26] and in so doing utilize the heavenly powers to defeat the evil forces: those who have broken the *mamitu,* or the covenant, that exists between the heavens and the earth and who use supernatural power for malicious ends.

> The speaker identifies with the stars in order to become a messenger of the heavenly court. But there are other reasons, as well, for his identification with the gods of the night sky, the stars, and it is noteworthy that his transformation into a heavenly body belongs not only to the social sphere but at the same time also to the individual sphere. The actor is not only a messenger who takes on a social role and functions on a socio-cosmic level but also an individual who participates in a ritual and is thereby psychologically transformed.[27]

The purpose for this type of "ascent" therefore is practical and prophylactic rather than purely spiritual, for instance, in the sense that we understand the practices of the later *merkavah* mystics. The exorcist identifies with the astral realm and assumes "the guise of a star"[28] in order to contribute to the social realm by protecting others from the machinations of evil witches; what Abusch admits, however, is that such an experience must have its psychological component and generate effects on the psyche of the exorcist. This is amplified by the nature of the rites performed according to the *Maqlu* text, which requires that the exorcist stay awake all night and into the dawn — imitating the "wakefulness" of the stars — and remain outdoors, on the roof of his building, in the company of heaven. The incantations are directed upward, toward the stars.

The priests in the Opening and Washing of the Mouth rituals call down the power of the stars, the *me,* into the statue as a means of "charging" it, imbuing it with the divine force. In the rites of the *Maqlu* text, however, the exorcist ascends to the heavens and joins the company of heaven, partaking directly of the *me* himself.

As the priests perform elaborate sacrifices in complicated formulae — imitating, perhaps, the writing of the stars in the sky with a terrestrial "writing" composed of the numerous bowls of offerings specific to selected stars, planets, and constellations — he communicates with the heavens but never leaves the earth; the exorcist deliberately identifies himself with the heavens and becomes (however temporarily) a star. The priests were able to read the signs of the heavens and to interpret their meaning: the gods spoke to them through the medium of the constellations and other astronomical phenomena. The exorcist depended on direct experience of the heavens and on self-identification with the stars in order to wield the necessary power to defeat evil magic. According to Abusch, this entailed a "shaman-like" ascent to "both the heavens and the netherworld" to effect this transformation.[29]

This idea of ascending to the heavens, and specifically to seven heavens, is reflected in the *merkavah* texts of the Jewish mystics. While some have argued that this idea was relatively recent and came from Hellenistic sources, others have argued just as compellingly that this "technology" was derived from the Babylonians. If it was, in fact, a legacy of the Babylonian religion, then we have in our hands a clue as to the *merkavah* practices themselves and the various mystical and occult methodologies that derived from them. We have, therefore, a clue to the origins, techniques, and purpose of modern occult practice and theory.

Part Two

Merkavah Mysticism and Ascent

From an engraving published in 1624 by Daniel Stolcius in his *Viridarium Chymicum*. Note the seven stars above and the two cherubim.

T HE PURPOSE OF part 2 is to provide an analysis of the Jewish mystical technique known as *merkavah* or *hekhalot* mysticism, particularly with reference to the Dipper asterism and its associated stars. We will examine the Book of Ezekiel, as well as some relevant *merkavah* texts, and documents found among the Dead Sea Scrolls. We will end with a discussion of the constellation Ursa Major and the Dipper asterism as it is relevant to the overall structure of celestial ascent.

Chapter 3

The Vision of Ezekiel

The term *ma'aseh merkavah*, often translated as "works of the Chariot," refers to a specific mystical practice based on an interpretation of the first chapter of the Book of Ezekiel in the Hebrew Bible, the *Tanakh*. In this chapter, a mysterious vehicle is revealed to the prophet Ezekiel while in exile in Babylon. We are told that Ezekiel is near the banks of a river Chebar when, to the north, appears

> ... a whirlwind ... a great cloud, and a fire infolding itself, and a brightness was about it, and out of the midst thereof as the color of amber, out of the midst of the fire.
>
> Also out of the midst thereof came the likeness of four living creatures. And this was their appearance: they had the likeness of a man. And every one had four faces, and every one had four wings. (Ezek. 1:4–6)

After a lengthy description of the four creatures — the cherubim, which is a reference to the same cherubim that were carved atop the cover of the Ark of the Covenant in Solomon's Temple — and descriptions of angelic beings, there is another lengthy description of a wheeled vehicle (later referred to as the Chariot) and above this there is a throne or, to be more specific:

> And above the firmament that was over their heads was the likeness of a throne, as the appearance of a sapphire stone: and upon the likeness of the throne was the likeness as the appearance of a man upon it. (Ezek. 1:26)

Thus, what we have is a *likeness* of a throne and a *likeness* of an *appearance* of a man upon it.[1] Ezekiel falls upon his face and hears a voice speaking to him. This voice is full of recrimination against the children of Israel, which is interspersed with episodes of Ezekiel being transported amid the noise of the wheels of the vehicle. In chapter 8, he sees the appearance of the man once again; the throne reappears in chapter 10; and the Lord appears to Ezekiel continually through the rest of the chapters until by chapter 40 and for the rest of the book Ezekiel is shown the dimensions of a new Temple.

The essential characteristics of the Book of Ezekiel are thus the vision of the chariot, the cherubim, and the throne, and these compose the environment in which the voice of God is heard and a being that seems to represent the presence of God is seen. This environment is the background against which the prophecies of Ezekiel are received.

For some reason this unusual book became the focal point for generations of Jewish mystics who analyzed the book's contents in detail and expanded upon them to the extent that their written works would bear little resemblance to the original. This school of mysticism claimed to know the method by which Ezekiel obtained his famous visions and to be able to replicate these conditions and this method in order to duplicate Ezekiel's experience. Eventually, this school would become known as the "descenders to the Chariot" and the type of mysticism they practiced known variously as *hekhalot* (palace) mysticism or *merkavah* (chariot) mysticism.

There are a number of factors contributing to this vision that we should analyze, based on what we have seen in the earlier chapters. In the first place, this takes place in Babylon about the time of the destruction of the Temple of Solomon. Second, Ezekiel specifically states that he is standing by a river and looking north. Third, there is a chariot and a throne in the vision. Fourth, Ezekiel is himself a priest of the destroyed Temple. These are all elements that are crucial for an understanding not only of Ezekiel's vision itself but also of a continuous thread in the western esoteric tradition that has resonance with other ecstatic flights in other cultures, all of which may help us to understand the nature of spiritual transformation.

Ezekiel

The opening lines of the Book of Ezekiel are quite specific as to the date and place of the famous vision. It occurs during the fifth year of the captivity of King Jehoiachin, on the fifth day of the fourth month, which corresponds to July 28, 593 BCE. The place is Babylon, by the banks of the river Chebar. This last is a bit more problematic as it could be any one of several rivers, but is now thought to be the man-made canal Kabar which connected the city of Babylon with the city of Nippur, the most sacred city in the land of Sumer, which was dedicated to the god Enlil and which contained the holiest shrine in Sumer, the Ekur or "Mountain House." Further, what is important is the fact that the vision takes place at the riverbank, and that modern scholarship is of the opinion that Ezekiel lived at Nippur where there was a large concentration of Jewish exiles, some of whom were involved in the building of the canal as slave labor. We may remember from the previous chapter that the statues of the gods of Babylon were taken to the banks of rivers to be consecrated. They were transported there on wheeled carriages.

While this may or may not be relevant, it is at least consistent with what will follow.

Jerusalem fell to the Babylonians in the year 586 BCE and thus seven years after the vision of Ezekiel. However, the Babylonian king, Nebuchadnezzar, had already captured more than three thousand Jews and brought them to Babylon in the year 598 BCE, killing King Jehoiakim and putting the king's son, Jehoiachin, on the throne. This measure lasted only three months before Nebuchadnezzar changed his mind and brought another ten thousand Jews captive into Babylon in 597 BCE, including Jehoiachin, who remained in prison for another thirty-six years. The vision of Ezekiel takes place during this time. Jerusalem had not yet been utterly destroyed as it would be in 586 BCE, but much damage had already been done. The Babylonian king had murdered and enslaved many Jews and decimated the kingdom of Israel even before he sacked Jerusalem, destroyed the Temple, and removed its sacred treasures. He was known as a vicious and cruel tyrant and feared by everyone from the Egyptians to the Chaldaeans (the residents of Sumer, the biblical Shinar).

Ezekiel himself is described as the son of a priest, Buzi, which would make Ezekiel himself a priest, as the role is hereditary. Ezekiel's visions include a prediction of the destruction of the Temple as well as a detailed description of the new Temple that would be built in its place, a description that may have influenced Herod when he rebuilt the Second Temple in the first century BCE. As a priest, he would have had access to information that laypersons would not have had and he would have been proficient in liturgical practices, hymns, and sacrifices. In other words, he was a ritual expert and learned in religious doctrine. His vision, therefore, was not that of a layman or a rural Jew dazzled by the opulence of Solomon's Temple but that of an insider.

Babylon in the early sixth century BCE was at the height of its power and wealth; it had become a virtual empire by the year 625 BCE at the time of the fall of Nineveh and remained strong until the year 539 BCE when it fell to the Persians and began a gradual decline. Later, in 331 BCE, it would fall, finally, to Alexander the Great and nearly disappear as a political entity after Alexander's death when the Seleucid empire rose to prominence.

But at the time of Ezekiel, it was a place of marvels, ostentation, and extremes. One of its most notable features — to a displaced nation mourning the loss of its Temple — was the ziggurat, the famous temple complex discussed in the previous chapter and identified with the Tower of Babel in the Bible. The cities of Babylon were surrounded by walls and gates, and excavations have shown that some of these gates were decorated by marvelous figures, half-man and half-bird, known to archaeologists as "griffin demons," as well as half-man, half-lion figures and half-man, half-bull figures, many of these with wings.

Thus, the physical environment in which Ezekiel found himself had many notable features that were different from those he would have seen in his native Judah. The ziggurats with their several — as many as seven — levels; the processions of the gods in chariots to the banks of the river; the strange half-animal, half-human creatures that were depicted on gates, on tablets, and on ornamentation. He was also in a state of distress; he was a captive in this strange and brutal land, and he was unable to worship at the Temple in Jerusalem, which meant that he was unable to fulfill the requirements of his profession as a priest, and his obligation as a Jew. He was in a twilight zone between the land he had lost and the land where he lived as a captive, neither one thing nor another, a citizen of nowhere and the worshiper of an invisible God with a missing Temple.

The Book of Ezekiel may not have been completely written by him; there are portions that are thought to be later interpolations. However, the basic elements of the book are believed to be genuine and certainly appear to have the stamp of authenticity, especially as the date and place and circumstances of the first vision are so specific and the vision itself so bizarre as to be beyond any reasonable attempt at creating a literary device or pious allegory.

After the first three verses, which establish the date and place of the vision, the fourth verse begins "And I looked and behold a whirlwind came out of the north, a great cloud, and a fire infolding itself, and a brightness was about it, and out of the midst thereof as the color of amber, out of the midst of the fire."

Thus, we have an extra piece of information: the fact that the whirlwind comes out of the north.

The fifth and six verses tell us "Also out of the midst thereof came the likeness of four living creatures. And this was their appearance; they had the likeness of a man. And every one had four faces, and every one had four wings."

The four living creatures are described as having the faces of a man, a lion, an ox, and an eagle. And they had the "hands of a man under their wings on their four sides" (verse 8). So we have a creature that is part man and part lion, ox, and eagle. Four faces and four wings. This description could easily be attributed to the appearance of the Babylonian griffins we have already described.

The vision goes on to relate the appearance of wheels and of wheels within the wheels; these wheels had the ability to leave the earth, for as it says in verse 19: "And when the living creatures went, the wheels went by them: and when the living creatures were lifted up from the earth, the wheels were lifted up." For, as it says in verse 20, "the spirit of the living creature was in the wheels."

Ezekiel goes on to describe a "firmament" above the heads of the living creatures, and "above the firmament that was over their heads was the likeness of a throne, as the appearance of a sapphire stone: and upon the likeness of the throne was the likeness as the appearance of a man above upon it" (verse 26).

After listening to a voice tell him what to say to the house of Israel, Ezekiel returned to the captives by the banks of the river Chebar and sat there for seven days; at the end of the seven-day period, God spoke to him and told him to perform a number of actions and warned him of the destruction that was to come to Jerusalem.

In chapter 8, the vision comes again as before: the same presence as in the first chapter. This time Ezekiel is taken by the hair of his head and lifted up "between the earth and the heavens and brought... in the visions of God to Jerusalem, to the door of the inner gate that looketh toward the north" (verse 3).

In verse 5 of chapter 8, Ezekiel is told "lift up thine eyes now the way toward the north. So I lifted up mine eyes the way toward the north, and behold northward at the gate of the altar this image of jealousy in the entry." Ezekiel is thus told that foreign idols have been brought into the Temple, polluting it.

And in verse 14 of chapter 8, we read that Ezekiel is brought "to the door of the gate of the Lord's house which was toward the north; and behold, there sat women weeping for Tammuz." This, of course, is a reference to the mourning rites for Tammuz/Dumuzi, the husband/lover of Inanna/Ishtar who was condemned to his fate in the Underworld: a clear and unambiguous reference to the Babylonian religion that, according to Ezekiel, was then being observed in Jerusalem and even at the Temple of Solomon itself.

By verse 16, we read that twenty-five men could be seen facing the east and worshiping the rising sun, an "abomination" according to verse 17.

Something that certainly stands out quite clearly is the constant reference to the north in all of these verses — and in others to follow in the Book of Ezekiel. In fact, when the east is mentioned it is associated with rituals of the sun and therefore is an abomination. Ezekiel begins by facing the north from where the vision arrives. He is then taken on a tour of Jerusalem and the Temple, and always by the north gate and facing the north.

Then, even more mysteriously, in chapter 9, verse 2, we read that "six men came from the way of the higher gate, which lieth toward the north, and every man a slaughter weapon in his hand; and one man among them was clothed with linen, with a writer's inkhorn by his side: and they went in, and stood beside the brasen altar." They are told to go through the city of Jerusalem and mark the foreheads of those who lament the decadence and abominations, but to slay all the others who do not have that mark, beginning the massacre at the sanctuary of the Temple.

Chapter 10 begins with the appearance once again of the throne and the living creatures, explicitly referred to as the cherubim now throughout the chapter, with a reprise of the original vision. When the cherubim appear this time, however, they take up positions on the east gate of the Temple, where the twenty-five men were worshiping the sun. God then chastises the twenty-five and foretells of their impending doom, after which Ezekiel is brought back to Babylon and the vision left him and he began to speak to his fellow captives about the future of the people of Israel.

The episode of the six men is intriguing. They arrive from the north, the same direction brought constantly to Ezekiel's attention, but this time they bring death and destruction with them. The mark on the forehead of the righteous recalls the mark of Cain in Genesis and the mark of the Beast in the Apocalypse. The man with the inkhorn is evidently one of the six and not an extra man; indeed, he is expected to reach under the wheels of the cherubim and take burning coals, with which he sets fire to the city.

In every vision, however, Ezekiel finds himself returned to his place among the captives in Babylon. Thus, he faces north along the river and sees the chariot and the throne and the cherubim. He has a vision, usually quite explicit, and visits Jerusalem and the Temple. He then returns to captivity and relates what has transpired. This is the template for the procedure known as the "ascent to the Chariot," sometimes referred to, problematically, as the "descent to the Chariot."

It can be seen from this brief description that Ezekiel does not have a vision of seven heavens. This comes later and is an important addendum to the basic structure of the ascent literature. Further, the northerly direction is not stipulated in the *merkavah* texts either, although it was the most important focal point for Ezekiel himself, as was the northern gate of the Temple.

Also, while the description of the cherubim, the wheels, and the rising up from the ground seem to indicate a wheeled vehicle and hence a chariot, the word "chariot" itself is not used. Chariots are first encountered in the Bible in Genesis 41, where they are associated with the Egyptians and in this case with Joseph, who is given a chariot by the pharaoh. Chariots are usually mentioned in the context of engines of war and defense. They are mentioned several more times in the Bible, usually in large numbers either seized from an enemy or purchased through taxation. A king, of course, would ride into battle on his own chariot and just as often there would be a second chariot accompanying him in case it became necessary to abandon the first. It is pure speculation on my part, but the sight of two royal chariots when there was only one king could have given rise to the idea of "two powers in heaven" or even of Enoch/Metatron as a secondary power to God, sitting on his own throne in his own chariot.

In most respects, this basic template of Ezekiel's famous vision could be seen as borrowing heavily from Mesopotamian sources, from the chariot and Throne of God to the cherubim (griffin demons) that surround the chariot. The mythology of Sumer and Babylon, as we have seen, places importance on the north and on the northern constellation Ursa Major as symbolic of immortality and divinity, as well as of the divine power of *me*. Ezekiel's vision begins with a whirlwind arriving from the north, and the rest of his visions are similarly concerned with the north in various contexts.

Soon the people of Israel would be released from their captivity by the Persians and would return to Jerusalem. Centuries of intrigue and politics would follow. A new Temple would be built, and dissension would take place as the position of high priest became a bargaining chip, with disregard for the ancient establishment of a hereditary priesthood and replacing it with political appointees. In that environment, various messianic and apocalyptic sects would arise in the land. One of the most famous, if least understood, of these was the community that occupied a small encampment along the Dead Sea: the brotherhood of Qumran.

Qumran

We no longer expect to rebuild the Temple at Jerusalem. To us it has become but a symbol.

— Albert Pike, *Morals and Dogma*, 1871, Charleston[2]

When scholars such as the late Gershom Scholem began the first large-scale investigation of Jewish mysticism — from the early forms of *hekhalot* and *merkavah* documents to later Zoharic texts and post-Zoharic texts and movements — an initial difficulty lay in dating the materials under discussion and thereby establishing when Jewish mysticism first made its appearance in the culture. This remains an important and somewhat contentious point when it comes to determining whether Jewish mysticism influenced Gnosticism, or Jewish mysticism was a development of Gnostic thought. Scholem himself favored early, rather than later, dating (third to sixth century CE) for such texts as the *Sepher Yetzirah* and the *hekhalot* literature, basing this view on internal textual evidence rather than on the physical documents themselves since few were to be found dating earlier than the eleventh century CE. Other commentators since that time have favored later dating of the texts, although they admit that the ideas contained in them are ancient.

With the discovery of the Dead Sea Scrolls in 1947, however, we find ourselves in a better position to evaluate the existence of a *hekhalot* form of
Jewish mysticism that dates to the first century BCE–first century CE, and
to analyze the importance of these beliefs for later forms of Jewish mystical
practice and belief. In addition, we are faced with practices that clearly an-
ticipate the destruction of the Second Temple by building a "third Temple"
in the heavenly realms in the years prior to 70 CE.

Historical Background

Israel in the first century of the common era was an occupied territory. The
Romans considered it a colony and enjoyed an uneasy relationship with
the Jewish leaders. To make matters worse, the priesthood at the Temple,
rebuilt in elaborate and magnificent style by Herod the Great about 9 BCE,
were not descendants of the priestly bloodline but had consolidated secular
and sacred power into a single dynasty. These were the Hasmoneans, more
commonly referred to as the Maccabees.

The revolt of the Maccabees has been celebrated in the Bible and in the
liturgical calendar of the Jews. We can summarize the salient elements of the
first and second centuries BCE as follows.

In the century after the death of Alexander the Great in 323 BCE the Hellenic empire, both cultural and political, had extended far into the Middle
East, and Israel was no exception. Military struggles for control of the region
between the Egyptians and the Syrians led to the domination by Hellenized
Egyptians of Palestine by 301 BCE, and this remained the status quo until
the invasion of the Syrian King Antiochus III in 201 BCE, replacing the
Ptolemaic rulers with the Seleucids. Antiochus III permitted his Jewish sub-
jects to live according to their own laws; however, with the presence of the
Seleucids in Palestine, Jerusalem was in the process of becoming another
Hellenic capital.

Although Greek influence had been felt in the region since at least the
fourteenth century BCE, by the time of the Seleucid dynasty the process
of Hellinization had become complete, at least in the cities. Rural Jews,
who went to Jerusalem only to sell their products or to attend the holy day
celebrations at the Temple several times a year, remained relatively aloof
from Greek cultural influences. Urban Jews, however, reached various levels
of accommodation with the new paradigm to the extent that they were
interpreting Greek religion in terms of Judaism and Judaism in terms of
Greek religion and philosophy, giving rise to the appearance of Hellenistic
Judaism: a synthesis of Jewish religion and thought with borrowings from
Greek philosophy. Greek became the *lingua franca* of the region, and one
could not be considered educated if one did not speak it. This process would

reach its culmination in the phenomenon of Gnosticism, but before then a series of revolts against the Seleucids would change the complexion of Jerusalem and of Israel in general.

By the second century BCE, the priesthood in Jerusalem was in the process of becoming increasingly Hellenized. This had profound implications for the future of the Jewish religion, since the Hellenizers were interested in bringing Judaism into line with the pagan cults of Greece and its neighbors. With a new Seleucid king, Antiochus IV (also known as Epiphanes), ascending to the throne in 175 BCE, matters reached a boiling point. Antiochus IV decided to auction off the position of the Temple's high priest. This prize was awarded to Jason, a man who was not a member of the hereditary priesthood but a noted Hellenizer who turned Jerusalem into a Greek *polis*, putting it under Greek law and thus reversing the promise of Antiochus III to keep Jerusalem Jewish.

The final straw came in December of 167 BCE when Antiochus IV introduced pagan idols into the Temple and established sacred prostitution as part of the Temple apparatus. Previously, Hellenizers among the Jews had gone so far as to reinterpret the God of the Jews as another Zeus or Baal, and with that came the beginning of acceptance of the worship of these foreign gods; with the start of the persecutions of Antiochus IV, however, this "reinterpretation" was carried to its logical conclusion. The Temple had now become a pagan cult center, and all Jewish laws were abrogated, including kosher laws and circumcision, and all under penalty of death.

In order to combat this infamy, a Jewish family organized a revolt against the Seleucid rulers and their Jewish collaborators. This was the Hasmonean family, led by Judah the Maccabee ("hammer") and his four brothers. Beginning in the countryside, they managed to secure Judah for the opposition. In December of 164 BCE, they took Jerusalem itself and reconsecrated the Temple. This event is celebrated in the Jewish festival of Hanukkah (a word that means "rededication").

The war against the Seleucids and their Hellenized Jewish collaborators was not over yet, however, and the conflict continued until 152 BCE, when a Hasmonean brother, Jonathan, assumed the role of high priest of the Temple of Jerusalem to general acclaim and acceptance. The problem with this development was that the Hasmoneans were not hereditary priests, but the general population viewed the priestly families — the Zadokites, named after the high priest of the Temple in the time of David — as part of the problem.

It is true that many Zadokites were supporters of the Hellenic "reforms," whether out of genuine belief or because they felt they could consolidate their political position with the foreign rulers. Others, however, staunchly opposed the Greek and other foreign influences and insisted on maintaining Temple purity and the valid line of hereditary, priestly succession. The

Zadokites were referred to in the Scriptures and elsewhere by their more familiar name, the Sadducees, a derivative of "Zadok."

The other important Jewish sect at the time was the Pharisees. This group does not appear until the time of Jonathan, the Hasmonean high priest, and seem to represent an anti-Hellenistic movement of religious purists who were nevertheless interested in obtaining political power for themselves. They were generally opposed to the Sadducees, whom they understood to be unrepentant Hellenizers, although at times they were known to form loose alliances with them when it was convenient or expedient to do so. It is to the Pharisees that today's rabbis trace their spiritual lineage and not to the Sadducees, a fact whose importance becomes pertinent to this discussion.

Gradually, the Hasmonean rulers themselves came under criticism for their decadence and tendency toward those same Greek ideas and cultural attitudes that they had so vigorously opposed. By 63 BCE, of course, the political situation would have to be revisited because that was the year the Roman Empire took control of Palestine, replacing more than a century of Seleucid rule.

The antagonism between the Hasmoneans, the two groups of Sadducees — those who supported the Hasmoneans and those who did not — and the Pharisees would now be played out against a backdrop of Roman imperialism. It is within this complicated and contentious historical context that we encounter the Qumran group. Knowledge of this group and their famous library, what we call the Dead Sea Scrolls, came to light only in 1947 with the discovery of the Scrolls in a cave near the Dead Sea. It has taken years to translate the Scrolls and much scholarship has been directed toward deciphering their meaning and judging their importance for a clearer understanding of the Second Temple period. Among the Scrolls were found many of the books of the Bible, some of them in their earliest known incarnations, as well as other, nonbiblical literature and Apocrypha, including the Enochian texts, making the discovery of the Dead Sea Scrolls one of the most important finds in centuries of biblical scholarship. The Scrolls have perhaps raised more questions than answers, and paramount among these questions is the identity of the Qumran sect itself. Some are of the opinion that they were the mysterious Essenes, referred to in Josephus. Others believe they were Samaritans. And still others that they were a dissident sect of Sadducees, Zadokite priests, who opposed the Hasmonean oligarchy in Jerusalem.

Based on examination of several important documents found in the Scrolls[3] it is obvious that the Qumran group took the idea of ritual purity quite seriously and chastised the Temple priests for their lack of understanding of the halakhic[4] laws. They seemed to have created their own group of priests on the banks of the Dead Sea and enforced a strict regimen of purity.

People desiring to join the sect had to go through years of probationary status and could not eat or drink with the members until their purity status had been maintained and verified. One of the ritual points emphasized by the sect, and noted especially in the famous Halakhic Letter, is the contamination of pure water by pouring it into an impure vessel. The Qumranites believed that even if the vessel containing the water was pure, and even if the water itself was pure, if it was poured into an impure vessel the water would not only become impure but the vessel containing the pure water would itself become polluted. In other words, the impurity would "travel" up the flow of water into the pitcher, contaminating everything in its path.

This idea was taken to its logical conclusion in the induction of new members to the sect. It was only after a long period of study and observation that the new member was allowed to eat the pure food of the sect; after another year or so of novitiate, the member would finally be permitted to drink the pure water. This may be a demonstration of the ritual purity law discussed in the Halakhic Letter, for if an impure person drank the pure water would this not contaminate *all* the water of the sect?

Ideas and practices such as these, as well as their notorious opposition to the Hasmonean priesthood, have been used to characterize the Qumran sect as a group of dissident Zadokite priests: hereditary sacred rulers of the Temple. What is missing is definite proof that the Qumranites had hereditary priests among their number, for they did initiate others into the sect who were presumably not hereditary priests. Were they perhaps led by a Zadokite, who relaxed the rules on the sacred bloodline by enforcing a rigid set of purity laws?

One of the pieces of evidence used to support the idea that the Qumranites saw themselves as the lawful priests of the Temple is their preoccupation with the Temple itself and the visualization — there is perhaps no other word for it — of a heavenly Temple, populated by the members of the sect who are joined by angelic hosts in the Sabbath services. This "virtual Temple" has become the focus of a great deal of study, and it clarifies a number of important points that were previously mentioned in our discussion of the vision of Ezekiel and the *merkavah* texts.

Emergence of the "Virtual Temple"

We may safely say that it was Scholem who introduced the world to the texts of what would be called *hekhalot* and *merkavah* mysticism: that pre-Zoharic form of Jewish mystical practice and belief that is characterized by the terms *hekhalot* (or "palaces") and *merkavah* (or "chariot").[5] Based on interpretations of the Book of Ezekiel as well as on the Enochian literature, this system uses the idea of seven palaces or chariots as a structure for attaining communication with God. Some of the more famous texts include the *Hekhalot Rabbati* and the *Hekhalot Zutarti*. *Third Enoch* is also usually included in the *hekhalot* canon. How the texts are to be used is a subject of some controversy (as a meditative schema? as a ritual magic process?) and the dates of the texts are also subject to debate. Many scholars agree that the most authoritative of the *hekhalot* texts were written before the creation of the Zohar in Spain of the thirteenth century CE, perhaps as early as the second century CE. Just how old these texts really are — and how old is the system they represent — is a question that, if answered, will provide scholarship in this field with important new evidence for the existence of a secret form of worship and mystical practice that may have been inherited from the Babylonians during the Jewish Captivity and Exile in that country in the sixth century BCE.

Therefore, it was with great interest that traces of this literature were identified among the texts associated with the Qumran community, specifically with the Songs of the Sabbath Sacrifice. If it can be shown that *hekhalot*-type documents existed in the Dead Sea Scrolls corpus, then we are a long way toward understanding what the system means and how it was meant to be employed. Just as importantly, we may be able to trace its origins either among normative Jewish practice of the pre-Christian period or as something foreign to Judaism that was adopted by certain sectarians during the Captivity.

The *Hekhalot* and *Merkavah* Practices

Briefly, the *hekhalot* and *merkavah* practices are techniques that are designed to provide the practitioner with a vision of the heavenly realms: specifically, of the Throne of God located in a heavenly Palace or Temple. The term *hekhalot* refers to a series of seven palaces (sing. *hekhal*) that constitutes the structure of the vision; that is to say, one proceeds from one palace to the next, like levels in a computer game, until one approaches the Divine Throne. The term *merkavah* translates as "chariot," and it represents a series of seven chariots or, alternatively, a single chariot that is divided into seven chambers. This refers to the vision of Ezekiel (Ezek. 1 and 10), which consisted of the appearance of God (or a God-like being) sitting on a throne that was also a chariot, with various supernatural beings, the cherubim, in attendance. This vision may have been a confabulation of memories of the First Temple of Jerusalem with that of the temple architecture seen in Babylon, where Ezekiel was captive.

Those who dared to imitate Ezekiel and attempt to see the vision for themselves are sometimes described as "descenders to the Chariot," a term that is itself enigmatic, but that may be a somewhat more recent designation.[6] The practice was considered dangerous, and even the biblical vision of Ezekiel itself was something that was not permitted to be discussed freely among the Jews of the rabbinic period after the destruction of the Second Temple in 70 CE.[7]

It is the author's suggestion that the practices covered under the general rubric of *hekhalot* and *merkavah* mysticism had their foundations in the Second Temple period, and that there is evidence in the Dead Sea Scrolls that would support such a contention. Further, it is the author's belief that the destruction of the First Temple was such a traumatic experience for the Jewish people that the Second Temple could be viewed only as a poor substitute, particularly as the essential Temple implements and relics, most notably the Ark of the Covenant, had disappeared after the sack of the Temple by the Babylonians and *are never referred to again*. The disappearance of the Tablets themselves would have constituted a breach in the physical connection enjoyed between God and the Jewish people and would have contributed to (if not instigated) the mystical practices of envisioning a divine Temple, a Temple of the (sacred and purified) imagination: one that could not be sacked or destroyed. Indeed, with the disappearance of the Temple and its implements, the need to locate the Temple in another realm of experience would have been strong. It became, in essence, a phantom limb of the Jewish people.

This concept would have lent itself easily to the extramural philosophy and mentality of the Qumranites, who already disagreed with the Second Temple practices current at the time and who seemed to regard the Hasmonean priesthood as illegitimate. Their eschatological and mystical works — represented, among others, by the Songs of the Sabbath Sacrifice and the Temple Scroll — would seem to support an idea that they had already given up on the Second Temple (had seen it as basically nonexistent for their purposes) and were busy creating a mental and spiritual version of the Temple in their rituals, their daily practices, and their scriptural writings. As Carol Newsom writes in her critical analysis of the Songs of the Sabbath Sacrifice (Sabbath Shirot):

> The Sabbath Shirot differ from many of the contemporary texts which refer to the heavenly temple in that they devote much more attention to the details of the structure of the heavenly sanctuary, its priesthood, holy vestments, etc.[8]

This would indicate a desire to imagine the Temple as clearly as possible, almost in the manner of the medieval "theater of memory," which was itself a mental practice associated with mysticism and the occult.[9]

Rachel Elior seems to concur with this idea when she writes:

Ezekiel...transformed the ruined Temple into a heavenly Chariot
Throne with cherubim, wheels, and sacred creatures, facing the four
corners of the earth, similar to their plastic representations drawn and
sculpted in the Temple.... In the Second Temple period, a time of controversy and strife, the Zadokite priests, who play a key role as divinely
nominated priests in Ezekiel's vision of the future (chapters 40–48),
revived the priestly prophet's Merkavah vision, perpetuating the angelic sacred service in the supernal Heikhalot [sic]. They engineered
the mystical and ritual revival after being deprived of their right to
minister in the sanctuary as high priests, toward the end of the first
third of the second century BCE.[10]

Thus we have a disenfranchised priesthood, removed from the physical
Temple, re-creating its glory in their ritual, in their ecstatic visions, and in
their imagination.

The Songs of the Sabbath Sacrifice

The Songs of the Sabbath Sacrifice number a total of only thirteen songs in
even the most preserved of the scrolls, which would seem to indicate that
there were only thirteen ever written, and these for the first thirteen sabbaths
of the year (which contains fifty-two weeks and hence fifty-two sabbaths).
They were to be sung or recited on the sabbath — one song for each succeed-
ing sabbath — and a kind of spiritual excitement would build from sabbath
to sabbath as the songs became increasingly joyous, reached a peak at the
seventh sabbath, and then gradually wound down to the thirteenth (with
the sequence presumably begun again on the fourteenth sabbath, although
this has not been proven).

An examination of the text of these songs[11] indicates that the congregation is expected to concentrate on the specifics of the Temple and its
priesthood during the cycle of thirteen psalms. The first sabbath song addresses the concept of the priesthood and its purity, and thereby the purity
of the Temple. The second sabbath song compares the angelic priesthood to
the human priesthood, thus establishing a connection between the earthly
and the heavenly realms. The third sabbath song is too fragmentary to describe with any certainty, and the fourth sabbath song aside from references
to "strong warriors" and "councils of rebellion," is also fragmentary. Only
the very end of the fifth sabbath song has been preserved, with references to
"a war in heaven" along with the "mustering of angelic hosts," themes that
appear to be common to Qumranite eschatology.

It is with the sixth and seventh songs that we approach something close to
the mysticism of Ezekiel and of the *hekhalot* and *merkavah* traditions. This

is to be seen not only in the descriptions of the Throne of God and of the Temple itself, along with its angelic priesthood, but also in the repetition of the number seven in various contexts. What we see in these songs is a kind of group meditation on the *hekhal* and *merkavah* (indeed, the plural for *merkavah* — *merkavot* — appears in the seventh song) that may be the forerunner of the mystical practices that would be written down as individual techniques in later centuries.

A look at some relevant hymns is in order:

The sixth song, from 4Q403 1 i 1–4:

Psalm of exaltation by the tongue of the third of the chief princes, an exaltation <of His faithfulness to the King of angels with its seven wondrous exaltations; he will exalt> the God of the lofty angels seven times with seven words of wondrous exaltations.

Psalm of praise by the tongue of the fou[rth] to the Warrior who is above all [heavenly beings] with its seven wondrous powers; and he will praise the God of power seven times with seve[n] words of [wondrous] prais[e. Psa]lm of [th]anksgiving by the tongue of the fif[th] to the [K]in[g] of glory with its seven wondrous thanks[gi]vings; he will give thanks to the God of glory s[even times with seven wo]rds of wondrous thanksgivings.[12]

This series of exaltations continues for the remainder of the sixth song. What is noteworthy is the constant repetition of the number seven, a number sacred as well in the *hekhalot* literature with its emphasis on seven chariots, seven palaces, seven chambers, etc., and the idea of seven "words," a concept that will reach greater fulfillment in the *hekhalot* texts with their *voces magicae* and the words of power associated with each of the seven levels of the divine presence.

The twelfth song is even more specific in its imitation of the details in Ezekiel's vision:

4Q405 20–21–22, col ii:

[They do not delay when they arise ... the deb]irim of all the priests of the inner sanctum [...]

By [strict ordinance they] are steadfast in the ser[vice of ...] a seat like His royal throne in [His glorious debirim. They do not sit ...]

His glorious chariot(s) [...] holy cherubim, luminous ophanim in the de[bir ... spirits of godlike beings ... purity] ... of holiness, the construction of [its] cor[ners ...] royal ...] the glorious seats of the chariot th[rones ... wings of knowledge ... wondrous powers ...] truth and righteousness, eternal ...] His glorious chariots as they move ... [they do not turn to any side ... they go straight ...][13]

This song continues in much the same vein, reinforcing many of the more startling images of Ezekiel, including the appearance of streams of fire, of wondrous colors, the wheels of the chariot, etc. The importance of these songs rests in the recitation of Ezekiel's visions as liturgical texts, meant to be recited aloud even though they contain no discernable theological or spiritual instruction, and even though Ezekiel's visions would themselves be considered too dangerous to discuss in public by the rabbis. This indicates either a degree of recklessness that we are reluctant to assign to the Qumranites or an earnest approach to the Divine that they deemed necessary due to their circumstances as a group cut off from the physical Temple in this time so close (as they saw it) to the End of Days.

Schiffman argues that even though the *Songs* contain many elements that are identical to later *hekhalot* literature — extending even to the prose style, such specifics as the seven archangels and the multiplicity of sevens, and the overall content — he does not believe that the *Songs* were intended to be mystical texts but rather mere descriptions of the heavenly Throne and the angelic hosts, perhaps to be recited in liturgical settings.[14] An argument against that position may be that the *Songs* were intended for a group experience rather than individual mystical practice, and that the later *hekhalot* literature was an adaptation from the group work for personal use (thus secret, i.e., beyond rabbinic authority). If we are to accept the general view that rabbinic Judaism is a survival of Pharisaic Judaism and that the mystical technology of *hekhalot* and *merkavah* practice was proscribed by the rabbis, then we may wonder if the Qumranites, arguably more Sadducean than Pharisaic, had developed or preserved this technology as a reaction to what they saw as the degeneration of Temple practice under the Hasmonean priesthood, and the *hekhalot* literature as a survival of priestly Judaism versus rabbinic Judaism. Indeed, such a focus and concentration on the Temple, the divine Throne, the *cherubim*, *ophanim*, and *merkavot* indicate a longing for the priestly service rather than a less emotional and more pragmatic acceptance of the loss of the Temple (either to the Hasmoneans, who were not in the legitimate Sadducean bloodline, or to its actual physical destruction by the Romans in 70 CE).

Scholem has argued that the language of the *hekhalot* texts is diametrically opposed to that of the Talmud:

It cannot be denied that this "polylogy," or verbiage, of the mystics, these magniloquent attempts to catch a glimpse of God's majesty and to preserve it in hymnical form, stands in sharp contrast to the tendencies which already during the Talmudical period dominated the outlook of the great teachers of the Law. They could not but feel repelled by it, and in the Talmud one early encounters a strong dislike for extravagant enthusiasm in prayer.[15]

Thus, we can see that we are dealing with two different camps with two entirely different approaches to spirituality, yet both operating within the paradigm of Judaism: the legalistic/pharisaic/rabbinical/Talmudic strain versus the mystical/Sadducean/Qumranite strain. But does the kind of Jewish mysticism we are discussing find a manifestation in the centuries-later *hekhalot* technology?

Other Approaches

Rebecca Macy Lesses has compared the purity obsession of the Qumranites to that of the "descenders to the Chariot" of the *hekhalot* workings.[16] In a chapter entitled "Ascetic Preparations for Hekhalot Adjurations" she notes that the *hekhalot* mystics had to maintain a strict state of purity for a fixed length of time for they were going to be in the company of the angels. Although the length of time required of the *hekhalot* mystics was finite and depended only upon the performance of the required rituals, the purity required of the Qumranites was permanent and extended throughout their life as members of the community. This purity extended especially to sexual relations and to seminal emissions, which were considered impure and polluting,[17] and both were concerned with being in the presence of angelic forces who were therefore pure for they did not eat, drink, or engage in sexual intercourse. Indeed, Lesses has traced this impulse toward purity to one common problem faced by both the *hekhalot* mystics and the Qumranites: "the inaccessibility of the holiness of the Jerusalem temple."[18]

From a different perspective, Naomi Janowitz has analyzed the language of the *hekhalot* literature, treating specifically the text known as *ma'aseh merkavah* ("The Work of the Chariot"), and has pointed out the peculiarity of its syntax:

> The systematic violation of normal language use, that is, phrases and other linguistic combinations that are not predictable according to ordinary rules of language, is found throughout the [*Ma'aseh Merkavah*]. ...Phrases often are not used to build sentences, words often are not used to make a standard sentence, but instead are used in a variety of unusual phrases.[19]

Compare this to Schiffman when he writes of the Songs of the Sabbath Sacrifice:

> The peculiar literary style of these texts is typical of later *Hekhalot* literature, demonstrating that behind these later mystical texts is a long

tradition.... When we analyze the text's sentence structure, characteristic of later *Hekhalot* texts as well, we find frequent use of participles,
a startling paucity of verbs, and chains of nouns that frequently defy efforts to parse them into discrete phrases and clauses. Such unstructured
syntax leaves a strange impression on the reader, a sense of spiritual
intoxication stimulated largely by the constant flow of praise.[20]

This type of writing indicates either the existence of a specific literary
genre or writing *designed to elicit a specific response*. The fact that both the
Songs and the *ma'aseh merkavah* (for instance) utilize a very similar, if not
identical, literary technique indicates that they were used for a very similar,
if not identical, purpose. Both were focused on the Temple and a vision
of God in his glory, surrounded by his angelic priesthood. Both utilized a
nonnarrative style, building up tension by the use of phrases and nouns
that were not tied together in any formal sentence structure but that were
designed to cause a break in the normal flow of conscious thought, thought
that was projected outward and upward: in the direction of a Temple that
did not exist on earth.

Both these texts contain highly charged, emotional prose/poetry and create an environment of sanctity and ecstatic vision. These are not texts that
elaborate upon the Law, or repeat biblical tales of the prophets or the history of the people of Israel; they are not narratives or instructions. Rather,
they are staccato chants of praise, reinforcing the link between human beings and angels, between the earthly priesthood and its divine counterpart,
reinforced with ritual purity and asceticism, and a palpable sense of longing
for the lost Temple that was their birthright and their responsibility to their
faith and to the people of Israel. It is a throwback of five hundred years
to the Babylonian Captivity and the vision of Ezekiel on the banks of the
Chebar River, a vision tormented by the loss of the greatest treasure Israel
had ever possessed: the Ark of the Covenant and the Temple of Solomon.

To the Qumranites, it is proposed, the loss of the Second Temple was
already apparent; to the "descenders to the Chariot" who came later, the
Third Temple had already been built.

Chapter 4

Ezekiel and the Apocalypse

Shortly after the destruction of the Second Temple by the Romans in 70 CE, and decades after the death of Jesus, a text was composed that more than any other in the canonical literature duplicates many of the themes of the vision of Ezekiel. Coming out of the environment of the Jews who were followers of Jesus — and allegedly written by one of Jesus' apostles, John — the Book of Revelation, or Apocalypse, demonstrates a fixation on bizarre images and cryptic references. Like the Book of Ezekiel, it is a book of prophecy and warning. It is the source of one of our most famous biblical references: the Mark of the Beast, which is "the number of a man; and his number is Six hundred three-score and six" (Rev. 13:18).

It is also a text obsessed with the number seven. Chapter 1, verse 4 consists of the statement, "John to the seven churches which are in Asia; Grace be unto you, and peace, from him which is, and which was, and which is to come; and from the seven Spirits which are before his throne." Thus, we immediately have the image of seven spirits before the throne. In verse 12 we read of seven candlesticks. In verse 13 we learn of the appearance "in the midst of the seven candlesticks one like unto the Son of man"[1] who is described as holding in his right hand "seven stars" (Rev. 1:16). The seven stars are identified as "the angels of the seven churches" (Rev. 1:20).

By chapter 4, we read that "a door was opened in heaven" and "immediately I was in the spirit; and behold, a throne was set in heaven, and one sat on the throne" (Rev. 4:1–2). Before the throne were burning seven lamps of fire, "which are the seven Spirits of God" (Rev. 4:5).

The author of the Apocalypse then goes on to describe the cherubim, much as Ezekiel had described them, except that in John's version the cherubim have six wings rather than four. Otherwise, they are virtually identical: a lion, a calf, a man, and an eagle.

In chapter 5, we read of the famous book of seven seals. In chapter 8, of the seven angels and their seven trumpets, etc., etc.

Much ink has been spilled in an attempt to identify all of the themes and decode all of the cryptic utterances of the Book of Revelation. In addition, several films have been made in the last few years that have Revelation as their theme and that focus on the End of Days and the Final Judgment.[2] The prophecies of the Book of Revelation are a major concern of the Christian Evangelical movement, which has given us the concept of "Rapture": the moment when the righteous will be directly and immediately transported to heaven without warning, leaving the rest of us behind — a modern Christian version of the descent to the Chariot.

If we see the Book of Revelation as being firmly in the tradition of Ezekiel and referencing many of the themes in the Song of Sabbath Sacrifice as well as in the later *merkavah* literature, then we can posit a kind of continuum of ideas that helped to form later Christian and even Gnostic concepts of heaven and the means of getting there. John was self-consciously imitating the Book of Ezekiel in many ways, from the vision of the throne in heaven and the cherubim to the dire warnings given of desperate times to come. What is perhaps missing from Ezekiel but present in Revelation is the use of the number seven and its association with spirits, angels, and the heavenly throne, a concept that may have been borrowed from the teachings of Qumran, which themselves may have been inherited from a somewhat older source.

Playing the Sevens

There is one biblical precedent for the importance of the number seven, and that appears in Genesis. In chapter 1 of Genesis we learn how God created the world in six days and in chapter 2 how God rested on the seventh day. This became the biblical template for the week of seven days, with the Sabbath day, the day of rest, falling on the last, the seventh, day. Most of the rest of the Old Testament usage of seven as significant comes from this divine institution of the seven-day week as emblematic of creation itself.

This is a construction most western people take for granted. It seems obvious and self-evident: weeks have seven days. Yet other cultures around the world did not, and many still do not, use the same type of calendar as was and is used in the West. There are calendar systems with multiple ways of calculating "years," some of which have weeks of five days (for instance). Some calendars are purely lunar-based, which give thirteen "months" during a single solar year rather than the twelve solar months to which we are accustomed. One the island of Java in Indonesia one can have as many as three calendars running simultaneously: the solar Gregorian calendar, the lunar Islamic calendar, and an indigenous Javanese calendar with a five-day week. Thus, a four-week month consisting of seven days per week is not a given; it is an invention.

That is not to say that the number seven does not have special significance, even for cultures that do not share our calendar system. The fact that some cultures viewed the number seven as sacred or important in some way regardless of the fact that their calendars did not reflect this is extremely relevant to our study and, in fact, helps to prove it.

Much of what we use in our everyday calculations of time and numbers has been inherited from the ancient Middle East. They are conventions. For instance, the 360-degree circle is a religious convention: it was a sacred number to the Babylonians, six times the perfect number sixty. It could just as easily have been a 100-degree circle, or a 365-degree circle or any other number.

The same is true of our week. It was noted that the moon completes its cycle of new moon–full moon–new moon in about 28 days. The sun went through one sign of the zodiac in about 30 days. But the year had a little less than 365 days. That meant that the lunar cycle would give us 13 "moons" or months in one solar year of 365 days. That was a pretty big disconnect between one calendar and the other, with the result that Jewish, Islamic, and many Asian calendars, all of them lunar-based, do not have holidays falling on the same solar calendar day every year. Thus, Passover, Hanukkah, Ramadan, and Chinese New Year always fall on different days and months each year (although, within the context of their respective lunar calendars, they always fall on the *same* day each lunar year).

If a lunar month consists of twenty-eight days, then a sensible division of those twenty-eight days would seem to be four weeks of seven days each. It could just as easily have been seven weeks of four days each, or two weeks of fourteen days each, etc., but the four-week/seven-day model stuck. However, that is really only good for the lunar calendar. A solar calendar, consisting of thirty-day "months," could have been divided differently into five weeks of six days, or six weeks of five days, etc., etc. There still would have been five days left unaccounted for each year, and efforts were made to include intercalary days (days that fell between two years and were observed as a holiday) in the older calendars to make them "come out right."

The point of all this is to demonstrate that the choice of a seven-day week is really rather arbitrary and was by no means universal. Elaborate calendrical schemes of interlocking "years" of various lengths were developed by the Aztecs and the Mayans, for instance, to account for a wide variety of astronomical phenomena.[3]

In the West, however, the ancient civilizations of the Middle East gave us our basic calendar system and eventually the twelve months as well as the twelve signs of the zodiac on which they are based. There was still tremendous tension between the lunar and solar calendars, however, and this led to some conflict between the Qumran sect mentioned in chapter 3 and their Hasmonean counterparts in Jerusalem, for the latter used the lunar calendar that is now employed by the Jewish people while the former used a solar calendar to compute the same religious holidays such as Passover and

Yom Kippur (the Qumranites do not appear to have celebrated Hanukkah, another piece of evidence to show that they were either anti-Hasmonean or, as some have suggested, Samaritans who did not observe Hanukkah either). Thus, calendars were serious business at that time and represented hardened religious positions. The division of time into sacred time was just as important as the division of space into sacred space, i.e., the geographical area of the dimensions of the Temple.

The Babylonians understood temples to be not only sacred space — what anthropologist Victor Turner called the *temenos*[4] — but also a cosmological system representing sacred time, as well. As the sun rose in the east and set in the west, it rose at the eastern gate and set at the western gate of the temple. The temple became a place where time and space met, where one experienced four dimensions and not only three. When holidays were celebrated at the temple, this space-time continuum became even more pronounced as the *temenos* became charged with the *me* of the stars at a specific time on a specific day in that very specific place.

In the Book of Revelation, the Throne of God is in the heavens, and it is surrounded by the seven Spirits, which are also seven "lamps." The sacred space of the earthly temple is duplicated in the heavens or, rather, vice versa with the human agents of the gods — the priests — replicating the celestial order on earth. This mutuality between heaven and earth is acknowledged by the famous opening lines of the Emerald Tablet of Hermes Trismegistus, probably the inspiration for the *Corpus Hermeticum,* which was translated in Italy in the fifteenth century: "That which is above is like that which is below, and that which is below is like that which is above, for the performance of the wonders of the one thing." It had been repeated in the famous charge of Jesus Christ to Simon Peter: "Whatsoever you bind on earth shall have been bound in heaven, and whatever you loose on earth shall have been loosed in heaven" (Matt. 16:19). As such, we have both pagan and Christian precedent for the idea that there is a link, a covenant, a connection between the earth and the heavens, between terrestrial powers and celestial forces. The *imitatio dei* was also and most clearly an *imitatio coeli:* if one could forge a link between the human operator and the actions of the stars, then one became as a god.

On a technical level, this was accomplished by identifying sacred space and time and if necessary by organizing and manipulating space and time so that it was a perfect image of the celestial order, bringing terrestrial objects and actions into alignment with the stars, and thus consecrating it. Thus, to the *temenos* of Victor Turner we must add an *eventus:* the sacred space is nothing without sacred time, and the co-incidence of sacred space and time results in an *eventus,* a sacred event that partakes of both species.

We associate Mecca with the birth of Islam; it is a sacred space, particularly the Ka'aba, and it is the focal point of prayer five times a day, and of pilgrimage one month a year. The town of Bethlehem is sacred as the birthplace of Jesus, an event that was identified as taking place on December 25 (although we know now this date is in error) and aligned with the pagan celebrations connected with the Saturnalia and with the rites of Mithra. Dealey Plaza, in Dallas, Texas, is sacred in the sense of popular religion as the site where a president was martyred on November 22, 1963. Sacred places are made sacred by events that take place in time; there is a relationship between them that transcends three dimensions, and even, it could be argued, four dimensions for scriptural literature is replete with instances of prophets traveling vast distances while "in the vision," only to return a moment later, believing they had been gone for hours, days, or even years.

To the Qumranites, the sacred calendar was associated with the Temple sacrifices. The problem was that they did not have access to the Temple in Jerusalem. Either because they had abandoned Jerusalem due to the decadence of the cult practices there, or were asked to leave, is irrelevant to this argument. What is important is that we have a group of priests who have no sacred space. Yet they are obsessed with the Temple and its rituals. For whatever reason the physical Temple is lost to them, but they create forceful and beautiful liturgies that celebrate the Temple in ecstatic terminology focused on the number seven and the visualization of beings and objects in groups of seven throughout. This is a theme that is picked up again and amplified in the Apocalypse of John.

The number seven has often been thought to refer to the seven "planets," which the ancients considered as Mercury, Venus, Mars, Jupiter, Saturn, the Sun, and the Moon. The latter two are not planets, of course. The sun is the star around which our solar system revolves; the moon revolves around the earth as its satellite. Yet it is often assumed that the ancients considered these seven identical in their basic nature as planets. This was due to the fact that the planets are seen to "wander" in the heavens against a backdrop of the fixed stars of the zodiac. They were seven anomalies and therefore were grouped together as a set.

That the ancients did not consistently identify the sun and moon as planets among planets, however, can be demonstrated by a look at some of the cylinder seals and other art of the Sumerian, Akkadian, and Babylonian periods. In addition, groups of seven stars are clearly depicted on other seals, and these are sometimes thought to refer to the Pleiades. The *Epic of Gilgamesh* refers to seven ancient antediluvian beings, the Seven Sages, or *apkallu*, who helped build the city of Uruk and who are definitely not identified with the seven "planets." The Seven Gods, or *sebittu* ("the seven"), are also a feature of Babylonian religion and are invoked as protection against demons. As these various incarnations of seven do not refer to planets and are not associated with planets, we must look elsewhere for possible correspondences.

In the Book of Revelation, the Seven Spirits are not identified with planets. The sun and moon appear in other contexts, however, and are nowhere linked with these seven angelic beings who surround God's Throne.

What is probably most telling in a modern context is the identification of the Book of Revelation with the Book of Ezekiel by such influential occult or "New Age" authors as Eliphas Levi — one of the more important gurus of the occult renaissance that took place in the mid-nineteenth century — who discussed this comparison in a book published after his death and entitled *The Mysteries of the Qabalah or Occult Agreement of the Two Testaments.* The "Two Testaments" of the title refer to Ezekiel and Revelation.

This book is largely a commentary on the two texts in the form of illustrations and brief remarks. The illustrations themselves are enigmatic, and those appearing in the commentary on Ezekiel depict various Assyrian images as well as one of Nergal, the Babylonian god of war, thus establishing the connection between Ezekiel's vision and his Babylonian environment. There are references to the Kabbalah, of course, as well as to the Sephirotic Tree.[5]

The commentary on Revelation is equally cryptic in places. There is a seal on one page entitled "The Moon among the Seven Planets" which doesn't seem to make sense if the moon was considered one of the planets. It shows a crescent moon surrounded not by planets but by seven stars.

Levi did point out one other obvious point of similarity between Ezekiel and Revelation, and that is both books finish with detailed descriptions of a new Temple in a New Jerusalem. If we consider that both authors *also* describe the same fantastical cherubim, a divine throne, and what can only be characterized as a celestial ascent, we are then forced to accept that Revelation is a self-conscious imitation of the Book of Ezekiel. If so, it perhaps offers us the first real *merkavah* text, especially as Revelation adds the mysterious insistence on the celestial importance of the number seven, a phenomenon that will become much more pronounced in the *merkavah* tradition of later centuries.

Ezekiel's vision took place after the loss of Jerusalem and the loss of the Temple, which would soon be destroyed by the armies of Nebuchadnezzar, the king of Babylon, where he was held captive. John's vision took place after the second loss of Jerusalem and the second loss of the Temple. Both visionaries imagined a new Temple and a new Jerusalem. Was the Apostle John, putative author of Revelation, a descender to the Chariot?

Had John indeed been a "descender," then we would have a convenient Christian model for this otherwise uniquely Jewish practice. Unfortunately, we may never know for certain. There is even controversy surrounding the authorship of Revelation and most especially the coded and cryptic references in it. But everything in Revelation seems to happen in sevens — seven spirits, seven angels, seven trumpets, seven seals, seven cups — a number that was prefigured in the Songs of the Sabbath Sacrifice of the Qumranites and their secret society on the banks of the Dead Sea. The theme recurs in the *merkavah* and *hekhalot* literature as essential to understanding the structure of heaven and how to approach God's Throne.

Therefore, it would be wise at this juncture to look at the *merkavah* texts themselves in some detail to see what they are trying to tell us.

Chapter 5

Ezekiel's Vision as
Template for Mystical Ascent

According to Kabbalah authority Joseph Dan, between the day of creation and the year 1960 only three books had been published on the subject of *merkavah* mysticism.[1] These were a book by Hugo Odeberg, a Swiss priest who lumped the *Sepher Hekhalot* (one of the "canon" of *merkavah* texts) with the biblical Apocrypha, thus ensuring that it would be viewed as outside the Jewish mainstream; a work by Heinrich Graetz, who dismissed Jewish mystical practices as nothing more than corrupting influences from Islamic sources in the Geonic period; and, of course, the seminal work by Gershom Scholem, *Major Trends in Jewish Mysticism*, which first appeared in 1941. Up until the nineteenth century, then, the *merkavah* practices were virtually unknown outside of small circles of Kabbalists who were not publishing in academic journals but instead actually practicing the technique of "descending to the Chariot."

With the publication of Scholem's work, however, the floodgates were opened and more and more works began to appear on this fascinating and somewhat controversial subject with a flurry of books and articles in peer-reviewed publications struggling to interpret this literature and to understand its relevance for Jewish and Christian studies. With the discovery of the Cairo Genizah at the end of the nineteenth century followed by the discovery of the Dead Sea Scrolls in Israel in 1947, new impetus was given to serious scholarship on the subject of what came to be known as "ascent literature": texts dealing with the idea that one could say the right prayers or perform the correct rituals or otherwise engage in mystical practices — chanting, weeping, or other forms of the *dereglement de tous les sens* — and thereby ascend to the heavens to the very Throne of God.

References to heavenly ascents were not unknown prior to the nineteenth century, however. St. Paul refers to "a man in Christ" who ascended "to the third heaven" (2 Cor. 12:2). In the Qur'an, oblique references are made to an ascent of the Prophet to the seven heavens; it is described in more detail in the Hadith as the *Mi'raj*.[2] The Enochian literature itself was emblematic of many of the themes encountered in the more formulaic *merkavah* texts, such as the structure of the heavens, the divine Throne, and the enigmatic figure of Enoch himself, the one who lived for 365 years and "walked with God" and "he was not, for God took him" (Gen. 5:22–24), thus implying that Enoch ascended to heaven in bodily form. In the New Testament, the Epistle of Jude states that Enoch was "the seventh from Adam" (Jude 14). These two numbers give us some pause, for 365 of course is the number of days in a solar year; 365 was also the number given to the Gnostic archon Abraxas, or Abrasax, since the numbers of his name (in Greek numerology) add to 365. Further, the depiction of Abraxas was virtually identical to that of the Mithraic deity Chronos, or Time: a fitting comparison. The statement that Enoch was the "seventh from Adam" only serves to reinforce what has already been said about the importance of the number seven in biblical and Babylonian literature.

Enoch has been identified with an important *merkavah* figure, Metatron, the "Angel of the Presence," who seems to represent an "angelized" Enoch. If Enoch, a human being, was brought to heaven bodily (as was, we should remember, the Prophet Elijah) then the precedent was established for human interaction with the Other World.

It should be recognized that Genesis itself provides us with several examples of the impossibility of humans "storming heaven" and ascending to the throne. The Tower of Babel is probably our best example of the futility of the ascent; but the story of the Garden of Eden is another example. When the Serpent tempted Eve and said, "Ye shall be as gods" (Gen. 3:5), he suggested the possibility of sharing in the divine power; yet Eve's attempt to do so was met with the expulsion of both her and Adam from Paradise. It would seem that God frowns on human initiative where bodily assumption into the celestial regions is concerned.

Such would be the conservative theological response to the *merkavah* literature and one reason why these practices were proscribed by the rabbinic authorities. The only times that humans successfully attained the celestial heights was when God specifically initiated the process, such as in the ascent of Moses up Mount Sinai to meet God and receive the commandments, or God taking Enoch or Elijah to heaven, or appearing to Ezekiel by the banks of the Chebar.

That humans can "storm heaven" on their own initiative is the foundation of the *merkavah* literature, however, even though this position seems to test the limits of Jewish law. The early Jewish commentators specified that the Book of Ezekiel could not even be discussed, along with the Book of Genesis and the Song of Songs. *Merkavah* techniques were specifically forbidden, and the example of the "four who entered the Pardes" is given as a warning of what might happen to those who dare to approach God directly.

The Garden

In chapter 2 we read of the Babylonian ritual of the Washing of the Mouth that took place at several different sites: the house of the craftsmen, where the statue of the god was made; the riverbank; the garden; and then, finally, the temple, itself. In the course of this three-day ritual, the statue was transported on a wagon or chariot.

This seems to duplicate many of the themes we encountered in the vision of Ezekiel and what we will find in the subsequent *merkavah* texts, save one: the garden. We do not know where Ezekiel was located at the moment of his vision, save that it was by the banks of the river Chebar in Babylon.

Yet the single most famous warning against using the *merkavah* techniques is that to be found in the Tosefta (the "supplement" to the third-century CE Mishnah that represents the "oral tradition" of the Torah, a tradition hotly debated and discussed from the period of the destruction of the Second Temple in 70 CE to about 200 CE). This is recorded in the story of "The Four Who Entered the Pardes."

Pardes is itself a problematic term. It has been translated variously as "garden" or "orchard" and considered the root of the word "paradise." According to the Tosefta, four famous first-century CE rabbis "entered the *pardes*," a phrase considered equivalent to entering Paradise. Of the four, one went insane; one died; one turned apostate or heretic; and the last, Rabbi Akiva, returned alive and survived the ascent. It was used as a cautionary tale regarding the *merkavah* techniques, and if the Tosefta is indeed as old as the second or third century CE, then the *merkavah* techniques, by implication, are at least as ancient.

What is compelling is the relationship that has been created between two different concepts of the Other World: one, a garden and the other, a place in the heavens. As the *merkavah* texts became more articulated and complex, we see that the *pardes,* or garden, is indeed a metaphor for the seven heavens, and the travel of the four sages is equivalent to the ascent — or descent — to the Chariot.

Within the context of the Babylonian religion, the connection is clear: the statues of the gods were consecrated — charged, animated — in the garden before their transport to the temple. The only time the statues were outside of the temple were during days sacred to their calendar, when they were carried in procession on chariots, or in the three days during the Washing of the Mouth ceremony. During the latter, the statues were in the open air, in the garden near the riverbank. This is purely speculation, based on the evidence of the Babylonian texts themselves, and on the fact that the Jews were held captive in Babylon, plus the fact that there was constant traffic of the Jewish sages between Babylon and Palestine during the first century CE.

But imagine the scene: four Jewish sages, curious about the pagan ceremony, wander into the garden where the rites are being performed. One dies, and another goes mad. One, perhaps on seeing the statue, raises the question, "Are there two powers in heaven?" and becomes a heretic; only the fourth is able to keep his wits and leave the garden of the ritual without either losing his life, his mind, or his soul.

Of course, there is no evidence that Rabbi Akiva and the other three sages were ever in Babylon or ever witnessed the Washing of the Mouth ceremony, or even that the ceremony took place while they were alive. What we are examining is not historical fact anymore, but religious and mystical allegory. Most authorities on this section of the Tosefta agree that there is no *historical* evidence for the entry of the four sages into paradise: it is accepted as a kind of metaphor for the dangers of mystical practice. The core text of Kabbalism, the Zohar itself, analyzes the Bible in terms of allegories, codes, metaphors, and mystical allusions, many of them based on numerological games and inspired wordplay. What we cannot ignore, however, is that the vision of Ezekiel took place in a country where cherubim, in the form of griffin-demons and other entities, were already known, where the gods traveled in chariots, and where the sacred locus associated with immortality was at once the temple of the immortal gods and the northern sky's circumpolar constellations.

The first time we encounter a garden in biblical sources, of course, is in Genesis and the Garden of Eden. The Garden is specifically identified as located somewhere in Mesopotamia, where four rivers converge, of which two, the Tigris and the Euphrates, are well known and still exist to this day. The identification of the other two is somewhat more difficult, but recent satellite photography has suggested that these two missing rivers converged somewhere a little south of present-day Iraq in the waters of the Persian Gulf, indicating that Eden may have existed on land that has since been submerged.

However, Eden is located in Mesopotamia and not in the land of Israel, or Egypt, or anywhere else. In fact, it is located precisely in the region of Sumer and Babylon. It is probably too much of a stretch to suggest that the garden where the Washing of the Mouth ceremonies were performed in Nippur — where it is thought Ezekiel and the other exiles lived — and the Garden of Eden or the *pardes* might be related. In fact they are most likely not the same. Yet the symbolism of a garden where the gods dwell and from which Adam and Eve were expelled is suggestive and tantalizing in view of this new information.

Adam and Eve attempted to become "as gods" and were cast out of the garden. Four Jewish sages attempted to reach God in the garden and only one survived intact. In a Babylonian context, the gods are invoked in a garden and brought down into statues in a ceremony we know was kept secret because of the injunction at the end of one cuneiform text, which admonishes the reader that this information "is for initiates only." This has a parallel in the sacrifice of the Catholic Mass, in which Jesus is similarly invoked into the bread and wine to transform them into his body and blood. During the epiklesis prayer in the Orthodox Church, this is accomplished by invoking the Holy Spirit in a prayer that is recited *sotto voce* — i.e., it is a secret prayer that is not spoken aloud in front of the congregation — and the bread and wine are transformed, transubstantiated: the essential nature or substance of the bread and wine undergoes a spiritual change. One assumes, although, again, it can't be conclusively proven, that if the Washing of the Mouth ceremony was for initiates only (i.e., for the priesthood of the temple), then intruders would have been dealt with harshly, particularly during the reign of a tyrannical and vicious ruler such as Nebuchadnezzar at the time of Ezekiel. The method of transformation, of making a god out of a stone statue, is a sacred secret. To trespass this rite, to show up unannounced and uninvited, is to court censure or worse. In the old days of the Catholic Mass, there was the unequivocal command: "All catechumens depart!" This was to prevent those studying for initiation into the church, the catechumens, from observing the ritual transformation. This act took place, for the Babylonians, in the garden. For the Egyptians, in the tomb of the pyramid. For the Christians, in the sanctuary of a church. For the Jewish mystics, however, there was no such externalized transformation of a statue, a corpse, or of bread and wine; the transformation that took place was internal and happened while one was still very much alive.

Re'iyyot Yehezkel

One of the oldest[3] of *merkavah* writings is the *Re'iyyot Yehezkel*[4] or "Ezekiel's Vision," based specifically on the first chapter of Ezekiel and expanding on this theme by describing ascending levels of heavens and their respective chariots for a total of seven.

Re'iyyot Yehezkel begins with a midrash on the opening lines of the Book of Ezekiel and proceeds to a description of Ezekiel as complaining to God concerning his plight as a captive in the land of Babylon. God then "opened seven compartments down below," and Ezekiel gazed into them. These are seven levels of what may be called the Underworld: *Adamah* (ground), *Eretz* (earth), *Cheled* (world), *Neshiyyah* (forgetfulness), *Dumah* (silence), *She'ol* (the pit), and *Tit ha-Yaven* (miry clay). These are interesting because they reflect to a degree a Sumero-Babylonian myth concerning the seven levels of the Underworld that mirror the seven heavens above, into which the goddess Inanna/Ishtar descended only to rise again after vanquishing the evil Queen Ereshkigal.[5]

The vision then proceeds to one in which God reveals to Ezekiel the Primordial Waters and a mountain beneath the sea "from whence the sacred vessels of the Temple will be restored in the future"; an interesting gloss that deserves more attention than we can give it in this space.

Finally, the vision proceeds to that of the seven heavens, and it is here that the vision becomes more complex and articulated, although by no means as complex as some of the later *hekhalot* literature. The scenario is, however, quite revealing, for Ezekiel sees his vision reflected in the river Chebar, and this is compared to a man at a barbershop, looking at his reflection in a mirror and seeing the king pass by on the street outside, reflected in the mirror's surface.[6] In other words, we are told directly that Ezekiel is looking at a vision of the heavens above reflected in the surface of the river. This could be a clue as to the meaning of the phrase "descended to the Chariot" since it makes more logical sense to "ascend" to the Chariot; but if one has to look down into a reflecting surface in order to "ascend," then the paradox is, somewhat, resolved.

The practice of looking into a mirror for reasons of prophecy and vision has parallels in other magical contexts, from the use of a pool of ink by Egyptian magicians to the use of an actual mirror by medieval and later European magicians.[7] In the case of the Elizabethan magician John Dee, use was made of a polished "shew-stone": a piece of Aztec obsidian that Dee used for gazing into and receiving messages from Elsewhere.[8]

The names of the seven heavens are given next, and they are *Shamayyim* (heaven), *Shemei ha-Shamayyim* (heaven of heavens), *Zevul* (meaning undetermined), *Araphel* (darkness), *Shehakim* (the skies), and *Aravot*, with the last heaven named the "Throne of Glory." There are also seven chariots, and it appears from the text that there is one chariot — *merkavah* — in each of the seven heavens, and each of these chariots has its own name.

The distance from the earth to *Shamayyim* is given as five hundred years, and this holds true for every distance thereafter. As Ezekiel travels from one to the other, he is given new, albeit brief, instruction as to the meaning of the name of each of the heavens, as well as that of each of the chariots. The only stage along the journey that becomes decidedly theurgical is the heaven of *Zevul*. It is at this stage that the "Prince" is said to reside, and one of the names given to him is Metatron, along with a number of mantric words of power. Metatron, as we have seen, was the angelic Prince previously known as Enoch.

However, between *Shehakim* and *Aravot* there is another stage, that called *Makhon*, which is a region of "snow and storehouses of hail, the dreadful punishments reserved for the wicked and the rewards for the righteous." *Makhon* does not merit a *merkavah*, and no more is said of this stage along the way, but it does add another five hundred years to the journey.

This concept of an intermediate stage before final apotheosis was reasserted in the schema of the Hermetic Order of the Golden Dawn, which posited an "Abyss" between the *sephira* of *Chesed* and that of *Binah,* between the lower seven *sephiroth* and the supernal triad.[9] This "Abyss" was said to be the realm of *Da'ath,* the *sephira* of Knowledge, sometimes called the "eleventh *sephira.*" Oddly enough, this idea of *Da'ath* and the Abyss was a focus of the false Messiah Jacob Frank.[10]

Once Ezekiel has arrived at the seventh heaven, the Throne of Glory above *Aravot,* the vision abruptly ends. The purpose in God's giving Ezekiel this vision was so that Ezekiel could return to the people of Israel in captivity and relate the vision to them exactly as he experienced it. The intention, then, was to both warn Israel and give Israel hope for the future: a promise that their lot in life would improve and that God had not forgotten them.

The basic structure of the *Re'iyyot Yehezkel* is repeated in many other *merkavah* texts, such as in the text called by Scholem the *Ma'aseh Merkavah* and reprinted in Janowitz.[11] As mentioned previously, it is difficult to get Kabbalah scholars to agree on a date for any pre-Zoharic Kabbalistic text, but we can safely assume that both the *Ma'aseh Merkavah* and the *Re'iyyot Yehezkel* did not appear later than the sixth century CE and were probably much older. While they were known to Jewish Kabbalists from Spain to Palestine, there is no evidence to show that they were known to Christian scholars or philosophers. They existed largely only in manuscript and in Aramaic or in Hebrew dialects from Palestine and Babylon. Some occult texts were even written in Arabic and sometimes in Arabic but using the Hebrew alphabet, thus making translation even more difficult for non-Jews.

The basic pattern, however, remains the same throughout. There is a schema of seven stages—either seven chariots, or seven palaces, and sometimes both—that must be traveled in the course of the "descent to the Chariot." Each stage has a different set of characteristics, different angels to be encountered, different divine names to be recited as if they were passwords. Eventually, one finds oneself before the Throne.

The Throne

Thus saith the Lord, The heaven is my throne, and the earth is my footstool. (Isa. 66:1)

No doubts are possible on this point: the earliest Jewish mysticism is throne-mysticism.
— Gershom Scholem, *Major Trends in Jewish Mysticism,* 44

Scholem's statement that "the earliest Jewish mysticism is throne-mysticism" says perhaps more than he intended. The tradition of throne mysticism goes back thousands of years in the Middle East, even as far back as ancient Sumer. In a cuneiform text we read of the throne of Enlil:

> He sets up his dais in the mountain mist.
> He rotates it in heaven like a rainbow,
> He makes it roam about like a floating cloud.[12]

The throne of Enlil floating in space like a rainbow or a cloud is consistent with Jewish ideas of a heavenly throne. In fact, this aspect of the ascent literature has been studied by scholars interested in the roots of Jewish mysticism, seeking answers in Babylon and Sumer. The idea of a divine throne was commonplace throughout the kingdoms of the Middle East; the throne was believed to have special powers, to represent the king (or, in this case, the god) when he was not physically present. Further, to sit on the throne was tantamount to usurping that power for oneself.

Depictions of thrones are among the most ancient images to be found on the cylinder seals of Sumer and Babylon. Gods are routinely shown sitting on thrones. To Scholem and other writers on Kabbalah, the terms "throne" and "chariot" are often interchangeable. The term for chariot is *merkavah,* as we have seen, but the word is often used as if it meant "throne" in various texts and traditions. When the king appeared before his people in public, outside of his palace, he would be seen in a chariot, which would then take the place of the stationary throne: i.e., it would become a throne in motion. Scholem refers to "throne mysticism" in his *Major Trends,* but from that point on refers to *merkavah* and *hekhalot* ("chariot" and "palaces") literature. The *merkavah* was the core vision, to be seen after passing through the *hekhalot.* One "descends to the Chariot" and not "to the Throne," although finally one comes before the enthroned Image.

This idea of God sitting on a throne like a king has influenced thousands of years of Jewish literature and Christian iconography. The image of an old, bearded white man in kingly robes sitting on a throne in the skies above the earth — being attended by angels and deciding the fate of humanity — is inescapable in western religious art. It represents a transcendent God, a God above humanity as much as he is above the earth. A God who is unapproachable except, perhaps, in full prostration, groveling as an ordinary subject does before an emperor or other monarch. The immanent God, the God who is everywhere, in all things, is a problem for normative Judaism and is much more likely to be found in the Kabbalah, which enjoys an interplay between transcendence and immanence. The ascent literature, the idea that one could perform the correct rituals and say the right incantations and then approach God directly, seems to be an attempt to bridge that difference, to accommodate both points of view. By placing God at the end of a series of seven heavens, on a divine throne and surrounded by angelic forces, one acknowledges the transcendence of God: placing God so far out-side human experience that he might as well not be here. It is a quaint sort of anthropomorphism, this ideation of a kingly God, but it places God within some kind of reach, makes of God an accessible idea; and that accessibility is what implies immanence, for if a solitary mystic, anywhere on earth, can, in the privacy of his room in the middle of the night, approach God using the ascent technology, then he is demonstrating that God is accessible from anywhere. This might not be the same as saying that God is immanent, but it's the next best thing: a human, using human abilities and force of will, is able to see God. That tangential point between God and human — the point characterized as the seventh heaven, the heaven of the Throne — ex-ists everywhere. A human being can reach that heaven and return unscathed. It makes of God an immanent Being, immanent in Time as well as Space, because present *now* and *here*, while maintaining a degree of transcendence because *not* now, *not* here unless the correct technology is employed.

In ancient Babylon, the statue of the god served as the contact point between the earth and the heavens: it could be seen and touched. The Jewish God was invisible, knowable only through His actions, like a planet we discover because of the wobble it introduces in the orbits of others. But the Jewish God had a Temple, an Ark, and a Holy of Holies. Although invisible, the presence of God was approachable in Time and Space. His throne was the Mercy Seat over the Ark. And the Torah, the written word, written not on cuneiform but on parchment, was the Word of God, the Law of Moses, and the Shekhinah, the presence of God among the people of Israel. The Word itself was held in such high esteem that the Jews considered their language, Hebrew, to be the language of God: a point that would be picked up later by the Christian Kabbalists of fifteenth-century Florence. With the destruction of the Temple in 70 CE, the text would replace the image for all time. The text was paramount, and the physical Temple — the image, we have to say, of God's House if not of God himself — passed away into a kind of oblivion, its walls, its divine service, and its sacred throne to be reborn in the rituals of dissident priests at Qumran and Kabbalists and would-be prophets in Provence, Safed, Gerona, Fez, Poland, Germany, and the Ukraine.

The Babylonian Connection

While Ezekiel may have been influenced by Babylonian religion in the sixth century BCE, what evidence exists for the continuation of Babylonian spir-itual and mystical themes into the first century CE, when the Qumran texts were fresh and when the Mishnah was being composed?

Actually, there is evidence from a number of sources that the rites of ancient Babylon were still being performed and their scriptures still familiar, even as late as the Qumran period of the first century BCE– first century CE. Traces of the *Epic of Gilgamesh* have been identified in the Book of Enoch from Qumran Cave number four, specifically in the section called the Book of Giants, which appears to be a later addition to the Enoch material and which betrays its associations with the Gilgamesh story.

The *Enuma Elish*, the Babylonian creation epic, also survived, and evidence for the worship of Marduk (in its later incarnation as Bel or as Bel-Marduk) and the recital of the *Enuma Elish* during the *akitu* festival (normally celebrated during the New Year) has been shown to have lasted until at least the first century CE in Babylon as well as in other areas of the Greco-Roman Empire at the time.[13] This claim has been supported by archaeological as well as epigraphic evidence, and its importance cannot be overestimated for understanding the phenomenon of the *merkavah* literature and its associated practices, for while the *merkavah* texts obviously form an essential part of Jewish mysticism, its practice was strenuously opposed by the Talmudic authorities.

We are faced with the possibility that what Scholem considered the basis of Jewish mysticism was, in fact, a tradition borrowed from the Babylonians during the time of their captivity and that — although molded and shaped in terms of Jewish religion and themes — it represents a continuation of a Sumero-Babylonian cultus, much in the same way that Christianity can be considered a Jewish "sect," or Buddhism an extension of Hinduism by other means. It also raises some important questions about mysticism in general, its "esoteric" nature, and its somewhat antinomian atmosphere. Does mysticism represent a current of religious and spiritual thought and practice that is essentially alien to organized religion, a practice or a technology that is *sui generis,* that only has accretions of the "host" faith or religion?

As we have seen so far, there are several elements of Sumero-Babylonian religion hidden within the vision of Ezekiel and, even more to the point, within the Enochian literature and the later *merkavah* texts. While we can identify individual ideas — such as the ascent, the throne, even the cherubim — as having Babylonian and even Egyptian analogues, can we go so far as to conclude that the entire practice itself of ascending to the Chariot is a manifestation of a technology that was already ancient when Ezekiel was sitting by the banks of the river Chebar?

If so, what is this technology? How was it originally conceived? What does it look like if we remove the sectarian and dogmatic elements and show it only in its most austere, naked form?

Excursus 1

Celestial Ascent
in Middle Eastern Mysticism

And He it is Who has made the stars for you that you might follow
the right way thereby in the darkness of the land and the sea. Indeed
We have made plain the signs for a people who know.
— Qur'an, Surah 6, "The Cattle"

The early Christians were not the only ones to be influenced by Jewish
ascent ideas. The idea that there are seven levels in heaven is reflected in
Islamic scriptural sources as well, in both the Qur'an and the Hadith. In
particular, there is the famous story of the *Mi'raj*: the ascent of the Prophet
Muhammad into the heavens from the site of what is now the Dome of the
Rock in Jerusalem.

As many readers no doubt are aware, the Dome of the Rock sits atop
the remains of the Second Temple. The story of the *Mi'raj*, also known as
the Night Journey and Ascension, has the Prophet leaving on his trip to the
heavens from that spot in Jerusalem, and therefore it has become a sacred
site to Muslims. This identification of the Jewish Temple with the Islamic
Prophet's celestial ascent is pregnant with spiritual implications. Further, as
the Prophet ascends the seven heavens, one by one, he meets the Jewish
prophets at each level.

The story is told several different ways in that collection of sayings and
episodes from the life of the Prophet known as the Hadith, and it is also
referenced in the Qur'an itself.[1] If we take the Hadith as a starting point, we
find that the Prophet was presented with a white quadruped, something in
size between a donkey and a mule, either after prayers at the Ka'aba (known
as the Sacred Mosque) or while asleep or in a state between waking and
sleeping; he mounts the creature and is transported to the Remote Mosque
(i.e., the Temple in Jerusalem), and from there ascends to the seven heavens.
However, before this ascension takes place, he is given a choice between two
vessels, one of wine and one of milk. He chooses the vessel containing milk
and is congratulated for this. In another Hadith the Prophet's heart is removed from his chest and washed, and then replaced before the Ascent takes

place.[2] This theme of the Prophet's chest being opened by an angel, Gabriel, and his heart removed is repeated in other places in the Hadith, and is surprisingly reminiscent of the shamanic initiation experience as recounted in Eliade's work on shamanism. This scenario of having one's internal organs removed and washed normally takes place as a prelude to ascent or full "initiation." In this case, the process is consistent with what we know of Siberian shamanistic techniques. It is another link in the chain of evidence associating ascent literature with shamanic initiation and making the connection between this type of initiation experience and the importance of the number seven, as in seven celestial levels with immortal beings assigned to each level.

According to the Hadith, Adam was the gatekeeper of the first gate or first heaven; at the second heaven, he was greeted by Jesus and John; at the third heaven, Joseph; at the fourth heaven, Enoch; at the fifth, Aaron; at the sixth, Moses. At the seventh and final heaven, he was greeted by Abraham himself. What is interesting about this lineup is the presence of Enoch, who is a minor figure in the Torah, deserving of only a single sentence in Genesis, but who is the model for Jewish ascent literature and often identified as Metatron. His presence in this list is therefore suggestive.

All of the celestial personalities identified in the *Mi'raj* are, of course, Jewish. The intention here is to identify Muhammad as the rightful (and final) successor to the line of Jewish prophets from Adam, the first man, through Enoch, Joseph, Aaron — including Jesus — to end with Moses and finally Abraham. In the Jewish ascent texts, the celestial gatekeepers are angels, with, in some texts, Enoch sitting on the heavenly Throne at the end. In the *Mi'raj* version, it is an angel, Gabriel, who is the psychopomp leading Muhammad up the seven levels.

The Islamic tradition represented by the *Mi'raj* identifies the Ka'aba in Mecca with the Temple in Jerusalem, naming one the Sacred Mosque and the other the Remote Mosque, a north-south axis of sacred sites. There is a sacred rock in the Ka'aba and another at the Temple, for which the site is called the Dome of the Rock. Yet the ascent does not take place from the Ka'aba, the Sacred Mosque, but from the Temple, the so-called Remote Mosque, the most sacred Jewish site in the world. Thus, we have the same themes in the Islamic version that we have studied in the Jewish version: a complex of ideas that associate the *Jerusalem* Temple with seven heavens and celestial ascent. This ascent is used as evidence that the Prophet Muhammad has divine blessing and is the legitimate successor to a line of Jewish prophets that includes Jesus. It is also used, paradoxically, to criticize Israel and to cite the destruction of the First and Second Temples as punishment for their impiety.[3]

One commentator has proposed that the use of the number seven in the Qur'an is often vague and means "*seven,* or *more, several* or *many,*"[4] but in the case of the *Mi'raj* the use of the number seven is unambiguous: there are seven heavens and seven divine gatekeepers.

Another group that incorporates the number seven in a celestial context is a controversial sect whose members may still be found in Iraq and lately in larger numbers in the West as refugees from the Iraq and Afghanistan wars: the Yezidis.

The Devil-Worshipers of Iraq

Such is the notion of the sacredness of the number seven, an idea which belongs to the common stock of the ancient inhabitants of Mesopotamia. The Yezidis have seven sanjaks, each has seven burners; their cosmogony shows that God created seven angels or gods; their principal prayer is the appeal to God through seven seihs; the sceptre engraved on the front of the temple of their great saint has seven branches. This reminds us at once of the Sabians who adored seven gods or angels who directed the course of the seven planets.
— Isya Joseph, *Devil Worship,* 133

Considered by their neighbors to be heretics at best or devil-worshipers at worst, the Yezidis are a Kurdish people who practice a strange religion that seems to be an amalgam of Islamic and Christian concepts. They have a unique scripture and a belief that the Fallen Angel of Christian and Muslim tradition will return to heaven in the future; they thus revere this Dark Angel and consider themselves specially chosen to follow it into heaven as its devotees.

They have two scriptures, the Book of Revelation and the Black Book. The latter has a description of the creation of the world and includes the statement that God "made the form of the seven heavens, the earth, the sun, and the moon,"[5] which makes it obvious that the latter three are not included within the idea of the seven heavens. This may seem like a mild point to make, but many have assumed that the seven heavens are an allusion to the sun, moon, and five visible planets. This Yezidi text makes a distinction between the seven heavens and the luminaries.

In addition, God creates seven angels at the time of creation. The first is Taus Melek, the chief angel and the one depicted as a peacock in Yezidi iconography. Taus Melek is also referred to as Azazil, which is the Azazel of the Jews, thus reinforcing the demonic nature of Taus Melek, for Azazel is the demon of the wilderness according to Leviticus (16:10ff.) and appears as the scapegoat in the Jewish liturgy for Yom Kippur, bearing the sins of the community on its back as it is sent into the wilderness. Azazel may be one of the *se'irim*, the hairy-goat demons also referenced in Leviticus (17:7).

The other six angels are Melek Dardael, Melek Israfel, Melek Mihael, Melek Azrael, Melek Semnael, and Melek Nurael. At a later time, God created Gabriel,[6] which may be a nod to Islamic tradition. The seven angels are referred to in the Black Book as the seven gods, and they reign over earth for one thousand years each. The classification of the Yezidi hierarchy is also based on the number seven, and includes the *sheikh*, the *emir*, the *kawwal* (musician), the *pir* (in charge of the fasts), the *kochak* (religious instruction), the *fakir* (instructor of children in music), and the *mulla* (who teaches religious instruction to children, guards the sacred books, and "attends to the affairs of the sect").[7] The Yezidi religious practices combine elements of Islam and Christianity, as well as Judaism. They practice a form of Eucharist, in which Jesus is invoked. They practice baptism, which is obligatory, and circumcision, which is optional. They do not pray five times a day or face Mecca when they pray; yet, their secular language is Kurdish while their sacred tongue is Arabic. They revere the Prophet Muhammad, but not as the Muslims do. And, of course, there is the problem of worshiping a graven image: the peacock *sanjak*, or standard.

How the peacock came to be a symbol for the Yezidis is not clear, as peacocks are not native to Iraq or Kurdistan, but to Sri Lanka (the former Ceylon). Critics claim that the peacock is a symbol of pride, and that therefore the god worshiped by the Yezidis is, indeed, Satan who, according to tradition, committed the sin of pride and was cast out of heaven. To the Yezidis, however, the scriptural reference tells us that Melek Taus came across a piece of paper in God's secret chamber, a place that had been forbidden to him. On this paper was written the commandment that one should worship God and none other. When God created Adam, he commanded Melek Taus to worship him, but the angel refused on the basis of the written commandment. Thus, it was not a sin of pride but of disobedience that caused the angel to be cast out of heaven: disobedience in entering the secret chamber and disobedience in refusing God's commandment to worship Adam, a disobedience in the latter case based on a written text (thus perhaps placing oral instruction over written commandments?). However, according to Yezidi tradition, Melek Taus is loved by God and God would not permit him to remain forever outside heaven. None of this answers the question about the peacock, however.

Considering that the Yezidi religion seems to be a deliberate amalgam of many different religious traditions we will have to wait until more field work is done among the existing Yezidi population and more textual analysis is accomplished on their sacred books. This will be difficult, since the

Yezidis typically do not wish outsiders access to their sacred rites or to original copies of their writings. One cannot blame them, for among all the persecuted populations of Iraq there are probably none so oppressed as the Yezidis. One thing is certain, however, and that is that the number seven has the same significance for the Yezidis as it does for the Jewish mystics: it signifies the heavens, and the Yezidis believe that both Jesus and Melek Taus descended from, and ascended to, that sacred space.

The theories about the origin of this group are controversial. The Yezidis claim an ancient lineage, of course, but documentation is scant. Some have proposed that they are descendants from Zoroastrians, but that seems untenable. There is not very much in their religion or ritual that is consistent with Zoroastrian practice. Yet they are quite unique in so many respects that speculation on their true origins is unavoidable. They would seem to be Kurdish since they speak that language, but they have little in common with their fellow Kurds in terms of religious or cultural practices. As Kurds, they would not be Semitic, but rather belong to the Indo-European language group that numbers the Iranians (Persians) among them and hence the accusation of being Zoroastrians.

A Persian-Hindu Mystic

One of the founders of an important school of Islamic mysticism was the Persian sage Abu Yazid al-Bistami (804–74 CE). He is credited with being the first Islamic mystic to formulate a concept of celestial ascent and, indeed, he is reported to have gone on his own *Mi'raj*.

Oxford University Professor of Eastern Religions R. C. Zaehner investigated the stories of Abu Yazid and found evidence that this inspired Sufi mystic obtained his startling philosophy of oneness with God — to the extent that he often claimed to *be* God — from a convert to Islam from Vedantin Hinduism. Zaehner traces the influence of specific texts of the classical Hindu scriptures, the Upanishads, through the utterances of Abu Yazid, a Muslim.[8]

Abu Yazid's grandfather was a Zoroastrian, but his teacher in mysticism appears to have been a convert to Islam from Hinduism, Abu Ali al-Sindi. Zaehner makes the case that there was more Hinduism than Islam in Abu Ali al-Sindi and his teachings. One of Abu Yazid's most infamous utterances — Thou art That — is used as evidence that his instruction was perhaps less Muslim than Indian, since it is an unfamiliar locution in Arabic or Farsi, but is a direct translation of the famous Sanskrit phrase *tat svam asi*, which is found in the *Chandogya Upanishad*. Further, Abu Yazid's ideas of mystical union with God are much closer to the Indian concept than the Muslim, for in the former there is the image of an almost sexual embrace whereas in Islam such would be considered anathema.

It is Abu Yazid's own account of ascension that preoccupies us here, for several reasons. In the first place, it is the first such instance to have been recorded since the Prophet's own ascension and therefore should be examined for similarities and differences. In the second place, it is the ascension of a Sufi mystic who was trained by a convert from the Vedanta, and that alone would make it something of interest. We have been looking at similarities in approach to celestial ascent among Egyptians, Babylonians, and Jews, and now we have a prelude to our study of the same subject in India using the convenient "bridge" of Abu Yazid.

To the Sufis, there is a sevenfold descent and a sevenfold ascent.[9] The descent describes the creation of the world as a series of emanations (similar to the Jewish idea of creation represented by the *Sepher Yetzirah*). The descent begins with (1) the divine essence itself, a unity, that then reveals (2) its Nature, in a (3) world beyond form, through (4) the world of imagination, the (5) world of spiritual perception, the (6) world of forms, and finally the (7) world of nature, the created world we experience.

In order to attain communion with the Divine, one begins at (7) which is the (1) of the ascent, the world of Nature and the Body, represented by Adam; then proceeds to (2) the realm of the senses, represented by Noah; to (3) the realm of the heart, represented by Abraham; then, powered by the upwelling of the purified heart, one proceeds to (4) the very edge of "super consciousness," the beginning of the dissolution of the ego and the personality, that is represented by Moses; as the ego dissolves in the ocean of superconsciousness it enters the realm of pure spirit (5), the realm of the prophet David; after this, there is only (6) the realm of inspiration, represented by Jesus; and finally (7) the realm of truth, represented by the Prophet Muhammad.

The Sufis point out that the prophets named in the seven steps up the celestial stairway are the prophets of one's own being; i.e., it is the Adam of one's self that is experienced at the first level. It is the connection between us as individuals and the archetypal Adam of scripture. Within each of us there exists a correlate to Adam, to Noah, etc., a meeting-place between who we are in a complex, mixed state of consciousness and the ultimate realities represented by the prophets who are in states of unity. These states are the rungs on the ladder, and they must be approached one at a time, in their appropriate order, because the psychological processes they represent are delicate and interconnected.

In order to perform this celestial ascent, the mystic must be in a state of spiritual preparedness. To do this, the mystic ordinarily follows the guidance and instruction of a sheikh, a spiritual master who can gently move the mystic away from outward fixations toward inner stillness. The powers of concentration must be developed in order to still the interior commotion of the mind. This is virtually identical to Indian teachings on meditation.

The sheikh, in Sufi terms, is a link in a golden chain of initiatory succession, going back to the Prophet himself. The sheikh initiates the seeker, and this initiation is a death and rebirth in the Sufi tradition as it is in other traditions around the world. In Indian terms, he would be called a guru, perhaps: a "teacher."

In addition to concentration, other tools are provided. These include meditation (*fikr*), invocation (*zikr*), and contemplation (*shuhud*). The mystic retreats spiritually from the world in a kind of sensory deprivation as exterior concerns are eliminated until there is only the sheikh, the mosque, the Qur'an, and prayer. Many Sufi orders have their own mantra, called a *wird,* a line of the Qur'an perhaps that is recited endlessly in order to attain a heightened spiritual state, joining one's own heartbeat to that of the Divine heart. This is similar to the Jesus Prayer recited by Eastern Orthodox monks, a short invocation of Jesus that is recited so often it begins to regulate heartbeat and autonomic function, leading the monk into a trance state.

Certain Sufi sects, of course, engage in other forms of "derangement of the senses," including music and dance, of which the famous "whirling dervish" is an example. It is important to realize that a period of purification and prayer precedes the active mystic quest, in Sufism as in *merkavah* mysticism or in virtually every other form. The "derangement" could be dangerous, even life- or sanity-threatening, if the body and the mind have not been purified of toxic substances.[10]

In the case of Abu Yazid, we have very little information as to the amount or type of preparation he had undergone before experiencing his own celestial ascent. It is reported that he felt himself to be a bird, flying upward through the heavens, seeing both heaven and hell but ignoring both and seeking the truth behind them.

> Then I ascended to the Second Heaven and saw winged angels who fly a hundred thousand times each day to the earth to look upon the saints of God, and their faces shone like the sun. When I had reached the Seventh Heaven one called unto me, "O Abu Yazid, stop, for you have arrived at the goal," but I paid no attention.... I continued to cross seas upon seas, until I reached the greatest of seas, upon which stands the Throne of the All-Merciful, and I went on swimming therein, until I beheld, looking from the Empyrean to the earth beneath, the Cherubim and those who bore up the Throne.[11]

It goes without saying that the references to the vision of Ezekiel and to the *merkavah* texts are remarkable and consistent.

As he flew higher and higher, he had a vision of the "tree of eternity," which has no end and no beginning, and he identified it with himself. This caused him great consternation, for he knew that he could not know God completely as long as an "I" remained, i.e., as long as he was Abu Yazid and something separate from God.[12]

This may have been the motivation behind some of Abu Yazid's more controversial behavior, as in his insistence that he and God were the same: an utterance (along with other behavior) that caused him to be expelled from his hometown seven times over the course of his life. As long as he was considered a madman, he was safe; like the famous Sufi character Nasruddin, a madman can say anything, even the most threatening truths, and remain unscathed. His self-identification with God was not necessarily the ravings of a madman, however, but the expression of a sublime and noble truth. Whether or not this "truth" could or should be accepted by his co-religionists, however, is another matter entirely. Orthodoxy has always had a difficult time dealing with the mystics, the fakirs, the descenders to the Chariot. Unauthorized access to the Divine is always frowned upon by the religious bureaucracy of whatever era, whatever land. To be fair, the technology of mysticism is dangerous. What may be even more dangerous is the content of the visionary experience itself.

Part Three

Ascent in Non-Abrahamic Religions

北斗九星圖

瑤光

右弼

左輔

開陽

玉衡

天璣

天權

天旋

天樞

A Chinese diagram of the Northern Dipper, showing the two additional "invisible" stars.

WHILE WE HAVE DISCUSSED the nature of celestial ascent in Egypt, Babylon, and Israel, with an excursus into some Islamic ideas and practices, we now turn our attention to non-Abrahamic religions and practices, including those of Africa and the Afro-Caribbean religions, and Indian and Chinese mystical ascent techniques. We begin, however, with a brief overview of shamanism: possibly the repository of some of the oldest (and nontextual) ideas and methods of celestial ascent.

Chapter 6

Ecstatic Flight in Shamanism

Shamanism is generally considered to be a worldwide phenomenon,[1] but subject to multiple variations. We can isolate many different ways in which shamanism is manifested, and the stories and legends that inform its theology, from culture to culture. A difficulty found in older attempts to quantify shamanism, Eliade's, for instance,[2] is the desire to equate the mythologems (the stories that surround the experience and that are representative of localized, cultural factors) with the techniques. This, in fact, might not be a valid approach for understanding what Eliade called the "archaic techniques of ecstasy"; instead, approaching shamanism as a technology, something out of cognitive science — actually what Eliade implied by his subtitle and a theme on which his colleague Ioan Couliano expanded[3] — might be preferable to interpreting it as a purely religious or purely psychological process, or some combination of the two. It might prove more valuable in the long run to start with the technology and then see how these techniques were interpreted in the light of indigenous theologies.

Eliade's definition was exclusive of what he called "sorcery," yet the term *shaman* itself comes from a Tungus word meaning "sorcery." This simple decision caused Eliade to exclude from his definition a wide range of practices that others might have included as shamanism. The link between the kind of ecstatic flight that Eliade envisioned and the practices of occultism and magic that fall under the generalized rubric of "sorcery" can be found in the grimoires, or occult handbooks, of the Greco-Roman world, in the Nag Hammadi library of Gnostic texts, and in the equally formalized practices of Chinese shamans.[4] While it would appear that the goal of the *merkavah* texts, for instance, was the experience of appearing before the divine Throne — an experience we might describe as purely spiritual or transformative in nature — so many of these texts linked the ascent with the attainment of supernatural powers that to separate the magical from the mystical in this area might be ill-advised. The idea that the right word or the right seal before an angel would "force" that angel to let you into his palace or chamber during your ascent implies that human beings have the potential to command the angels. This power could be applied not only during the ascent, therefore, but also during more mundane activities. Thus, we see the names of the angels inscribed on talismans, amulets, and the other impedimenta of occult practice, what we might call "practical *merkavah*" in imitation of Scholem's phrase "practical Kabbalah."

While we in the West, after centuries of Christian and especially Catholic domination of the religious and scientific discourse, have become accustomed to separating magic from religion, and religion from science, in order to think as the ancients did, we have to ignore those intellectual and largely theoretical distinctions and enter a world where magic, religion, and science were a single discipline, and where "knowledge" was an all-encompassing term containing spiritual data as well as data on the natural world. Cosmology was inextricably linked with spiritual concepts and with ideas gleaned from scriptural sources. One could painstakingly draw a picture of a plant, an herb or flower, and detail all of its component parts in precise fashion, but when it came to describing how the plant grew or why one plant was different from another, one was reduced to supernatural speculations. The same was true for describing the nature of the celestial orbits, the revolutions of the planets, the essence of the stars. In order to think like the ancients, to think with cherubim, we don't have to abandon our scientific knowledge and technological advances, but we do have to accommodate what Cotton Mather in another era called "the wonders of the invisible world." While we may feel secure in the knowledge that the earth revolves around the sun, we have to realize that we behave *as if* the sun revolves around the earth: our very language forces us to do that, for we speak of sunrise and sunset when the sun does neither. The difference between our intellectual understanding of the cosmos and our emotional response to it is profound; we may understand how cancer functions in the destruction of a loved one's liver, for instance, but on another level we interpret that event as something more than mere pathology. Why *that* person, at *that* time? "Who sinned, this man or his parents, that he should be born blind?" (John 9:2).

Therefore, it won't be that difficult for us to enter the world of the shaman. We, as human beings, still live there in some part of our consciousness, in some chamber of our hearts. It's the ghost in our twenty-first-century machine, the reason why some live and some die, why some get rich and others struggle with poverty; it's spontaneous regression, miracle cures, winning the lottery, and the light behind the eyes of a newborn baby's knowing smile. We may say, statistically, that such-and-such a percent of us will develop heart disease in our lifetimes; but when we get it, we always ask, "Why *me?*" Especially when our next-door neighbor doesn't. We may realize the dangers of automobile travel, but if we get into an accident it becomes a cosmic event that changes our lives. We do not have intellectual responses to disease, death, war, poverty, and oppression when it happens to us. We seek meaning, relevance, the reason why it was us and not someone else. Saying it was the "luck of the draw" doesn't satisfy, doesn't help us get up in the morning to face a new day with the knowledge of new, unseen forces at work.

The shaman is the interpreter of these events and the manipulator of reality itself. In order to perform that function for society, the shaman must ascend to the heavens and make contact with That which rests outside our world. It's a vantage point for looking down and seeing the big picture, for seeing how each event is connected to every other event. The shaman is transformed by this experience, but only after he or she goes through the pains of hell. The shaman experiences death, dismemberment, and all the horrors that life has to offer. The shaman lives an entire lifetime in days, weeks, months, or even years — experiencing all the dangers, sadness, pain, and isolation of life and the ultimate isolation of death — so that he or she returns with the knowledge of how things really work.

In most *merkavah* texts, this refers to the dreaded sixth level, the level just before the Throne. It's the level where complete dissolution of the personality is threatened. In the *Re'iyyot Yehezkel*, it's the level between the sixth and the seventh, *Makhon*, where snow and ice are created: the dangers of the environment, of the world outside the descender to the Chariot. The things that can tear the shaman apart. The world as its own motivation, its own rationale, separate from linear cause-and-effect processes because we cannot fathom how our individual moral action can result in a hurricane, a tornado, an earthquake, war or disease or famine. The acceptance of this level, the surrender to the forces of nature — which are really metaphors for the nonhuman, inhuman forces for which we have no name, no category — is a prerequisite for admittance to the last and highest level, that of the Throne. It is an acknowledgment of the Unknowable, the Uncontrollable; in a sense it is death. In another sense, it is a return to infant status prior to the rebirth that takes place on the seventh level where the shaman comes into the Light.

It is initiation.

There are many examples of shamanic initiation that are not identical to the type of initiation we encounter in Masonic societies or other, more urbane forms. Masonic initiations take place within the normal course of mundane events; an evening set aside for the ritual observances, the recitation of the appropriate information. There are many forms of shamanic initiation, however, that take place outside normal life with the shaman leaving society for a length of time and becoming immersed in the total experience for however long it will take. While the goal of the Masonic initiate is to return to society a more powerful, more aware individual — virtually the same goals, in a very general way, as those of the shaman — the Masonic initiate obtains this power from a social group and the "power" that is bestowed within a group ritual. In the shamanic initiation under discussion, power comes as an effect of the psychological transformation taking place under extreme forms of emotional and psychic distress, a situation that the Masonic initiations duplicate in more sedate form by the use of blindfolds, restraints, and the creation of a solemn atmosphere. What takes place in formalized ritual in the Masonic and other secret societies of the West occurs *in situ* with the shaman. Hallucinogenic drugs might or might not be employed; days and nights spent alone in isolation in the forest or jungle; trance states: a derangement of the senses that is created and maintained for as long as is necessary until the shaman experiences his or her apotheosis. In the Masonic initiation, when the ritual is over (all the rubrics observed, the charges recited) the initiation is complete; the initiand is admitted into the brotherhood without any determination if a spiritual or psychological transformation has taken place or is in the process of taking place. The binding of the initiand within the group was the purpose of the rite. In the shamanic version, there is no completion until the initiation has "taken," for the shaman will be expected to demonstrate the newly won powers of healing, protection, and divination in a rigorous social setting. The Freemason is not expected to demonstrate supernatural abilities; the power the Freemason exercises is that of a member of a select and elite society with all the privileges and responsibilities that entails.

Of course, there are shamanistic societies in the world of an initiatory nature. Eliade details those of some Native American populations as examples of groups who initiate new members by miming the psychological tortures their Siberian counterparts undergo on their own: death, dismemberment, washing the internal organs and replacing them, etc. We are concerned here with those that emphasize ecstatic flight and celestial ascent, however, to ascertain degrees of correspondence with the ancient Egyptian and Babylonian systems on the one hand and those of the *merkavah* mystics on the other. Our intention is not to prove or disprove theories of diffusion or independent invention, but to discover enough similarities to create a working hypothesis of the technology being employed.

The Ladder

And he dreamed, and behold a ladder set up on the earth, and the top of it reached to heaven: and behold the angels of God ascending and descending on it. And, behold, the Lord stood above it.
(Gen. 28:12–13)

And Jacob awaked out of his sleep, and he said, Surely the Lord is in this place; and I knew it not. And he was afraid, and said, How dreadful is this place! This is none other but the house of God, and this is the gate of heaven. (Gen. 28:16–17)

The famous dream of Jacob, the progenitor of the children of Israel, is of a piece with the ascent motifs we have studied so far. Jacob was in fear of his life from his brother Esau, who wanted to kill him because of his father's favor. He left the land of his father and traveled abroad in search of a wife as well as to escape his brother's wrath. He came to a deserted place and made a pillow out of stones and slept. This could be seen as a parallel to Ezekiel, who was also in exile and also in some distress and fear for his life. Jacob's exile was in part due to a trick he had played: he put on a hairy garment to make his blind father believe he was Esau, who was considerably hairy, in order to receive his father's blessing. Ezekiel's exile was due to the sinfulness of the people of Israel (at least, that is how Ezekiel interpreted it). Sinful actions led to the exiles of both these men. This is in some contradiction to the self-imposed exile of Moses and his people from Egypt, which was due not to the sinfulness of the Jews but to their enslavement by the pharaohs. The exile of Moses led to his receiving the Law from God on Mount Sinai; the exiles of Jacob (before Moses) and Ezekiel (after Moses) led to their visions of God and promises of future glory.

Jacob was in exile from his father's land and family for a period of twenty-one years, a number that is the equivalent of seven multiplied by three; he waits to marry Rachel for seven years; when he is finally reconciled with his brother, Esau, at the end of his exile, he bows down before him seven times. There is no indication in Genesis of the number of steps in the ladder to heaven; the Zohar connects the ladder with the *sefiroth,* the ten emanations from God that are his creation, with the base of the ladder identified as *Shekhinah* (or *Malkuth*) and the top of the ladder with *Yesod,* "heaven" being identified with *Tifareth.*[5] The Zohar is specifically Tantric in this regard as well, showing a connection between this ladder and themes of circumcision, the phallus, and the "foreign wives" of King Solomon: themes that are amplified, in a peculiarly homoerotic context, in Wolfson.[6]

The idea of a ladder leading to heaven is not unique to Jewish scripture, as we have already seen. Until recent times, and among the Siberian populations, the ladder remains a central concept linking heaven and earth; moreover, the Siberian shaman is expected to climb this ladder in order to maintain connection with the Other World. That this ladder often consists of seven rungs is probably not coincidental.[7] Eliade links this concept with the Mesopotamians[8] and expresses the opinion that those systems that value the number nine for celestial purposes over number seven are more archaic, a position that seems speculative and depends on how one reads the available evidence. He references the Altaic shaman who "climbs a tree or a post notched with seven or nine *tapty* [notches], representing the seven or nine celestial levels"[9] and the "Cosmic Pillars of the Ostyak have seven incisions."[10] Further:

The Vogul believe that the sky is reached by climbing a stairway of seven stairs. The conception of seven heavens is general throughout southeastern Siberia. But it is not the only one found: the image of nine celestial levels, or of sixteen, seventeen, and even thirty-three heavens, is not less widespread.[11]

Thus, while for western religious iconography and what Wolfson calls the "hermeneutics of visionary experience"[12] the number seven seems of paramount importance when it comes to describing the distance between the earth and the highest heaven, it is by no means the only possible number employed by all peoples. The relationship between the number of heavens and the number of gods often seems artificial, however, as if an attempt was being made to force two contradictory elements into a coherent and consistent framework.[13]

What is consistent is the reliance placed on the shaman ascending from the earth to the heavens. A variety of strategies and implements are employed by shamanistic societies around the world, including ladders, ropes, stairways, etc.[14] In many cases, each "heaven" has a specific set of correspondences related to it. Among the Altaic shamans, for instance, the sixth heaven is the realm of the full moon[15] and the seventh heaven is the realm of the sun.[16] In this ceremony, the shaman uses a variety of "vehicles" to travel through the heavens including the soul of a sacrificed horse and a goose. In this example of an ascent, the shaman rises higher and higher, reaching increasing levels of ecstatic experience. The ascent is accompanied by the beating of a drum and the circumambulation of a pole set in the middle of the ceremonial space, representing the Cosmic Tree that connects the earth and the heavens.

The cardinal direction favored as the placement of the Ladder or the Cosmic Tree is the north. Again, according to Eliade:

> The Altaians conceive the entrance to the underworld as a "smoke hole" of the earth, located, of course, at the "Center" (situated, according to the myths of Central Asia, in the North, which corresponds to the Center of the Sky; for, as we know, the "North" is assimilated to the "Center" through the whole Asian area, from India to Siberia).[17]

He goes on to note that "the Altaic shaman successively passes through the seven underworld 'obstacles' (*pudak*). Indeed it is he, and he alone, who commands experiential knowledge of the underworld, for he enters it as a living man."[18]

This idea of the north as the "center" is indeed widespread among Asian populations. It is noted in China as well as India as we shall soon discover, albeit usually in an archaic or shamanistic context. Further, we can see that there is a tradition that the Underworld has the same number of levels as the celestial ladder, and that the shaman is a "living man" (or "woman" as the case may be) who is able to enter both realms. In the case of the shaman, such travel in both realms is to be expected of someone who claims supernatural powers. According to Christian tradition, even Jesus "descended into hell" on Holy Saturday, the day after his crucifixion, and then "ascended into heaven" after his resurrection. Mastery over both realms was the hallmark not only of Siberian shamans but also of the magicians of the Greco-Roman period as well as the sorcerers of medieval Europe. Grimoires such as the *Greater Key of Solomon* and the *Lesser Key of Solomon* gave instructions for summoning both angelic and demonic forces, respectively. What was missing from these medieval examples was any idea that the magician or sorcerer must have previous knowledge of the divine and infernal regions through a process of ascent and descent; yet, this is precisely what the *merkavah* literature suggests.

This is an important point for any discussion of New Age occultism; for the easy availability of translations of these grimoires in bookstore chains around the world implies that anyone who buys such a book is automatically empowered to raise demons or speak with the angels. The importance of the spiritual training and perfection of the magician — in terms of actual direct experience of the celestial regions by whatever means, *merkavah*-like trances brought on by intense prayer or shamanistic-type trances instigated by drumming or hallucinogens — is ignored. The popular media has contributed to this misunderstanding through the employment of ideas like those expressed in the archetype of the "sorcerer's apprentice," who only needs the right words or the correct seal to duplicate the supernatural prowess of his master.

That the seven palaces or seven chariots of the *merkavah* tradition represent an initiatory path should become obvious, especially when viewed alongside its Siberian and other Asian counterparts. The path taken first by the gods and then by dead kings in Egyptian and Babylonian religion was eventually traveled by ordinary living men and women; the fact that it had originally been viewed as a practice reserved for the gods or the dead meant that the journey would be dangerous for a living soul who would be surrounded by images and experiences totally out of the context of normal, everyday life and therefore presumably unable to negotiate the perilous shoals and withstand the unspeakable terrors such a journey would present.

Eliade makes clear, based on his reading of the literature of shamanism, that shamans were either selected because of hereditary factors or because the gods had chosen them. In other words, there was little or no self-selection, and, as it was for Jacob or Ezekiel, destiny was handed to the shaman on a platter. In the *merkavah* tradition, by contrast, the entire emphasis is on self-selection. This may not have always been the case, however. If we agree that this tradition began among the Zadokite priests of the Second Temple period, then it was originally a hereditary function as the priesthood was hereditary. With the loss of the Temple, however, it may have seemed that "all bets were off" and the way to the celestial regions open to everyone.

Indeed, the celestial regions themselves were in the "public domain," as it were. The heavens were above the earth, visible to everyone. If we accept, based on the evidence already presented, that the seven celestial regions refer specifically to the seven stars of the Dipper, then it would seem as if the template of divine ascent were within everyone's grasp.

Moshe Idel, in commenting on the shift from God selecting the human agent for his revelation to the human self-willed ascent to God, says:

> My thesis is that one of the major developments in post-biblical Judaism is the continuous growth of the apotheotic vector in the general economy of Judaism, a theophanic religion in its first manifestation, through the emergence and the flowering of some forms of Jewish mysticism.[19]

Apotheosis shifted the focus of celestial intercourse not only from God to man as initiator, but from the community to the individual. This may have been due, as mentioned above, to the loss of the Temple and the consequent inability of the Jewish people to perform the sacrifices as required and to observe the other halakhic stipulations defined in the Torah. The heavens may have taken the place of the Temple in this development; once the Temple had been "removed" from the earth, the emphasis was on the visualization of a heavenly Temple, one that was accessible to anyone, and the best image or icon of this heavenly Temple was one that could be seen from any spot in the northern latitudes: the constellation of Ursa Major.

Why not the seven planets? The seven planets could be considered the most logical frame of reference, and indeed in the Greco-Roman period and especially within the cult of Mithra that dominated the entire region for hundreds of years, initiatory rites of seven stages identified with the seven planets were quite common. As Idel points out, however,

> The rather widespread ascent of the soul through the seven planets found in Hellenistic and early Christian sources was alien to late antiquity Jewish sources, which provide a separate and independent model of psychanodia.... Despite the impact of astrology and of hermetic sources on various Jewish literatures, discussion of the ascent through the planetary system are few.[20]

Yet the number seven and its importance to this literature goes un-explained, even as it has not gone unremarked. It should be repeated that the seven stars of the Dipper would be a constant reminder of permanence with its implication of immortality, and the fact that they rotate around a central "pole" or "pillar" or *axis mundi* or Cosmic Tree — the area occu-pied by the North Star — would further emphasize their importance over and above that of the seven planetary spheres; literally "over" because the signs of the zodiac against which the planets move occupy planes that are lower on the horizon than the circumpolar stars. The privileged position of Ursa Major "above" the orbits of the planets implies a higher level in the celestial hierarchy.

Among shamanistic societies, perhaps, this was noted; certainly the uti-lization of pillars and poles as means of transporting the soul of the shaman to the heavens is a trope on the idea of the north "pole" and its function as the point in the heavens around which the entire universe revolves. In the case of shamanism, this ascent was clearly related to the transformation of the shaman from a "normal" member of society to someone "other": a person with privileged access to the supernatural worlds of the heavens and the hells.

Chapter 7

Celestial Ascent in Afro-Caribbean and African Religion

The study of Afro-Caribbean religious patterns is a controversial one, due in large part to the arrival of slaves to the region from various parts of Africa and the fact that they were brought to North America under severe duress, in chains, and their cultures suppressed by the demands of slaveowners and other hegemonic forces in the persons of the church and the state. While various authors have made a case for the survival of authentic African religious traditions even under these perilous circumstances, the appearance of syncretism has clouded the issue further: How much of what is practiced as religion among the Afro-Caribbean peoples is "purely" African and how much has been adopted or adapted from Christian and Native American sources? To assume syncretism is a political decision; it implies a colonialist perspective for some observers, as if the African religions themselves were not strong enough to withstand the power of Christian influences, or as if the Africans themselves were unsophisticated religiously and made a kind of hodge-podge of African and Christian beliefs and practices.

More recently, scholarship on this subject has shown that African religious ideas and practices survived relatively intact, in spite of all the pressures that would ordinarily have diluted or even eradicated them.[1] Our interest here is in the presence or absence of ecstatic flight in these practices, for such a study might help us understand the phenomenon even further. Eliade studied African sources only briefly and in passing in his *Shamanism*; there are only a handful of references to African beliefs and none to Haitian vodoun or to Santeria. Yet all the basic elements are there for a technology of ecstatic flight and celestial ascent. If there is no evidence to support it, then we must ask ourselves why? What is missing from our analysis?

The first religious phenomenon under discussion is Haitian vodoun, commonly referred to as "voodoo." To the popular imagination this is a cult of darkness, black magic, insistent drums, animal sacrifice, and possession. It would represent all that is evil and satanic from the point of view of a Catholic priest of the eighteenth century. Indeed, it would appear virtually identical to the fantastic tales told of the Black Mass with its heavy visceral and erotic overtones. Female priestesses, the presence of blood, dancing, animals, alcohol, ritualized sexuality — all conducted in the middle of the night, perhaps at a crossroads or a graveyard. Add to this mixture the practice of magic and the casting of spells, the infamous "voodoo dolls" and the zombie, and you have an African version of what the Europeans feared most: witchcraft; yet this was witchcraft with a twist, for its practitioners were not the next-door neighbors, the old women at the edge of the village, or any other European satanist but instead were black Africans. The racial component cannot be ignored, of course. The implication that Africans were less than human is manifest in the very condition of slavery; the imputation of savagery was inescapable. Thus it became almost inevitable that one would describe an arc of progression from African to European, from paganism to Christianity, from savagery to civilization, from witchcraft to monotheistic piety. Long before Darwin, the enslavement of Africans by Europeans represented a kind of sinister evolutionary outlook with Europeans representing the acme of human development and Africans at the other end of the scale.

All this made a sober and objective investigation of vodoun difficult, if not impossible. It is only in the past few decades that we have gained from more penetrating analyses of Afro-Caribbean religion in general and vodoun in particular. What has been discovered is the vibrant survival of African belief systems in the transplanted communities of Haiti, the Dominican Republic, Cuba, and other Caribbean nations. If there was any syncretism it was to be found in the borrowings of one African religion from another, rather than from Catholicism or Protestantism. While surface images might have led some observers to deduce a mixture of Christianity and African religion, a deeper look proved that African cosmological systems were intact.

In the case of vodoun, we are confronted with a system that mirrors those of the other celestial realms we have been considering. This can be observed in the rituals that take place in the Haitian "temple": the peristyle.

The peristyle itself is an image of the Haitian cosmos. There are four corners representing the four cardinal directions. There is a pole or pillar in the center, called the *poteau mitan,* representing the *axis mundi.* The *poteau mitan* reaches down into Vilokan, the world of the *loa* (the Haitian deities), and the *loa* ascend up the pillar to participate in the rituals. Where the *poteau mitan* enters the ground is the zero point between this world and the next; the priest or priestess officiating at the rituals touches the *poteau mitan* to summon the *loa* from below.

The use of the cross in Haitian religious iconography and in the creation of the *veve* — the seal or symbol of the appropriate *loa* or collection of *loas* — represents this idea of the peristyle at the crossroads of two worlds. This concept is made more complex by the fact that, like the Jews in Babylon, the Africans were exiles from their homeland. As the Jews identified the Temple with their race, religion, and homeland, the vodouisants identify Vilokan both as the abode of the *loa* and as their ancestral home. In order to have contact with the gods, the vodouisants must approach Vilokan through the medium of the *axis mundi*, the *poteau mitan*, in the center of the peristyle. Strangely, the locus of the Haitian homeland is under the earth: the gods travel up the pole rather than descend it. Thus, the "ascent" is not practiced by the faithful but by the gods themselves who arrive at the ceremonial site after being called.

Vilokan is perceived as a genuine mirror image of earthly life. It is opposite in every aspect. When it is daylight on earth, it is night in Vilokan. (This is very nearly an accurate description of the time zones that separate the Caribbean from the western coast of Africa, for when it is midnight in Port-au-Prince it is already dawn in Dahomey, Benin, Ghana, and Nigeria.) As in the Egyptian rituals of the dead, the Other World is considered a place of origin; and as in the rituals of Egypt and Babylon and those of the Jewish *merkavah* mystics, there are gatekeepers along the way who must be mollified.

In the case of vodoun, this means the Lord of the Crossroads: Legba.

In Legba, we have a constellation of values and characteristics that to some degree are reminiscent of those associated with the ascent literature of other cultures. Legba is identified with the *poteau mitan*, the pole that connects this world with the other. As such, he controls access to the other world. As is the case with many Haitian deities, Legba's attributes are complex. He is associated with the sun, and "moreover, in the ritual invocations addressed to him, one finds such words as *cleronde,* meaning circle of brightness, and *kataroulo,* meaning the four wheels of the sun's chariot as they roll on their daily path across the sky."[2]

Perhaps the reference to the lord of the gateway between heaven and earth having a chariot is only coincidental in this case and not meaningful. Legba is identified with the "regenerative life force,"[3] which is how he corresponds to the sun in this instance. He is also identified quite specifically with the phallus but is also identified with the womb: he is considered androgynous, and the entire peristyle is sacred to him, his phallus represented by the *poteau mitan* and his womb by the ground penetrated by the sacred pole. Iconography depicts him as being uncannily similar to the design of the "Fool" card in the Tarot Deck: an old man with a sack over his shoulder, leaning on a cane. The cane, we are told, is a phallic symbol and represents his creative energy and power.[4] He is known as the Master of the Great Way to Vilokan,[5] and the Catholic St. Peter is said to be the image of Legba, for in popular iconography St. Peter holds two keys, the keys to the gates of the Other World. The saint is also shown with a rooster, and roosters are sacrificed to Legba on one of the most famous days in the Christian calendar, All Saints'

Day or November 1, the equivalent of Halloween, when the gate is opened between the living and the dead.

This brings us to another aspect of Legba, which is Gede. Gede is the Petro equivalent of the Rada Legba. The Petro rites are different from the Rada cultus for they represent a different set of deities that are nonetheless similar in many aspects to those of the Rada, if a bit more violent and "dark." As the Petro counterpart to Legba, Gede rules the night as opposed to the day and is represented at times by the moon instead of the sun; yet the two *loa* are mirror-images of each other. Gede rules the land of the living-dead, which is a locale different from Vilokan, a concept that is a little difficult to comprehend. Perhaps it is easier to imagine Vilokan as a kind of heaven and the land of the living-dead as the Underworld, even though both places are considered to be located "below the earth." Ginen, the land of the living-dead, is a cold, watery abyss situated below the surface of the earth itself and approached through the cemeteries and graveyards. One of the manifestations of Gede is the famous Baron Samedi and Baron Cimitiere; this incarnation is the guardian of the crossroads between the living and the dead just as Legba is the guardian of the crossroads between this world and the next. The symbol for both of these deities is the cross.

The Haitian conception of the human soul may help us to understand how ideas of "ascent" and "descent" may be interpreted, because there is a definite correspondence between ideas of death and ideas of ascent: they both involve questions of the soul and immortality, and a destination somewhere other than this world. The Haitians believe that every human being has three souls: a *gwo-bon-anj* (*gros bon ange* in French, or "great good angel"), a *ti-bon-anj* (*petit bon ange* or "little good angel"), and a *met tet* (*maître tête*, "master of the head").

At the point of death, the *ti-bon-anj* leaves the body and ascends to a spot "higher than the sky,"[6] where, newly liberated, it continues an existence that seems to have no further contact with the living. This place "higher than the sky" is the equivalent of heaven for the vodouisants, but ideas concerning it seem rather vague and ambiguous. "Higher than the sky" would seem to indicate the furthest point north and be a reference to the North Star, but this is only speculation as there seems to be very little in the way of astronomical data in the theology of vodoun.

The *gwo-bon-anj*, however, will take its place in Ginen, the land of the living-dead. In order to do so, it must be freed from the corpse during the course of a special ritual called *desounen*, which can be roughly translated as "de-sounding" or "removing the sound" from the body. (This is an interesting elocution, for the vodouisants believe in the efficacy of the word as much as do the Kabbalists. To remove the sound from a body is to remove its voice: its soul, its spiritual force.) The body is washed, some of its fluids collected and buried in a place where no sorcerer may find them, and the spiritual forces are asked to leave. The outcome of this ritual is that the *ti-bon-anj* goes to heaven, the *gwo-bon-anj* and the *met tet* to Ginen; but this only occurs once the spirits have left the corpse and the *met tet* has entered the body of the priest who is performing the ritual. Thus possessed, the priest rushes outside the room where the corpse is being held and the *met tet* begins to speak through him to the community. Once the *met tet* leaves, the priest, called a *oungan*, is considered reborn, and the community reborn through him.

A year and a day after death, the *gwo-bon-anj* is "reclaimed" in another ceremony and brought back from Ginen. This spirit is summoned to reside in a jar, where it may be consulted by members of the family and the community. After the passage of years, the *gwo-bon-anj* is believed to gradually become a kind of *loa* itself, filled with power even as its identity (particularly the deceased's less attractive qualities) is just as gradually forgotten as its family members also begin to die off and with them all direct experience of the deceased's personality and history. Instead, only the good deeds remain as part of the community's collective heritage in a reversal of Shakespeare's "the evil that men do lives after them, the good is oft' interred with their bones." Thus we have two types of immortality: one, that of the *ti-bon-anj*, takes place in a distant heaven and is never heard from again; the other, that of the *gwo-bon-anj*, is manifest as a reclamation from the land of the living-dead and becomes part of the community, an act of reclamation that must be performed by the living.

Just as the corpse is washed after death, the living are also subject to a ritual washing at the time of their initiation into one or other of the various vodoun societies. This may be an allusion to initiation being a kind of ritualized death and rebirth, but that explanation does not help us understand further extensions of this rite. This bathing also is performed on objects and places — sacred sites, such as the sanctuary where the *oungan* keeps the ritual implements, and the implements themselves — not merely to purify them (although that element exists also) but also to charge them or consecrate them. This action is called *lave tet* ("washing of the head") and is performed on neophytes entering the service of the *loas* and upon anything else that might be used in ritual work.[7] That it is the head that is specifically washed is interesting, for this "washing of the head" as a means of consecrating or "charging" both humans and inanimate objects has resonance with the Babylonian Washing of the Mouth ceremony, which served the same purpose.

In fact, what we see as confusion between the Vilokan of Legba and the Ginen of Gede is reflected in the Egyptian and Babylonian concepts of the afterlife. There seems to be at least two types of existence after death: the immortality assured by residence among the gods, and the kind of immortality represented by the abode of the dead. The latter is obviously considered less desirable, for the souls of the dead must be "reclaimed" from Ginen in rituals specific both to Haiti and to Benin in Africa where these rituals originated. In both cases, something enduring is represented: the *ti-bon-anj* in "heaven" and the *gwo-bon-anj* in Ginen. And in order for their immortality to be assured, they must be separated from the physical body which, of course, dies and decays. The ritual agent, the *oungan,* is the essential force separating the spiritual essences from the physical, implying that human agency not only is required but also is capable of separating the two. During the quintessential phenomenon of the vodoun ceremony, the devotees are "possessed": their bodies are taken over by the *loas.* This may be evidence that the physical body is conceived as a vessel for the spiritual elements, which come and go: that there is a separation possible between the body and the spirit, thus implying the independent existence of the latter.

This separation can take place in one of two ways: naturally, at the time of death and with the proper ceremonies, and more violently during possession by the *loa.* Although possession of the vodouisant by the *loa* happens at the *loa*'s discretion, it normally occurs during the performance of a ritual that the *loa* are invited to attend; thus, once again, we witness the presence of human agency in the transit of *loa, gwo-bon-anj,* and *ti-bon-anj* to and from the human body. In the case of possession, this occurs during what the poet Rimbaud would call the *dereglement de tous les sens,* or the disorder of the senses. One may also acknowledge that death is itself the ultimate disorder of the senses, as the senses shut down and cease functioning. In the case of possession, this is a temporary state of affairs brought about by external forces as well as the internal preparedness or vulnerability of the devotee. In the ritual, the senses are disordered by the rhythms of the drums, the chanting, the nocturnal atmosphere with its suggestion of sleep and trance, and the ritual gestures themselves, which are pregnant with meaning on a deep, psychological level below the threshold of conscious thought or linear thinking. The drums themselves operate on the heart, synchronizing the heartbeat of the devotees with the rhythm of the drums so that a connection is made between the ritual performance and the autonomic nervous systems of the vodouisants; the autonomic nervous system regulates heartbeat as well as respiration and other functions of the body that are normally outside conscious control.

In addition, there is a strong sexual component to Legba, which is consistent with certain Kabbalistic ideas linking the Ladder (*climacus* or climax) with sexuality.[8] The idea of sexuality as a metaphor for spiritual "enlightenment" is nothing new, of course, and may be not only a metaphor but a clue to understanding what I am calling the "technology" of mysticism. Episodes of intense sexual activity are known to produce states equivalent to trance, what the twentieth-century British occultist Aleister Crowley called "eroto-comatose lucidity."[9] The more extreme Tantric sects of India also elevated sexuality and sexual metaphor to the realm of the intensely spiritual, including the acknowledgment of the relevance of the death state to the ascent, and managed to bridge the gap between the celestial hierarchy and the human organism in such a way[10] that we are forced to accept the validity of this thesis: that the celestial ascent is a well-known practice in cultures as diverse as Egypt, Babylon, Israel, India, China, and Africa where the basic symbolic structure underlying the ascent technology is amazingly consistent.

Next, we should examine the traditional African culture that most especially is concerned with astronomical observations. The discovery of their complex calendar system and ritual cycles was the source of much astonishment and speculation when their beliefs were summarized in a book published in 1976 to wide acclaim and positive reviews by everyone from Isaac Asimov to Erich von Danniken: *The Sirius Mystery.*

The Dogon of Mali

The premise of *The Sirius Mystery,* by Robert K. G. Temple, is that the astronomical knowledge possessed by a West African ethnic group called the Dogon might prove some of the wilder claims that the earth has been visited by extraterrestials at some point in the distant past. Temple's work is the result of prodigious scholarship, Temple himself boasting impeccable academic credentials with degrees in Sanskrit and Oriental Studies as well as being a colleague of the famous Sinologist Joseph Needham. Temple based his provocative study on a book published in France in 1965 entitled *Le renard pale* or "The Pale Fox" by two French anthropologists, Marcel Griaule and Germaine Dieterlen. Griaule and Dieterlen conducted an intensive study of the Dogon of Mali from the 1930s until the 1960s, research interrupted only by World War II. Their research came to popular attention in 1976 with the publication of Temple's work. Temple was able to put the astronomical knowledge of the Dogon into the context of Egyptian and Sumero-Akkadian religion and astronomy, an attempt that — had it been made by anyone less confident in the classical and historical source material — would have fallen on its face or attracted the mirth of academia. Instead, the reviews were respectful if at times cautious.

Along with *Hamlet's Mill,* Temple's *The Sirius Mystery* demonstrates that we must have a grasp of astronomy if we are to fully understand the religious scriptures of ancient peoples. In the case of the Dogon, we have an ethnic group that uses an "alphabet" of 266 letters; detailed knowledge of astronomy beyond the capabilities of anyone in the rest of the world until the nineteenth century; and a coherent cosmobiological system that anticipates that of Indian yoga or Chinese alchemy. In fact, the complicated religio-magical apparatus of the Dogon can only be called "Kabbalistic," a designation that is surprisingly reinforced by their veneration of the number twenty-two as the twenty-two "articulations" of the human body, a number that is immediately recognizable as that of the number of letters in the Hebrew alphabet and the number of the associated paths on the Tree of Life which is itself used as a diagram of the Primordial Man, Adam Kadmon, and thus "articulates" his body.

How the Dogon came by this knowledge is a mystery. They possessed no telescopes for penetrating the realm of the stars invisible to the naked eye, yet they had detailed knowledge of the Sirius star system: they knew it was a binary star, and that the smaller of the two stars was the heavier. This, and much additional information, led Temple to speculate on the source of the knowledge since no human civilization had access to the technology that would put this information into the hands of the Dogon. The Dogon themselves revere the sky and the heavens as the source of the information, and a strange creature — half-man, half-fish — who was said to have visited the earth from the heavens in the distant past. Temple associated this creature with Oannes, a creature who was said to have imparted the same type of information to the ancient Sumerians.

Thus, in the Dogon we have an example of a heavenly "descent": the arrival of a divine being from the stars who brings advanced knowledge to humanity. A complete analysis of Temple's work, and that of Griaule and Dieterlen, is of course far beyond the scope of this work. Instead, we should look for the correlations to the ascent literature specifically. The Dogon calendar system — based on their perfect number of sixty, like the Babylonian perfect number — and the detailed legends and mythologems of the creation of the world, etc., make for compelling reading and the above-referenced works are recommended for those who wish to take this premise further. For now, however, we should pay attention to the role that the circumpolar stars play in the Dogon cosmological schema. The importance placed on Sirius, the Dog Star, is suggestive of a link between the Dogon and the Egyptians, for whom Sirius ("Sothis") was an important indicator of the rising of the Nile every year. Sirius is the brightest star in the sky, and appears behind the rear boot of Orion ("Osiris"), the Hunter. Such attention paid to Sirius by the Dogon would indicate a profound concentration on the fixed stars that should include other constellations.

According to the Dogon, the world was created by Amma, the Supreme God. Amma is a combination of four "clavicles," joined together like a ball. Each of the four represents one of the four elements: fire, water, earth, and air. These four clavicles also represent the four cardinal directions. In this, the Dogon cosmology is remarkably similar to that we would find in the *Sepher Yetzirah* or other Kabbalistic texts. When Amma is shown as a diagram, it is an oval shape divided into four sectors, and in each of the four sectors there are eight signs, which are each subdivided into eight more signs, resulting in a total of 256 "complete signs of the world."[11] This number and the method of its calculation are remarkably similar to the 256 *odu* of the Ifa divination system of the Yoruba.[12] Even more startling is the similarity between this diagram and the so-called Enochian system of the Hermetic Order of the Golden Dawn, of which more later.

This ovoid shape, called Amma's Ball, eventually opened and the four cardinal directions were the extensions of the four clavicles. The ball opened "in the north" and the other directions were at first contained "within the north." This opening and the axis it created as it spun is specifically referred to as the "axis of the world" by the Dogon.[13]

According to the Dogon, creation took place as a series of explosions, one after the other for a total of seven stages and resulting in seven souls. These are "spiritual principles" which are "the consciousness and intelligence of every being."[14] The number fourteen then becomes important, for it represents both the heavens and the Underworld, as in the saying, "seven above, seven below, he spun fourteen worlds."[15] The diagram of these fourteen worlds is actually a spiral shape of seven ovoids, one atop the other, like a strand of DNA or the serpents in a caduceus. Each half of each ovoid represents a world. Should we superimpose a typical yoga diagram over the Dogon glyph, we would see the chakras and the sushumna line up quite neatly.[16]

An essential aspect of this cosmology is the *po*. *Po* refers to a type of seed grain that is sacred to the Dogon and represents a stage of creation. There were twenty-two *po* seeds in a spiral at the moment of creation, as depicted in a *yala*, or sacred diagram. They spun clockwise and then the force of their spinning caused them to burst. The second *yala* shows seven rays around a central dot, representing (perhaps) the moment that the spinning stopped and began in the opposite direction, as depicted by the third *yala* in this series, which shows a spiral spinning in the counterclockwise direction, the coiling up of Amma's "word." The word for "seven" in the sacred language of the Dogon is *soy;* "word" is translated as *so*. The word for seven, *soy,* literally means "this is the word."[17] Thus, there is an explicit relationship between the concept of seven, twenty-two, the word, and creation in the Dogon cosmology. The idea of the "word" is central to their creation story, for they believe that signs preceded things, that the idea of creation in the mind of Amma as words preceded its materiality.

At the end of creation, as the world axis was created and the four directions extended, the *po* coiled upon itself *in the north*.[18] Thus, we include this cardinal direction in our mythologem of the Dogon. More specifically, the Dogon refer to the North Star, or Pole Star, as the "eye of the world," sitting atop the *axis mundi*. The symbol of the Pole Star, like that of Legba and Gede of Haitian vodoun, is *a cross*.[19]

Even more incredibly, the Dogon also reference the stars of the Southern Cross — which occupy a position in the southern latitudes equivalent to that of Ursa Major in the north — as the opposite end of the *axis mundi*, calling it the "second eye of the world."[20] The Dogon therefore have a more complete, more comprehensive cosmological system that incorporates both hemispheres of the earth and of the heavens into a coherent whole.

The Dogon also have a tradition of celestial ascent and descent, although this is believed to have taken place as part of the creation epic. In this case, the progenitor of the human race, Ogo, who becomes the Pale Fox, descends to earth a total of three times from the opening in the sky above the *axis mundi*. He performs this descent in what the French anthropologists call "an ark": a vessel designed like a boat in some versions and like a box in others. In virtually every case the ark is divided into segments, or shows engraved lines representing a matrix divided into cells equaling the sacred number 60 as well as a depiction of the *po* seed. Ogo is the agent of disorder, as well as of individuality and human frailty. His opposite number, Nommo — the amphibious being or beings who came to earth from the stars — brought civilization and organization to the world. The pair of them are seen in cosmic struggle over the souls of humanity.

The priest of the Dogon religion is called a Hogon, which is a close approximation to the vodoun word for priest, Oungan. The Dogon people are found in Mali, in close proximity to the area of West Africa that saw slaves being collected for the long sea voyage to the Americas. In their divination systems and other elements of their religious beliefs and practices they show some similarities with the religions that arrived in Haiti, Cuba, and elsewhere in the Caribbean with the slaves from Dahomey, Benin, Nigeria, and other West African nations.

The recurrence of certain themes — the north, the Pole Star, the number seven, the *axis mundi*, ascent and descent to and from the north — is certainly suggestive of a baseline idea concerning the relationship between humanity and divinity. With the Dogon, we have much additional information that resonates with other sources such as the figure of Nommo with its similarity to that of the Sumerian Oannes, both of whom were amphibious beings who brought civilization from the stars. The employment of the number twenty-two in relation to creation and specifically to the "articulation" of the divine body is equally striking.

The identification of the number seven with the Pole Star and the *axis mundi* is relevant to our case, of course. There is no further qualification of how the Dogon made that connection, so we would be forced make a number of deductions based on the available evidence. Temple has offered evidence to show that the Dogon migrated from North Africa to their present location in Mali thousands of years ago; he speculates that the Dogon are the "cultural, and probably also physical, descendants of Lemnian Greeks who claimed descent 'from the Argonauts,' went to Libya, migrated westward as Garamantians (who were described by Herodotus), were driven south, and after many, many centuries reached the River Niger in Mali."[21] Temple believes that predynastic Egypt was the source of the Dogon sacred tradition concerning Sirius. While this cannot be considered proven, the sheer amount of scholarship that is represented in *The Sirius Mystery* is probative of larger issues at work in the field of the history of religion and religious studies. Both Moshe Idel and Ioan Couliano have written supporting a multi-disciplinary approach to the study of religion, one that would incorporate various other fields of academic endeavor such as archaeology, anthropology, psychology, astronomy, and the cognitive sciences. To this must be added biology and chemistry, as we will discover in the next chapter.

Chapter 8

Celestial Ascent in
Asian Ritual and Alchemy

> In the most general sense, it may be said that the luminaries collectively orient man. Thus, from one perspective, the "teaching" may be regarded as an orientation. To the extent that it does involve an orientation, it is for the purpose of a journey; a journey begun by the soul in the realm of darkness and eventuating in its return to the realm of light.[1]

Heretofore, this study has focused on Middle Eastern and African sources for examples of celestial ascent, showing some consistency in concept between the polytheist approaches of Egypt, Babylon, the Dogon of Africa, and the Vodouisants of Haiti on the one hand and the purely monotheist interpretations of the Jewish mystics on the other. For those searching for "origins" there is much food for thought in these approaches, for one could easily posit a single "source" for the idea of celestial ascent, perhaps in Africa and its Egyptian culture or just as easily in Sumer and Babylon. As mentioned previously, however, it is not my intent to defend either a diffusionist or an independent inventionist position in the material. My interest is certainly from the viewpoint of a historian of religion and particularly of mysticism, but I am certain that the question of "origins" will not be satisfactorily answered in my lifetime.

Rather, my interest is in the technology of celestial ascent, that is, celestial ascent as a mystical technique employed by cultures around the world. While it is tempting to speculate on the transference of ideas from one culture to the next, with every new discovery of a scroll or a lost library or a cache of cuneiform inscriptions we are forced to adjust our timelines and rearrange our matrix of connections. That there is, however, more than enough data on the nature of the mystical ascent itself to provide a working hypothesis as to how it is performed and what the implications may be for disciplines other than the history of religion is nowhere more obvious than in the celestial ascent literature of India and China.

India

India is the source of many of the world's most famous religions, from Hinduism and Buddhism to Jainism and Sikhism. Even Hinduism is itself an umbrella term for a variety of forms of religious expression. There are also different modalities in Buddhism, from the Vajrayana of Tibet to the Mahayana and Theravada forms represented by important temples in India, Thailand, Sri Lanka, Taiwan, Indonesia, and Singapore (among others). It could be said, however, that Hinduism is the root of most of India's religions, excepting, of course, Islam, and it is to Hindu cosmological beliefs and mystical practices that first we turn.

Vedic Cosmology

Unlike the Egyptian and Babylonian scriptures we have already considered, those of ancient India, the Vedas, are thought to be the oldest in the world that have been in continuous use. They date to about 200 BCE if we reference only the written versions or to about 1500 BCE if we grant that period as the beginning of the oral tradition. (The Egyptian and Babylonian scriptures have not been, of course, in continuous use except for the appearance of their themes in various, later, traditions such as those of the *merkavah* and possibly Gnosticism.) The problem with dating the Vedas is to be found in two systems of analysis. The first is paleographic analysis and is restricted due to the fact that these scriptures were written on very perishable media, such as the leaves of plants; thus the oldest actual Vedic manuscripts in existence date only to about the fifteenth century CE, about the time of the Florentine Academy and the discovery of the neo-Platonic literature in the West. The second is a form of analysis based on internal evidence and other historical references to the Vedas, which clearly show that they are of ancient origin. Since it is not our goal to trace origins, we will leave the debate as to the age and provenance of the Vedas to the experts. Our interest in the Vedas, and in Hinduism generally, is focused strictly on ideas of cosmology, astronomy, and ecstatic or celestial flight to determine if the "map" and the "vehicle" share any similarities or diverge in important ways, or add to our existing body of knowledge of the technology of celestial ascent. More importantly, the Asian sources will integrate the cosmological schemes we have investigated with individual, human correspondences in such a way that we can begin to appreciate how the "archaic techniques of ecstasy" function.

According to the various references in the Vedas to cosmology and the structure of the universe, it is clear that a mountain is envisioned as the center of the world, Mount Meru or Sumeru. (One may remark on the similarity of the name Sumeru with Sumer, and further note that the Sumerians made numerous references to mountains in their sacred writings even though Lower Mesopotamia is far from any mountain range.)

There are four main Vedic texts and the fourth, the Artharva Veda, is largely concerned with magic and charms.

In the Artharva Veda we read:

> Time, the steed, runs with seven reins, thousand-eyed, ageless, rich in seed. The seers, thinking holy thoughts, mount him, all the beings are his wheels. With seven wheels does this Time ride, seven naves has he, immortality is his axle. He carries hither all these beings. Time, the first god, now hastens onward.... He carries away all these beings; they call him Time in the highest heaven.[2]

This is from a hymn to Kala, or Time, but demonstrates the internal consistency of various familiar concepts: immortality, the number seven, the highest heaven, the first god, the axle, even the wheels of a celestial chariot. The reins, or *pasa*, represent "The Indestructible Permanent Laws of the Universe."[3] The seers themselves are seven in number and are mentioned in many other Vedic texts. They are the seven rishis, ancient gods "connected with the origins of man and the origin of knowledge."[4] They are identified as the seven stars of the Great Bear.[5]

> The stability of the world results from the rituals performed thrice daily, at dawn, midday, and sunset, by the seven seers, and the recitation of the sacred triple-song (*Gayatri*) by all the twice-born at the same hours.[6]

The names of these seers differ from one cycle of creation to the next; there are fourteen such cycles, called *manvantara*, each of which is equivalent to one "reign of Manu," or two and a half precessions of the equinox. Manu is known as the law-giver of humanity, and each reign of Manu is ruled by a different version of this Being. There are fourteen in number, and each rule a fourteenth of the day of the "Immense Being," Brahma. One day and night of Brahma is a *kalpa*, a unit of time. The current Manu is known as the Son of Brightness or the Son of Light. In the present or seventh *manvantara*, the seven seers were responsible for the creation of the Vedic hymns themselves, and their names are Atri (Devourer, Eater), Vasistha (Owner of Wealth), Kasyapa (the Son of Vision, also referred to in the *Markandeya Purana* as the Wine Drinker or perhaps Drinker of Soma), Gautama (the sage), Visvamitra (the Universal Friend), Bharadvaja (Skylark), and Jamadagni, the famous sage who was beheaded by a Kshatriya king over ownership of a celestial, wish-fulfilling cow.

The relevance of each of these seers is a matter beyond the scope of this work, as it would require a lengthy excursus into Vedic legends, hymns, and variants in the *Mahabharata* and *Ramayana*. What is of most interest here is the fact that the sages are identified with the stars of the Dipper and are believed to reside on those stars, that they are identified with creation itself, and with the division of Time. The legends surrounding Jamadagni are also pertinent, particularly one concerning his wife, Renuka.

Renuka was renowned for her purity and chasteness. She would go to the river every day to collect fresh water for Jamadagni to perform his morning rituals. She was able to collect this water in an unbaked clay pot: so great was her purity and devotion that the pot never broke or collapsed.

One day she was at the river as usual when she noticed one of the gods, the celestial musician, Citraratha, bathing and cavorting with his numerous wives; the scene distracted her for a moment with its lush eroticism. Returning to her senses, she collected the river water but the clay pot broke. She was devastated.

Jamadagni, using his powers as a yogi and seer, was able to see what had happened. He ordered his five sons to kill his wife for this dereliction, but all save the youngest refused. The youngest, Parashu-Rama, agreed, on condition that she would be reborn in purity and have no memory of what had transpired. This was accomplished.

The relevance of this story lies in the meaning of the name Renuka, which means "semen." The story is seen as a coded reference to Tantric yoga techniques pertaining to sexuality and the cultivation (and retention) of seminal fluid by the male.[7] If we go back and reread the story with this information, the meaning becomes clear. Even Parusha-Rama himself is identified as one of the chakras in the human body, the *visuddha* chakra located behind the forehead. The goal of this type of yoga, as we shall see, is the cultivation of sexual energy, diverting it from its normal, procreative function and raising it through the channels of the body to the uppermost chambers of the brain. In other words, it is a type of celestial ascent, a biological analogue to the *merkavah* practices. The breaking of the pot and the death and rebirth of Renuka have other resonances, as well, as would be familiar to students of Lurianic Kabbalah and its concept of the breaking of the vessels: an abortive first attempt at creation that gave us the broken shards, or *kelippot*, negative forces that must be reintegrated into creation.[8]

There are other groups of seven forces, or celestial beings, and they are all concerned with the division of Time and Space, with a focus on the north. For instance, the Marut ("the Immortals") are classified into seven groups of seven that dwell in seven spheres: earth, sun, moon, stars, planets, the Seers or Great Bear, and the Polestar (called here "The Changeless"). The names of the Marut associated with the Great Bear are: Idrs ("Such"), Nanyadrs ("Not Otherwise"), Purusha ("Man"), Pratihartr ("Doorkeeper"), Sama-Chetana ("Even Mind"), Sama-Vrtti ("Even Tendencies"), and Sammita

("Equal").[9] The name Marut itself is open to interpretation, but it is associated with the term *ma rud* which means "do not weep." It is uncertain why the Immortals — the guardians of the chalice of Soma, the celestial beverage of immortality — should weep at all. What is interesting about this identification between the Immortals, the Seven Seers of the Great Bear, and weeping is that it reflects one of the *merkavah* techniques for ascending to the Chariot, which is weeping, as referenced by Idel.[10]

The other names of the Marut are provocative as well: the Doorkeeper being the most obvious, but if we attribute Even Mind and Even Tendencies to the qualities needed for a successful ascent to the Chariot, then we may be able to understand the last term, Equal, as a reference to the mistake made by one of the Four who entered the garden: assuming that there were two powers in heaven and that Metatron was the equal of God. The terms "Such" and "Not Otherwise" are problematic because they are paradoxical; "Such" would seem to be another way of saying "Not Otherwise," but in this case what does that mean? It may be a significator of identity and single-mindedness, focus, of a state of union or of trance. The following Marut is called, simply, "Man," and it is Man who confronts the Doorkeeper who can be passed only in a state of Even Mind and Even Tendencies.

The preceding may seem whimsical, but as another glyph for the story of Renuka as an elaboration of the basic *merkavah* techniques it is at least consistent and may help us decode the technique for the celestial ascent.

Chakras and Tantras

It is well-known to students of yoga and of what is popularly understood to be Tantra that there are seven chakras, subtle energy centers, in the human body. These are usually depicted as seven wheels placed in various places on the center of the body, rising vertically up the spinal column from the base of the spine to the top of the head. The goal of one type of yoga, known as Kundalini yoga, is to raise the energy believed to be coiled at the base of the spine up through each of the chakras to end in the "thousand-and-one-petaled lotus" chakra at the very top of the head.

In Sir John Woodroffe's introduction to his translations of two important Tantric texts, the *Sat-cakra-nirupana* and the *Paduka-pancaka*, he refers to the *Saptabhumi,* or "Seven Worlds," stating, "The Saptabhumi, or seven regions (Lokas), are, as popularly understood, a exoteric presentment of the inner Tantrik teaching regarding the seven centres."[11]

The seven centers are the seven chakras, so what we have is an attempt to externalize the chakra system, projecting it onto the cosmos, which may be a reflex of an attempt to *internalize* the seven stars of the Dipper onto the body, bringing the body into alignment with ideas of immortality, immutability, and the Divine.

The essence of Kundalini yoga is to be found in the concept of energy. In the human body, this energy is believed to rest at the base of the spine in a coiled form. A Yogi or Yogini is able to locate this coiled energy within his or her own body and raise it up through the six chakras within the body to the level of the seventh chakra which is at the very top of the skull. "Energy" may be one of the most overused terms in the New Age movement, so we should perhaps spend a little more time explaining what the authors of the Tantric texts meant by the expression.

The word that Woodroffe translates as "energy" is the name of a Hindu goddess, Sakti. Sakti is the wife or consort of Siva, and their union is often immortalized iconographically as the male and female deities in the act of coition. Sakti, according to Woodroffe, is Power, whereas Siva is Consciousness.[12] Thus, the act of Kundalini yoga is nothing less than the application of Consciousness to Power: the deliberate act of will in raising the Serpent Power through the seven levels to attain the ultimate illumination.

Methods for doing this vary, but in the main they involve meditation, controlled breathing, visualization. It is a passive process when performed by a single individual, an introverted looking-within and a conscious raising of the power from chakra to chakra, with visualizations appropriate to each of the seven chakras including particular mantras, Sanskrit syllables, gods and goddesses, etc. In other words, the system bears a lot of similarities to that of the *merkavah* literature, which posits different angels for each of the seven heavens, different words to be used at each level, etc. In the case of Kundalini yoga, the system is much more articulated and defined; often, in the *merkavah* texts, there is a lack of detailed information on each of the seven heavens: they are merely places to get through on the way to the Throne.

Yet there is no escaping the fact that the seven chakras correspond to the seven *lokas* or seven *bhumis*: seven celestial realms. There is clearly an ascent up a pole or pillar — in this case, the *sushumna nadi* that runs from the base of the spine to the top of the head — through the seven localities to the ultimate goal. The Throne for the practitioner of Kundalini yoga is the thousand-and-one-petaled lotus. Siva sits on this Throne, just as Sakti is coiled at the base of the spine. The act of raising Kundalini is to bring the goddess Sakti to union with the god Siva, analogous to uniting the female Shekhinah with the masculine *Kether* in the Kabbalistic format. In both Kabbalah and Tantra, the ultimate goal is the uniting of the male and female essence in a sacred marriage, or *hieros gamos*. The mystic in both cases, through a process of discipline, concentration, and meditation, unites these two elements in himself (these practices have largely been written by men and from a male perspective), and this *unio mystica* causes an explosion of consciousness. In both cases, the process involves a celestial ascent.[13]

In a compelling study of sacred architecture, Adrian Snodgrass has pointed out that the human body, complete with its system of chakras, is referred to as a "chariot of fire": "The psycho-physiological complex of man's microcosmos is a chariot of fire, with wheels (*cakra*) set upon its axis (the *susumna*) as upon an axle."[14]

If we factor in the cosmological data — Mount Meru, the seven lokas, the seven rishis, the chariot — we find that both the *merkavah* mystic and the Tantric adept employ images of an *axis mundi*, a north polar direction, and seven stars with corresponding angelic or divine beings residing at each of the levels.

The modern critic will object that there are significant theoretical and philosophical differences between the two schools and that to insist on any but the most superficial resemblance would be to fall into the doctrinal error of universalism. This author most respectfully disagrees. I believe that the same format is basic to both systems, and that doctrinal or ideological differences between the two approaches are based on *interpretations* of the technical process and not on the actual process itself. In other words, first came the technique and then came the catechetical elaborations as attempts were made to fit the experiences within a socially acceptable framework. Indeed, Kabbalistic scholars such as Moshe Idel are on record characterizing the Zohar and other Kabbalistic works as Tantra.[15] While Idel bases this on literary analysis of the texts of Kabbalism, which are replete with religio-sexual or mystico-sexual imagery, my approach is based on the techniques themselves, using Tantric literature to explain Kabbalistic texts. This type of multi-disciplinary approach is admittedly more difficult but in the end far more rewarding, for it reveals a basic methodology at the heart of many disparate mystical texts, and this methodology is based on a shared understanding of the workings of the cosmos. To the mystics, "heaven" is a very real place: the spiritual abode of the gods is also the heaven we can see with our eyes in the evening. Night is truly the darkness we require in order to see the light.

The Kundalini practitioners are descenders to the Chariot in everything but nomenclature. They incorporate a scheme of seven levels and a gradual process of rising up these levels to attain illumination. Filtered through a thoroughly Hindu context, this may be difficult to see at first, but if we rely on the numbers and the schema we will always find ourselves on familiar territory. The map may be in a different language and the vehicle be a different model, but the technology is so similar as to be virtually identical. By shifting our emphasis away from theological arguments and critiques of doctrine and scriptural exegesis and toward the physical world in which the mystics find themselves, we can begin to read their scriptures and occult texts from a different and very revealing perspective; for while the desert may be a very different place from the rainforest, and while India may be a very different environment from Babylon or Egypt, and while monotheists may believe they have little in common with polytheists, the stars above them all are the same. They are identical. And the response of the mystics of many disciplines to the stars is surprisingly similar.

This is probably nowhere more in evidence than in the Buddhist shrine Borobudur in Indonesia.

Borobudur

There was virtually no reason why Borobudur should have been erected the way it was. It is situated on the island of Java in present-day Indonesia, about an hour's drive northwest of the ancient city of Yogyakarta. It was built during the famous Majapahit dynasty when Java was under the influence of the Indian religions of Hinduism and Buddhism. It is said that Borobudur dates to the eighth century CE; it is certainly one of the oldest and largest Buddhist shrines in the world and as such is protected as a United Nations World Heritage site. For many years, however, it had languished under a mountain of earth and vegetation, all but forgotten after an eruption from nearby Mount Merapi had covered it in volcanic ash. It was rediscovered in the nineteenth century, and slowly dug out of its premature burial to reveal the glories of an ancient culture.

It is a classic example of Vajrayana Buddhist architecture, an anomaly in Java since the prevailing form of Buddhism to be found there is Theravada (the form most associated with Thailand). Vajrayana is the Buddhism of Tibet, so it is interesting to find a Vajrayana temple so far from the Himalayas. What is more compelling, however, is the orientation of Borobudur.

The temple is composed of a series of square platforms topped by three circular platforms, and with a stupa, a shrine, at the very top. There are either five or six square platforms (depending on which source you use, and how one counts the platforms), and these are heavily illustrated with bas-reliefs depicting various elements of Buddhist doctrine. The practice to be employed in visiting the shrine is to walk from the bottom to the top, clockwise, with one's right hand touching the bas-reliefs and gaining insight into the human condition along the way. One begins with depictions of the various sins and ills to which humans are subject (or to which they subject themselves), and gradually comes to the life story of Buddha. Finally, at the very top, the bas-reliefs disappear and one comes upon a marvelous collection of seventy-two stupas, each containing a sitting Buddha. At the very top of the shrine there is the largest stupa and it is empty, symbolizing the state of nirvana.

Seventy-two is a suggestive number, for the Kabbalists use it as the *shem-ha-mephorash*, the seventy-two-lettered sacred name of God. Depending on how you count the levels of Borobudur, you may end up with a total of ten (counting the final stupa, the symbol of ultimate attainment, as the tenth). This would also be consistent with the Kabbalistic concept of ten spheres, or *sephiroth*, with the final, ultimate *sephira* being *Kether*, or the Crown: an unknowable and indescribable point of tangence between creation and Creator.

Borobudur is a representative in stone of the ancient Vedic idea of celestial ascent as contained within the *Satapatha Brahmana*. This text is concerned with the building of the sacrificial altar, a process that is designed to reverse the descent of spirit into matter and the subsequent differentiation of material substance; by building the altar, one brings together the disparate elements of reality into a cohesive and undifferentiated whole, thus providing a spiritual vehicle for the ascent to the heavens. Borobudur represents in visual form that process of ascent as the pilgrim gradually moves further from earth the higher she goes and loses the heavy materiality of mundane life to a more rarified state of spiritual awareness.

This form of celestial ascent is reinforced by the actual orientation of the temple to the precise point in the sky occupied by celestial north.

While most Hindu and Buddhist temples (and, indeed, the temples and churches of many other denominations) are oriented according to the four cardinal directions, in the case of Borobudur the "orientation" is slightly off: 1.5 degrees west of true north, to be exact. This deviation from true north represents the position of the North Star (Polaris) at the time Borobudur was erected, at the end of the eighth century CE. At this time, Polaris was only about eleven minutes above the horizon and slowly disappearing beneath it; in fact, it was only visible at all during a few months of the year, although Ursa Major was still visible above the horizon and its two "pointer" stars could have been used to locate the position of Polaris below the horizon.

Why this should be the case — why Borobudur should have been oriented toward Polaris, even though Polaris could hardly be seen in East Java at the end of the eighth century CE, when the temple was erected — is due to the influence of the Buddhist scriptures, and especially the Puranas, on ideas of divine cosmology. The Buddhist sages who traveled to Java from the north brought with them their own ideas concerning the structure of the cosmos, and these ideas necessarily included the many references to the seven rishis (the stars of Ursa Major) and the Pole Star as pivot point and central pillar of the universe. Since these are visible manifestations, and used for orienting temples and rituals elsewhere in Buddhist lands, they would have continued the practice in Java even though the stars in question were not as visible or were, in fact, in the process of disappearing altogether due to the precession.

Regardless of whether or not the stars were actually visible from the Javanese hills, they were important enough to immortalize for they represented ideas of constancy, immortality, and infinity; characteristics of the gods.

On the fourth gallery of Borobudur, in the northwest sector, one can see a depiction of the sun and moon and seven circles between them. Rather than assume that any grouping of seven celestial objects must refer to the seven philosophical planets (i.e., the five planets visible to the naked eye, plus the sun and the moon) this bas-relief shows that these seven celestial objects do not include the sun and moon and must, therefore, represent seven other objects. Due to the importance of the idea of the seven rishis and the role of the rishis in creation and bringing the dharma to the world, they occupy a sacred space in the architecture of both Hindu and Buddhist temples where the idea of "seven" as related to seven stars is quite clear and unequivocal. It is only when we confront the literature of western esotericism that the confusion of seven "planets" with seven stars becomes obvious and clouds many issues that would otherwise be quite apparent.

In another gallery, we have a very badly damaged bas-relief that depicts the birth of Buddha. In this frame, we see Lord Buddha walking on seven lotuses or, rather, that seven lotuses rose from his first seven footsteps: yet another allusion to seven and divinity. These are hints that are scattered among the icons of Borobudur, and certainly there are other allusions to other Buddhist concepts and doctrines that have nothing to do with the number seven or the constellation Ursa Major; however, there is no escaping the fact that Borobudur was created as a mandala of the universe, a cosmological diagram that incorporates within itself Buddhist and Hindu ideas concerning morality, ethics, and spirituality. In other words, it is not only a physical cosmos but a moral cosmos; it is a plan for celestial ascent that emphasizes not only the schematics of the seven stages of initiation but also the spiritual qualities necessary for successfully completing such an ascent. It also depicts, at the final and ultimate level of the shrine, the inability of human beings to describe or explain the nature of this apotheosis: the eerily empty stupa at the very top.

Whereas the goal of the *merkavah* mystics in their celestial ascent was simple—to stand before the Throne of God and experience the divine presence—the goal of the Buddhist was more ambitious: a permanent change in spiritual status, beyond apotheosis, an annihilation of the self and return to Nothingness. However, the Kabbalistic texts themselves are conscious of this aspect of divinity when they refer to the "area" above *Kether* (the highest of the ten *sephiroth*) as *"Ain"* or *"Nothing."* While the *merkavah* mystic did not attempt to achieve a state of nothingness, it would be rash to assume that the descent to the Chariot was somehow inferior to the Hindu or Buddhist forms. With the emphasis on community and social responsibility that permeates the Jewish scriptures, we might be tempted to say that the Jewish mystic was already conscious of a duty to adopt the "Boddhisattva vow" of *not* attaining the ultimate stage of spiritual progress so that he might be able to act as a channel and conduit for the divine presence for his community of believers. The descent to the Chariot, while structurally very similar to the celestial ascent of the Hindu and Buddhist mystics, was designed to enable the Jewish mystic to ascend and descend, to come back to the community with special insights and powers that would enable him to improve the spiritual (and mundane) lives of his people while at the same time maintaining a link with the Divine that legitimated the process and reinforced the faith of his fellow Jews. As representative of a people whose survival was always in question, the Jewish mystic could not afford to become completely swallowed up in the mystical experience, to become separated from the life of his (small, isolated, and vulnerable) community forever. Further, messianic ideas and movements always threatened the status quo; the most famous of these movements ended in apostasy and heresy (Sabbatei Zevi, Jacob Frank, and even the movement that developed around the slain Jesus Christ). Instead, he could be expected to bring back gifts that the community could use: the ability to heal, to dispel demons, and otherwise to manipulate the harsh reality that everywhere and at every time threatened to destroy the fragile shtetls and ghettos. It was, if anything, a more practical approach to an extremely impractical idea and it was mirrored in another Asian culture that duplicated almost exactly the *merkavah* techniques of its Jewish counterparts.

China

As did the other ancient civilizations above the equator, China also revered the Ursa Major constellation and most especially the seven stars of the Dipper. More to the point, the Dipper was thought to be a seven-stepped ladder to the Northern Palace: the abode of the Immortals. The image of the Dipper was used as a template for the celestial ascent by Chinese Daoist mystics, and the Dipper appears on various seals and talismans used to ward off evil and ensure longevity. Thus the similarities between the Chinese celestial ascent and those of the *merkavah* mystics, the Babylonian and Egyptian priests, and the Hindu Tantricists, among others under discussion, are too numerous to ignore. But just as the Hindu methods presented us with an expanded and more articulated form of ascent technology, the Chinese methods will give us another dimension of this important mystical technique, one that ties it in with a peculiarly western phenomenon: alchemy.

The Chinese had developed a cosmological scheme that shares many similarities with those of the ancient Middle East and India. They understood the importance of the four quarters, or four cardinal directions of north, south, east, and west, and these were considered the domains of spiritual forces. They divided the four quarters into four celestial and four terrestrial versions. Thus, the north in heaven was the entranceway to the abode of the Immortals, but the terrestrial north was the entrance to the Underworld and the abode of the dead. They posited an *axis mundi* that ran from the center of the earth to the center of the heavens, i.e., to celestial north and the Pole Star. To the Chinese, the seven stars of the Dipper were seven deities: one had to know the names of each of the gods as well as the appropriate passwords in order to "go" from one star to the next, ever upward, in the quest for the Northern Palace and the Celestial Garden of the Immortals. Furthermore, divine spirit or "essence" flowed from the stars of the Dipper; bones and sinew, on the other hand, were creations of earthly forces.

The vision of Ezekiel would be comprehensible to the Chinese of the Han and Shan dynasties in its particulars: the vision comes from the north, there are four heraldic creatures representing the four corners of the universe, there is a chariot and a throne, and on the throne a divine being. From the perspective of a Chinese alchemist, the vision of Ezekiel could be nothing other than a vision of the gods of the Dipper. Even more so, the texts of the *ma'aseh merkavah* share greater similarities in the idea of an ascent up seven levels, different spiritual forces at each level, divine names and words of power appropriate for each, etc. As we will see, the Chinese alchemists had a procedure, practiced in one form or another for centuries, that is virtually identical to the "descent to the Chariot" and that opens up for us another level of understanding of the nature of this practice.

To the Chinese mystics and alchemists — who were operating at the same time as the Jewish sect of Qumran was initiating members and writing letters to the priests of the Temple in Jerusalem — there are two forms of what they call alchemy: inner alchemy (*neidan*) and outer alchemy (*waidan*), terms that could also be translated as "inner elixir" and "outer elixir" after the name of alchemy itself, which is *jindan,* or literally "golden elixir." The earliest references we have to anything resembling this form of alchemy is from the fourth-century-BCE records of the *fangshi,* the "masters of the method" or more commonly translated as "magicians." The historical data becomes more prevalent by the first century BCE in China, when alchemists were known to have been searching for an elixir that would grant immortality, an elixir that was created by transforming metals. By the fourth century CE, Chinese alchemy had become highly articulated with an emphasis on the parallel actions of the heavenly spheres and the internal bodily processes. Terminology that was commonly used for describing chemical processes and transformations had begun to be used to describe biological and psychobiological functions, states, and anatomy. The one was the reflection of the other, much in the same way that the Indian Tantricists believed that the cosmic structure of the macrocosm could be identified within the microcosm of the human body. While the Daoist alchemists of this, the *Shang Qing,* period visualized the gods and goddesses of the Dipper as residing in the heavens, they also understood that the heavens were reflected within the organs of the body. By controlling the actions of the human body, it was believed, one could exert control over the external world as well. Like a Jewish *merkavah* mystic, alone in his chamber in the dead of night, meditating and visualizing the seven *hekhalot* or palaces of heaven, the Chinese alchemist also retreated alone to a special, quiet chamber and visualized the seven stars of the Dipper. While the Jewish technology was identified with Jewish law and scripture, the Chinese technology was equally culturally encoded, in this case within a purely Daoist (and originally shamanistic) framework. Thus, if we try to compare the two techniques from the point of view of religious doctrine, we will not get very far; but if we strip the techniques of their cultural contexts we find that we have before us technologies that are virtually identical in form as well as function.

Someone critical of the "history of religions" school might insist that this doctrinal and cultural difference is everything: that you can't compare apples and oranges. I agree, to a point, while at the same time maintaining that both apples and oranges are fruit. It is this basic level of the practice that is of importance to this study, for it is the mechanism by which much religious and mystical experience is obtained, and from that experience, and from the commentators and theologians who come after, religions and schools of mysticism are born. The theory put forward in this thesis is that there is a correlation between this particular mystical praxis and astronomical phenomena: that the internal process imitates perceived external cosmological structures (structures, in this case, that are identical in form to everyone living in the northern latitudes and that thus provide a "universal" correlate). That is, of course, the theory behind the type of Chinese alchemy under investigation; it can also be applied to *merkavah* mysticism, in the opinion of this author and in light of the evidence being presented. The implications of this approach are profound, for they indicate that the different reactions that are recorded by different cultures represent nothing less than different perspectives on the same experience, an experience that is by its very nature ineffable and indescribable. Once we realize that the same technique is being employed toward the same end, we can then begin to appreciate the quality (and the necessity) of the variations of human reaction to this experience. In other words, the Chinese doctrines can be usefully compared to the Jewish texts, and the Egyptian to the Haitian, etc., each culture a lens through which the divine experience is filtered, for no direct experience of the Divine — no lens-free confrontation, stripped of any and all cultural, ethnic, political, environmental, and economic perceptions and biases — is possible.

The Daoist scholar Isabelle Robinet has clarified this approach in her own essay on Shang Qing alchemy published in 1989, when she wrote:

> In meditation practice, the active value of the image is first, not its theoretical or discursive importance. Mere philosophical propositions don't play a significant role in this context, because Taoism as a practice is essentially pragmatic.[16]

This is an advantage for our study, for this pragmatic approach will help us to reexamine the other forms of celestial ascent we have mentioned so far.

Celestial ascent was as much a feature of Daoist philosophy and mythology as it was of *merkavah* mysticism. The Yellow Emperor — Huangdi, the first Chinese emperor — was believed to have ascended to the heavens as is reported in the *Zhuangzi;* and he did this utilizing the same force or power that specifically keeps the "Northern Dipper" spinning around the Pole Star.[17] The same passage in the *Zhuangzi* refers to the mysterious mountain Kunlun, the *axis mundi* of the Chinese mystics.

The Pace of Yu

To understand the context within which the Shang Qing alchemists were invoking the powers of the Dipper, we must begin with the story of Tai Yu, or "Yu the Great," the founder of the Xia dynasty (twenty-first century–sixteenth century BCE), the first recorded Chinese dynasty. The legends surrounding Yu are numerous and rich in suggestive detail. He is credited with quelling the floodwaters of the rivers, an important attribute in a country that experiences severe flooding every decade or so. He is also credited with defeating barbarian hordes, establishing agricultural practices, exorcising demons, and creating the boundaries of the Chinese state. He is sometimes depicted holding a compass and square in his right hand, and a water level and chalk line in his left,[18] reminiscent of the symbols of a Mason or a builder of temples in the West. According to tradition, he founded the Xia dynasty in 2070 BCE. Stories and legends grew up around this enigmatic figure, and it appears from the historical record that he was more identified with the peoples of south China than with the north, and that shamanistic elements played a large part in the development of the corpus of ideas and rituals that surround his name. Part Moses, part Noah, he was associated with the beginning of Chinese civilization in many ways, from the building of dykes and levees to hold back the floodwaters, to the establishment of a lineage of nobility to rule the country, to his ability to communicate with beings both natural and supernatural. By the time the Celestial Master cult had penetrated to south China from north China around the time of the

Han dynasty (circa 200 BCE–200 CE) shamanistic ritual practices involving Yu the Great had become mixed with those of the Daoist practices of the Celestial Masters. Yu's peripatetic wandering around China had become expanded to include his wandering around the heavens as well. By the fourth century CE, and almost certainly much earlier than that, these wanderings had been enshrined in a mystical practice known as the "Pace of Yu."

The Pace of Yu has two important elements. The first is the relatively simple dance itself. As described in the writings of the fourth century CE Chinese alchemist Ge Hong in his famous *Baopuzi* ("The Master Embracing Simplicity"):

Stand straight. Move the right foot forward, leaving the left behind. Then advance the left foot and the right foot, one after the other, until they are both side by side. This is step one. Move the right foot forward, then the left, then bring the right foot side by side with the left. This is step two. Advance the left foot, then the right, then bring the left side by side with the right. This is step three. These three are the Pace of Yu.[19]

The second important element is the identification of this strange dance with the seven stars of the Dipper. It is not known when the Pace of Yu became coupled with the Dipper concept; it is likely that the Pace was originally a shamanistic dance intended to invoke spiritual forces and that it only later became identified with the Dipper. However, the Chinese texts have indicated that the dance represents a man limping;[20] if that is so, then we may have evidence of a somewhat older concept linking both the dance and the Dipper.

When one tries to walk in a straight line with a limp or with one leg shorter than the other, the straight line becomes a circle, describing a circumference around a central point. This is, of course, precisely what the stars of the Dipper do around the Pole Star. The theme of a limping man is to be found in various mythologies around the world, and often this concept is linked with ideas of antiquity, the northern regions, the Underworld, etc. We might say that the ancient Egyptian concept of the Thigh of Set may be linked to this idea: an animal or a human, wounded in one leg or deprived of one leg, would limp.

The Pace of Yu, therefore, is consistent with other patterns relative to the stars of the Dipper and actually represents in kinetic form the movement of its stars around the Pole Star. By the time of the Han dynasty, this had become official. Diagrams were created showing the Pace of Yu as an overlay on the Dipper asterism.

The alchemists of the Shang Qing school elaborated upon this technique with rituals that seem to prefigure those of medieval European ceremonial magic and that, indeed, may help to explain much of western esoteric practice that has remained mysterious so far.

Shang Qing Daoism

Shang Qing Daoism dates to the fourth century CE, specifically to the years 364–70, a period of seven years during which one Yang Xi received a continuing series of visions. These visions were said to have come from Immortals who had descended from one of the Chinese heavens, the Shang Qing. The result of these visions was a set of scriptures, which were expanded and commented upon by those who came after Yang and who formed the core of what would be known as the Mao Shan revelations, after the mountain retreat where the scriptures were kept and studied. These revelations constitute a large part of what is now known as the Daoist Canon, and contain everything from instructions for meditation and concentration to recipes for magical elixirs and other areas of alchemical interest.

One of the more interesting of these texts is the Sword Scripture. This contains a description of a ritual that should be performed by the mystic in which a sword is used as his proxy during the celestial ascent, standing in for the adept's body, which was believed to be transported to the heavenly realms. The Sword Scripture survives today only in fragments, many of which are concerned with elixirs and poisons; as in European alchemy, the difference between an elixir for immortality and a poison that would cause immediate death could be very thin indeed.

Another Shang Qing document records the celestial hierarchy. Known as *Concealed Instructions for Ascent to Perfection,* it has also come down to us as *Ranks and Functions of the Perfected and Other Powers.* Believed to be a fifth-century CE work, it lists seven levels of celestial hierarchy, from the absolute heaven of Jade Purity, to those of Supreme Purity (*Shang Qing*) and the Great Bourne (*Tai Ji*) in the north, the Great Purity in the east, the Nine Mansions in the west, the Cavern Heavens beneath the earth, and finally to the Citadel of Night in the terrestrial north, the abode of the dead. This seven-layered cosmological scheme may have been influenced by Buddhist ideas — as may have been the *axis mundi* of Mount Kunlun — but its focus on the north as the region of the highest heavens is consistent with everything else we have been investigating. It is also linked to the idea of celestial ascent; once again, the map of the cosmos is also an instruction manual for ecstatic flight.

This flight was itself called "Pacing the Dipper," and to perform this ritual a room was selected that was private, where the mystic would not be disturbed. On the floor of the room would be placed a carpet or length of silk upon which were traced the seven stars of the Dipper. After invoking the guardian spirits of the four cardinal directions, the mystic would then either physically walk, or pace, the diagram on the floor with the appropriate chants and prayers for each star, or would perform the ritual mentally while in a meditative posture in the center of the diagram. To "Pace the Dipper" one would use the same shamanistic dance known as the Pace of Yu, progressing from one star to the next in this fashion.

According to Chinese tradition, upon which the Shang Qing scriptures are based, there are nine heavens; this discrepancy is usually explained by the fact that the seven visible stars of the Dipper are accompanied by two invisible stars. These are sometimes depicted in diagrams of the Dipper. In addition, it is believed that there is an "invisible Dipper" that provides the ground or backdrop for the visible one. This idea of invisible stars has a long pedigree in China, and it is believed there are also invisible planets and that each visible planet has its invisible counterpart.

There are also five "poles" in the Chinese cosmological system, but they refer to the four cardinal directions plus the central pole or *axis mundi*. The Daoist magician or alchemist invokes the poles for protection before beginning his meditations in much the same way modern occultists of the European esoteric tradition invoke the four "watchtowers" in the cardinal directions as a prerequisite for any ritual performance. The four guardian spirits, or "emperors" in the Chinese tradition, will protect the body of the mystic as his soul leaves it to wander the vast spaces of the cosmos in search of secret knowledge and magic elixirs.

Several texts refer to the mystic as traveling heavenward in a divine carriage or vehicle; others have him simply flying in human form, without visible assistance. The idea that the soul could leave the body during ecstatic flight is something that is well-known to the *merkavah* mystics. In several reported cases, a *merkavah* mystic was known to be in a state of deep trance during the descent to the Chariot, and it was considered dangerous to wake him or to otherwise disturb him.

To the Shang Qing mystics, the focus of the ritual was on internal, interior processes. It was believed that the ecstatic flight took place without the use of chemical means, but rather concentrated more on visualization and meditation. The cosmological scheme was complex and detailed, and it was believed to be mirrored in the human body. It represented an interiorization of the alchemical process but one that simultaneously enabled the practitioner to climb the seven heavens and wind up in the Northern Palace, or Garden of the Immortals. The seven stars of the Dipper were real places to the Chinese alchemists, and even their astronomy reflected the circumpolar nature of their cosmological systems. Rather than the ecliptic-oriented focus of the Greek and Roman astrologers and astronomers, the Chinese divided the heavens using the North Star and the Dipper as starting points with the seven stars of the Dipper each in charge of four "stations" of the moon, for a total of twenty-eight lunar stations. The center of the Chinese geomancer's compass was a magnetic needle; in some depictions, the center is represented by the sign of the Dipper constellation. Everything else flowed from that, and the divine essence that is the unseen force in all creation came from the Dipper. Thus, the ecstatic flight of the Shang Qing alchemist was linked to immortality: a voyage to the stars that culminated in sipping from the source of Life itself.

This sipping was even more literal than one might imagine. It began with the doctrine of the "sprouts": through special breathing exercises and meditation, one's saliva became imbued with divine qualities. The sprouts are the "germinal essences" of the four poles.[21] They ascend to the heavens every morning from their germination points throughout the universe, from where they descend through the five sacred mountains of the five directions on earth — north, east, south, west, and center — and finally into the adept who is trained in their cultivation, performing the ritual at dawn when the *yin* and *yang* breaths are not yet separated, the time of the sprouts' greatest potency. Thus, the "germinal essences" perform a flight to the heavens and a descent to the earth; strengthened by consuming these essences, the adept can mimic their ascent to the celestial gates. By carefully following this procedure for a length of time, the adept eventually consumes only the sprouts, needing no other nourishment, and becomes lighter than air and able to fly.

Then the adept begins to visualize the topography of the four quarters of the heavens, imagining every detail of their respective landscapes, beginning with the geography closest to him and expanding further and further out until he is within sight of the sacred mountain of each of the four cardinal directions. Once he has attained this proximity, he is given an elixir to drink and returns "home" in command of the creatures of that Pole. (This visiting of a visualized site and returning empowered over it is a central feature of the *merkavah* texts, as well.)

Eventually, this concept of travel over vast distances extends to travel to the sun, the moon, and the stars. The sun and moon occupy important places in Daoist philosophy, as they do in virtually every other native religion. The sun in Daoism is considered reflective of the principle of *yang*, or active, masculine energy while the moon is correspondingly *yin*, feminine and passive. *Yin* represents the earth just as *yang* represents the sky. The number of attributions given to *yin* and *yang* are legion, of course, and many ancient and modern texts have been written elucidating their respective natures. The famous book of divination and philosophy, the *I Jing*, is concerned with just this interplay of positive and negative, *yang* and *yin*, forces in the universe.

The sun and moon are also the celestial beings that regulate the four celestial Poles through the four gates of the two equinoxes and the two solstices that represent in space what the four cardinal directions do on earth.

The adept will prepare an elixir made of pure water in which a talisman, representing the appropriate gate, has been dissolved. Drinking this will enable the adept to pass safely through the appropriate gate. At the same time, the sun and moon are visualized in their appropriate places in the adept's body, nourishing and empowering the interior organs, which are, after all, micro-cosmically resonating with their macrocosmic orbits. As the sun and moon are thus internalized, the adept's organs become externalized as the very stars themselves. Flight is then possible as the adept identifies himself with the cosmos; it then takes only the movement of the mind to propel him into the heavens.

When the Dipper becomes involved, the *rituale* becomes more complex and articulated. Rituals involving what the Chinese refer to as the Northern Dipper are ancient, existing long before normative Daoist practices and at one point becoming combined with Buddhist iconography and religion.

Perhaps the earliest Chinese god was Shangdi, the creator god who dwells in the Northern Dipper, which serves as his throne.[22] Worship of Shangdi goes back to the third millennium BCE, at which time, according to an ancient Chinese source, the philosopher Da Nao created the division of time into ten celestial stems and twelve earthly branches, thus giving rise to the cycle of sixty years that is the Chinese calendar. According to the text, Da Nao conceived of this division through observance of the motions of the Northern Dipper.[23] That measurement is associated with the Northern Dipper and with the Supreme God is, of course, a common motif in the West as well. In China, this identification is extended through the association of the "Mother of the Measure" as a goddess who resides on a lotus that is itself supported by the Northern Dipper (for longevity) and the Southern Dipper (for wealth). The Southern Dipper is identified as six stars in the constellation Sagittarius, which form an asterism very close in appearance to that of the Northern Dipper. While the Southern Dipper represents wealth, the Northern Dipper, consistent with the mythologem everywhere we find it, represents longevity, immortality, and the central pole of the universe.

The system for invoking the stars of the Northern Dipper reflects these ideas. In the Shang Qing school, the Northern Dipper consists of the same seven stars with which we are already familiar, plus the "invisible" stars of Fu and Bi. Fu is somehow related to the planet Mars, and Bi to the Polestar. They occupy a position similar to that of the sun and moon in ecliptical astronomy, but at a higher — circumpolar — frequency. They remain invisible to those who have not attained the requisite level of purity.

The Northern Dipper is the abode of gods; the seven visible stars plus the two invisible stars form a system containing nine heavens and a god for each. However, as mentioned above, there is also a mirror-image of the Northern

Dipper that is entirely *yin* or female. These "black stars" are inhabited by goddesses, the spouses of the nine gods of the Dipper.[24]

According to the Shang Qing school, the Northern Dipper provides a protective function for the adept. Since it represents immortality, it also represents the Underworld. It is simultaneously the seven levels of heaven and the seven steps down into the abode of the dead. This is consistent with the themes as represented in the Egyptian and Sumerian concepts of the seven levels.

In the Shang Qing text known as the *Jinshu yuzi*, one may ascend to the Dipper by sleeping on a mat on which the constellation has been drawn: "Meditating in this position, adepts visualize the essences of the nine stars turning into one divinity who comes down to receive them in a chariot."[25]

The most complex and complete form of this celestial ascent, however, is depicted in the method known as "pacing the net" or "pacing the Dipper," which is itself based on the Pace of Yu. According to Isabelle Robinet, this system was already in place by the first century CE,[26] thus making it contemporary with the Qumran texts. In this four-part ritual, the adept must circumambulate the stars of the Dipper counterclockwise; then pacing the stars beginning with the first star, one foot on each star, beginning with the left foot; then circumambulating the stars clockwise starting with the last star and beginning with the right foot; then finally pacing all the stars again, this time using both feet. In this way, the ancient shamanistic practice of the Pace of Yu has been grafted onto the Daoist theme of the Northern Dipper and the ideas of Chinese alchemy. The concept of stars having a protective function, and the use of the four cardinal directions to protect the body of the adept, plus the circumambulations and the celestial ascent, have all found their expression in the rituals of modern-day ceremonial magic as illustrated by the practices of such groups as the Golden Dawn and the witchcraft revival of the twentieth century known as "Wicca." What Shang Qing Daoism has to offer to this discussion is a more clearly articulated raison d'être for these practices, as well as an expansion of these themes to include alchemy and Tantric rites.

Chinese Alchemy as Biological Process

When one realizes that, according to the texts of Shang Qing Daoism, the Northern Dipper and the Pole Star around which it revolves represents ideas of germination and birth, one can extrapolate from this idea to the general themes of Chinese alchemy which focus on regeneration and longevity. The north may be the place where the sun dies on its daily course through the four cardinal directions, but it is also the place where the sun is reborn, to begin anew its diurnal motion. Thus, the north became a focus for Chinese alchemists who desired to imitate nature and find the sacred, hidden essence of life in the darkest, most remote place of the cosmos. Daylight was the time when nature manifested itself in all its glory: it was the time of expression, of showing the result of the natural processes. Night time, however, was the period when germination and conception took place. Night time was the period when one could see clearly the motions of the stars and the activities of the heavens and could imitate these events on earth.

Night was the time of secrets and things hidden; so was the earth, the underground world where it was believed metals "grew" like plants. Similarly, the internal organs of the human body were the loci where fabulous essences could be germinated and cultivated. Just as the north was simultaneously the locus of the highest heaven and of the Underworld, so the human body was linked to both heaven and hell. The body contained palaces where gods and goddesses resided, as well as fields where divine essences could be coaxed into an immortal harvest. Like the Tantric systems of India, the Chinese had located various locations in the human body that formed a network of energy and miraculous "metals" that could be manipulated through meditation and various physical and mental exercises, of which the Pacing of the Dipper was one variation. The body itself could be transformed, its longevity assured, by probing its secrets and allowing its inner nature to be revealed — all the time coordinating its actions with those of the heavens and especially the Dipper, since the Dipper itself was immortal.

> Though their common matrix was terrestrial, the rhythms of growth of the diverse vegetable and mineral species were complex protocols of time determined by a higher power. The interlocking patterns of their development in the earth met in the heavens, in the pure sphere of the eternal stars. . . . Since Han times at least, the stars had been recognized as embodying the essences of all things.[27]

This internalization of the celestial hierarchy means that the gods of the Dipper are said to reside in the heart, while the goddesses of the black stars reside in the head.[28] The heart is thus north, and the place of the element water from which all life begins; the head is *yin* to the heart's *yang,* the realm of the Nine Palaces. The Daoists placed importance on the head, heart, and kidneys; likewise they believed that the male adept should refrain from sexual activity or at the very least avoid seminal emissions. In this, of course, they are in agreement with the *merkavah* mystics, who similarly avoided seminal emission. The Daoist adepts, however, employed various physical practices to stimulate the production of semen while at the same time forbidding its emission. This included applying pressure to the perineum during sexual activity: this pressure would block the flow of semen during orgasm and cause it to discharge into the bladder. This was considered preferable to normal seminal emission during which the vital essence of the seminal fluid would be lost. Like controlling breath, this control of another bodily function was considered vital to the pursuit of longevity.

It would seem that a major doctrinal difference between Chinese alchemy and Jewish *merkavah* mysticism could be found in analyzing the ultimate goal of each practice. Both mystics wished to ascend to the heavens and both mystics employed similar devices for attaining that immediate goal. The Chinese, however, saw the utility of this practice in becoming immortal, while for the *merkavah* mystics it would seem that the descent to the Chariot was an end in itself. The documents tell a different story, however.

While the idea of the descent to the Chariot is enshrouded in mystery and awe, the *merkavah* texts themselves seem to reflect a preoccupation with mundane concerns. While physical immortality is not described in the *merkavah* texts — it would be doctrinally inappropriate for a pious Jew to contemplate such a goal — attaining a certain degree of perfectibility was not out of the question. In order to participate in the company of the angels, one had to become pure. Long periods of fasting, sexual abstinence, and prayer would precede the attempt to descend to the Chariot. The physical body had to be made subordinate to the will of the adept. He had to demonstrate control over bodily functions and desires, to regulate passions and appetites. The biological process that preceded the descent to the Chariot was the same for the *merkavah* mystic as it was for the Daoist alchemist. Even the physical surroundings of both were virtually identical: a sealed chamber in which neither mystic would be interrupted or observed; a meditative pose; a concentration on the seven levels and the words and gestures appropriate to each. The mystic would create an athanor in this fashion: the sealed furnace in which the chemical transformations would take place, the dross of the base human nature changing into something angelic, nearly divine. After all, the patron saint of the descent to the Chariot was Enoch: the human being who was brought to heaven by God and who became almost indistinguishable from an angel or a celestial lord. The imitation of Ezekiel was an attempt to reach the Throne of God in the heavens where human transformation was represented. The body itself was the laboratory in which this transformation would take place; the autonomous nervous system was the Net that the Tantricist, mystic, and alchemist alike "paced" during the celestial, ecstatic ascent. To the Babylonians, it was the ziggurat; to the Indians, it was Mount Meru; to the Chinese, it was Mount Kunlun. In every case, it was the *axis mundi* and at the very summit could be seen the Pole Star and the seven stars of the Dipper spinning eternally around it.

The Ainu

As a brief comment, we can look even further east, toward northern Japan and the race of the Ainu. Ainu origins are shrouded in mystery, and one of their core rituals is the *iyomande,* the "home-coming of the soul."[29] In preparation for this ritual, a bear cub is reared by a village. It is fed and much care is taken of this creature believed to resemble in many ways a human being. Once the bear has come of age, he is sacrificed in a brutal ritual that involves its torture and eventual strangulation. The bear's soul is sent off to the heavens to convince its parents that it has been treated well (!) so that it will return to be hunted once again.

The name of the dead bear, the soul of the bear thus sacrificed, is *chinukara-guru.* This means "prophet" or "guardian." It is the same name given to the Pole Star.

Part Four

Ascent and the Dipper in Modern Esotericism

The Seal of the Hermetic Brotherhood of Luxor (also the Hermetic Brotherhood of Light). Note the seven stars around the serpent and arrow in the center of the diagram and the four cherubim from Ezekiel's Vision in the four corners. The seven stars represent stars and not planets, as is obvious from the addition of the Sun and Moon symbols to the right and left, respectively. The placement is identical to that found at Borobudur.

THERE HAS BEEN A CONTINUUM of technology from the Dipper mysticism of the ancient Near East, Africa, and Asia to the modern western European esoteric tradition of the last two hundred years. The strains of this continuum are easy to discern. The basic iconography of the seven stars is duplicated in many of this tradition's writings and rituals, although never explicitly identified as such. Both the Dipper iconography and the *merkavah* technology have been retained, although in subtle forms and subject to a certain degree of misdirection. We will examine in particular the thread of this concept in the rituals and knowledge lectures of the Hermetic Order of the Golden Dawn and in its associated groups such as the Hermetic Brotherhood of Light, the Ordo Templi Orientis, etc. In the process, we will discover that there was a line of succession to the Golden Dawn from the Frankist movement of the eighteenth century, thus providing a Kabbalistic pedigree and channel of transmission for this ancient and sacred tradition. Finally, in an excursus, we will look at a key Rosicrucian document, *The Chymical Wedding of Christian Rosenkreutz*, for more evidence of this transmission.

Chapter 9

Origins of a Western Tradition

We have followed the idea of celestial ascent from Egypt and Babylon to India and China. The focus on the Northern Dipper (Ursa Major) and the Pole Star with regard to celestial ascent has been consistent in all of these cultures, as we have demonstrated. What has not been so obvious is a similar focus to be found in the esoteric and occult traditions of Europe and the West, which have typically placed more emphasis on the constellations of the ecliptic, the zodiac, through which the planets "move" every day. If we were to draw a picture of these two approaches to esoteric astronomy, we would see that they were roughly perpendicular to each other: the European, zodiacal approach would focus on the rising and setting of the stars and planets from the eastern horizon to the western, while the "Asian" approach would be on the circumpolar constellations that do not rise and set with the others but revolve around the Pole Star in the north. The first approach is terrestrially centered, with the rising of the sun marking the all-important east and the four quarters measured from that point. The second approach is celestially centered, with the Pole Star as the top of the world-axis in the north and the seven stars of the Dipper demarcating the twenty-eight lunar mansions and the quarters of the cosmos.

However, there is an esoteric tradition in the West that did place a strong emphasis on the circumpolar aspect of astronomy although it has not been considered as such until now. There has been some confusion and controversy over this particular field of religious history due to the utter lack of reliable documentation concerning its practices; it has, however, left us considerable iconographic material to consider, and this will help us to reveal its secrets.

The Cave of the Bull

Each of the planetary bodies presided over a day of the week, to each some one metal was consecrated, each was associated with some one degree in the initiation, and their number has caused a special religious potency to be attributed to the number seven.

— Franz Cumont, *The Mysteries of Mithra*[1]

135

David Ulansey has done a great deal of work in an effort to tear away the veil from the sanctuary of the Mithraic gnosis.[2] By emphasizing the celestial aspect of the Mithraic mysteries he has pointed scholarship in a promising direction. His work has focused on the iconography of the Mithra cult as it has appeared in Europe and the Middle East, as well as on the few available documents we have on the society that have come down to us from the pens of Christian and, hence, hostile authors.

Perhaps the first modern scholar to have written extensively about the cult of Mithra was the French historian Franz Cumont. Cataloging the archaeological evidence left behind by the cult, he was able to bring together the physical remains and tie them to the ancient writings of Origen and Tertullian, as well as to the sacred scriptures of the Zoroastrians and the Mazdaeans. On one aspect of the cult virtually everyone is in agreement: it consisted of seven degrees, sometimes depicted as rungs on a ladder, that would lead one to higher and higher states of enlightenment and understanding. These seven degrees were usually related to the seven "Platonic" planets: the Sun and Moon, with Mars, Mercury, Venus, Jupiter, and Saturn. The cult met in caves or in other lonely places, and their rituals were not written down. As in the case with the Eleusinian mysteries, what we know of their initiations is largely conjecture based on scraps of available evidence.

As the main competitor of Christianity in the final days of the Roman Empire, the Mithra cult had hundreds of sacred sites scattered throughout Europe and those parts of the Middle East under Roman control. Its origins are as shrouded in mystery as its rituals. Some historians, like Cumont, have insisted on a Persian, Zoroastrian source, while others are not so certain. In more recent times, it has been considered that Mithra was a syncretic deity composed of several different strands of indigenous religions. Cumont felt that the cult of Mithra was born in some tangential point between the religion of the Aryans of India and that of the Persians, and it is true that we can find traces of the word "Mithra" in the Zoroastrian scriptures, the *Zend Avesta*, as well as in the Vedas. The high priests of the cult of Mithra (as of the Zoroastrians) were the Magi, from which we derive the word "magician" and "magic." By the first and second centuries CE, the cult of Mithra had come into its own throughout the Roman Empire, including the British Isles as far north as Hadrian's Wall, and had become the cult of the Roman soldier. Indeed, one of the degrees of Mithraic initiation was called *milites*, or "soldiers." Prior to its adoption by the Roman legions, however, the worship of Mithra was ancient and had spread throughout the east from India to Assyria, declining in force only in those lands as other religions came to take its place. Gradually, the supreme nature of this god was reduced until it was mentioned only in passing, and in much degenerated form, in the sacred scriptures of the east.

While the religion itself lost its command over the masses of people, it never lost its romantic allure. It pretended, after all, to grand secrets and esoteric knowledge that could be conferred only through an arduous process of initiation. As one progressed up the seven levels of initiation, one became privy to greater and greater secrets and whatever these have been are lost to time. The only remnants of these doctrines are to be found in polemics by Origen and Tertullian and other writers of the period, and in Mithraic iconography.

One of the most arresting figures of the Mithra cult was the icon of Kronos ("Time"), the Mithraic Saturn. Various attempts have been made to identify the emblems and symbols with which this figure is usually identified. He is normally shown as a naked male figure with the head of a lion. Around his body can be seen the coils of a serpent, whose head then covers the top of the lion's head. In his hands are seen two keys, one in each hand. He has four wings — two on top, pointing upward, and two lower wings, pointing downward — and a thunderbolt design on his chest.

The thunderbolt design is interesting, for although it is identified as such in Cumont,[3] in appearance it seems so similar to the Tibetan *dorje* symbol as to be uncanny. The four wings immediately call to mind the wings of the *cherubim* of Ezekiel and the various supernatural beings of the Babylonians, from depictions of gods like Ninurta to the so-called griffin-demons, all of whom are shown with four wings in the same formation.[4]

In addition, the physical appearance of the two keys is suggestive. Cumont identifies them as keys to the "portals of heaven";[5] in the drawing accompanying his text, the key in the figure's right hand looks suspiciously like the adze used by the ancient Egyptians in the Opening of the Mouth ceremony.[6]

In fact, one could look at this figure, completely wrapped in the coils of the snake and holding two keys and a scepter, and imagine an Egyptian mummy. The snake itself has been identified by Cumont as representing the passage of the sun through the belt of the ecliptic. If we were to accept that Mithra is a solar cult and that Kronos is a representation of this in symbolic form, then it makes a certain degree of sense to accept this interpretation of the coils of the snake. However, there was another "snake" in the heavens, and the coils of this snake may point us in a slightly different direction.

In ancient astronomy as well as in contemporary science there is a constellation close to the Pole Star known as Draco, or "the Dragon." It separates the two constellations of Ursa Major and Ursa Minor, and thus lies between them and the Pole Star. In fact, its folds still wrap around Ursa Minor and in old manuscripts it is shown with both Bears as *Arctoe et Draco*, the Bears and the Dragon. Due to the precession of the equinoxes, in ancient times the star Thuban (from the Arabic for "basilisk") in the constellation Draco was the Pole Star, lying about 10' from due north in the year 2750 BCE, at the time the Great Pyramid was built and was possibly the star toward which the pyramid was oriented. When the Pole Star shifted from Thuban to Polaris one could say that the Dragon was "slain": it had lost its preeminent position as the very top of the *axis mundi*. This took place gradually over a long period of time, however. From about 1000 BCE to the Christian era, the position of "Pole Star" was relatively vacant as polar north shifted from Thuban to Polaris, passing briefly through Kochab in Ursa Minor about 1900 BCE and its companion Pherkad (the two stars, Kochab and Pherkad, are sometimes called the "Guardians of the Pole") until about 500 BCE, when Polaris began to occupy that role, getting gradually closer and closer to true north so that today it is less than one degree from that position.

It's not the intention of the author to weigh down this argument with a discussion of celestial mechanics. It is, however, critical for an understanding of how the ancients understood the structure of their cosmos that was, after all, the structure of their religious understanding as well. Many of the religious themes we have already encountered can be seen as coded forms of cosmological data, based on close observation of the skies over long periods of time. The rising and setting of the sun and the moon were obvious points of departure, for depending on the season they could be seen to rise and set at different places on the horizon. Thus, the solar year could be divided into four seasons, corresponding to the two equinoxes ("equal nights" when the hours of day and night are equal: the first day of spring and the first day of autumn) and the two solstices (when the sun seems to "stand still": the first day of winter, the shortest day of the year, and the first day of summer, the longest day of the year). These "quarter days" correspond to the first days of the present-day zodiacal signs of Aries, Cancer, Libra, and Capricorn. The "cross-quarter" days were days that were roughly midway between the quarter days, and were April 30, August 1, October 31, and February 2, corresponding to positions in the present-day zodiacal signs of Taurus, Leo, Scorpio, and Aquarius. Taurus of course is represented by the Bull; Leo by the Lion; Scorpio in a few Middle Eastern cultures by the Eagle; and Aquarius by a Man. These in turn refer to the four cherubim seen by Ezekiel in his famous vision and became symbols of the seasons that were reflected in the iconography of the Mithra cult. Further, April 30 is the pagan festival of Beltane, or Walpurgisnacht; August 1 is Lammas; October 31 is Samhain or Halloween; and February 2 is Imbolc or Candlemas: important pagan festivals in the cultus of western Europe and the British Isles and enshrined today as holidays in the neo-Pagan movement.

While the establishment of the seasons and the solar and lunar calendars was of primary importance to agriculture and for determining planting and harvesting cycles, consideration of the orbits of the planets was another matter entirely. Knowledge of their circuits through the heavens did not directly correspond to any pragmatic, mundane application. Even today, while we are aware of the passage of the seasons and the observance of "daylight saving time" in the northern latitudes, the transits of Venus, Mars, Mercury, and the other planets pass unnoticed and unremarked for most people. Yet those of us who are involved in navigation by land, air, or sea do become aware of the circumpolar stars and the position in the sky of true north, as that information is essential to survival when there is no other technological alternative at our disposal.

One could extrapolate, from the unquestioned importance of the solar and lunar calendars and the importance of the circumpolar stars, that the orbits and transits of any and all celestial bodies had some degree of relevance to the human experience. It was only a matter of determining what events they signaled or signed. In the case of Mars, its red color when seen with the naked eye was an easy determinant: red was the color of blood, and thus of human passion and violence. Jupiter was the largest of the planets, and therefore the significator of wealth or power. Saturn, as the furthest away and the slowest moving, was an Old Man and the symbol of Time, Wisdom, and even Judgment. Mercury, as the closest and fastest-moving, was the messenger and communicator. Finally, Venus was both the Morning Star and the Evening Star, rising and setting close to the sun as if its Bride. She could represent love and faithfulness on the one hand, and could also be a goddess of war on the other. "Hell hath no fury … " etc. These were still relatively fanciful designations, because their effect on affairs on earth were not as obvious as those of the sun and moon. They could be determined only through observation over a long period of time: Did Mars rise at a time of danger or war? Did Jupiter rise at a time when the prosperity of the nation was on the increase?

As the sun and moon rise and set at different places at different times of the year against the backdrop of the ecliptic and the zodiacal belt, so do the five planets. The sun in winter was a different significator from the sun in summer or spring. The same could be said for the planets. Eventually, a cosmic scheme was developed capable of interpreting all the possible combinations of luminaries, planets, and zodiacal signs.

This system was by no means universal. The solar calendar itself was somewhat problematic, even as late as the first century CE, when the Jews of Herod's Temple utilized a lunar calendar at a time when the Qumran sect insisted on a solar calendar. Religious differences in the application of Time to Space resulted in political differences as well. When the Roman Catholic

Pope Gregory reformed the solar calendar, those who were not under the control of the Catholic Church refused to accept it and maintained their loyalty to the old Julian calendar of the Roman period. This division of religious time versus civil time continues to this day all over the world; the Eastern Orthodox Church contains elements that call themselves "Old Calendar" and refuse to accept the Gregorian calendar, celebrating Christmas on Gregorian date January 5, which is actually Julian date December 25. Even those Orthodox who have since accepted the Gregorian calendar still observe the Jewish lunar calendar when it comes to computing the date for Easter.

Of course, Islam follows a lunar calendar as do the religions of Asia including Buddhism, Daoism, the religions of India, and other faiths. Indonesians are conscious of several calendars all running concurrently: the Gregorian calendar, the Islamic calendar, and one or two Javanese calendars.

These are all survivals of religious cosmologies of time and space, when the motions of the luminaries and the planets were considered sacred events and signs from an invisible God. If, indeed, the Great Pyramid was built with an orientation to the Pole star of Thuban, then we can readily agree that our most ancient recorded religions were celestial in nature and that sacred space was as essential as sacred time and just as carefully structured and imagined.

To the cult of Mithra of the Roman period, sacred space meant caves and underground temples where the light of the sun would never shine. While David Ulansey argues that the Mithra cult was formed around the Hellenistic discovery of the precession of the equinoxes — a discovery that is said to have taken place in the first century BCE — there is ample evidence that the ancient peoples were aware that the position of true north was a moveable feast. They may not have understood the precession scientifically, but they observed its effects in the movement of the star Thuban in the constellation Draco away from true north until our present-day North Star, Polaris, took on the role.

It is possible that the sacred ceremonies of the Mithra cult were not completely oriented toward a solar deity and that the seven-stage initiatory structure of the cult was not meant to represent the sun, moon, and five planets. The mithraeum — the temple of the Mithra cult — was normally underground, in darkness. It consisted of a *pronaos,* or antechamber, where it is believed the lower-ranked initiates waited during the performance of the rituals in the sanctuary. At the far end of the sanctuary was an apse, where the sacred images were kept and displayed. If this had been a solar cult, then one could reasonably expect that the mithraeum would be oriented east-west, with the entrance in the west and the high altar in the east. However, this does not seem to be the case.

In the diagram of the mithraeum of Heddernheim, shown in Cumont,[7] we find that the orientation of the temple is north-south, with the high altar and apse in the north. Other examples[8] show an indifferent approach to orientation, but so far the author has found none with an emphasis on the east as the place of the rising sun. If we remember that the title of Mithra was Sol Invictus — the Invincible or Unconquerable Sun — we may surmise that the natural sun of the ecliptic was not intended.

This is a difficult and contentious topic. Obviously, as the sun constantly "dies" and is "reborn" with each passing day, we may say that it is invincible and unconquerable; but the sun of the ecliptic may have been seen by the Mithraists as a symbol or representation of another sun, equally invincible and unconquerable: in fact, a "sun" that never dies but is immortal. That the Sol Invictus of the Mithra cult may be the Pole Star is possible if we consider that the current research of Ulansey and others proposes that the Mithraic initiates were aware of the precession of the equinoxes and that this phenomenon was enshrined in their rites. Not only would the movement of the sun through the signs of the zodiac be recognized as emblematic of the precession, but also of the displacement of the stars of Thuban, Kochab, and Pherkad as the North Star and their eventual replacement by Polaris. If, then, the true ("esoteric") nature of Sol Invictus was the Pole Star, then might not the seven degrees of Mithraic initiation really represent the seven stars of the Dipper?

The design of the mithraeum traditionally depicted the twelve signs of the zodiac and had representations of the seven planets, often as human figures of the gods associated with them. The main emblem, however, was that of the god Mithra either carrying a bull or slaughtering a bull, accompanied by a dog, a serpent, and a scorpion. We may recall that a slain bull was the central element of the Opening of the Mouth ceremony of the ancient Egyptians, and that the bull (or, more specifically, the bull's thigh) represented the Dipper. In both cases, the bull represents immortality; but in the Egyptian case it is specifically linked with the Northern Dipper asterism and the northerly direction. A search in the astronomical lore of the Middle East also reveals that one of the names for the Little Dipper (and now, specifically, for Polaris) was *Cynosura,* a Greek word meaning "Dog's Tail"; in addition, Ursa Major was sometimes referred to in ancient Egypt as the Dog of Set.[9] There is no correspondence in either of the Dippers for "Scorpion," except that the star Alcor in Ursa Major was believed by the Arabs to be a guardian against the bite of scorpions and snakes.[10] If we look at these constellations as a set, therefore, we have a Bull, a Dog, and a Serpent (Draco or its component star, Thuban): all of which were depicted in sacred art as elements of the *tauroctonous* ("bull-slaying") Mithra.

The seven degrees of Mithraic initiation from lowest to highest include *Corax*, or Raven, *Nymphus* (Bridegroom) or *Cryphius* (Occult), *Miles*, or Soldier, *Leo*, or Lion, *Perses*, or Persian, *Heliodromus*, or Runner of the Sun, and *Pater*, or Father. The first three degrees were considered the lower degrees, while the last four were those of the Participants: full members of the Mithraic society who were privy to the secret doctrines. This division of three degrees and four degrees recalls the structure of the Dippers, with three stars for the handle and four for the scoop. What is not obvious from the names of the seven degrees is any association at all with the seven planets, except possibly for *heliodromus* with its reference to the sun. Even *Leo* refers to a constellation and not to a planet. *Corax*, the Raven, also refers to a constellation — Corvus, the Raven — which used to be on the celestial equator and was thus one of the "zodiacal" signs in ancient times. The Serpent (in this case Hydra) and the Dog (Canis Minor) were also zodiacal signs at one point and, of course, Scorpio and Taurus still are.

The idea that the Mithraic initiation might not have been planetary in design is supported accidentally by the research of David Ulansey.[11] He postulates that the Sol Invictus of the Mithra cult refers to a "hypercosmic sun": i.e., a sun beyond the realm of the fixed stars. Thus, we are in agreement that the sun of the Mithraists is not the sun with which we are all familiar but a different sun. It is the statement "beyond the realm of the fixed stars" that provides the most food for thought, however.

If we posit that the "realm of the fixed stars" refers to the zodiacal belt, i.e., those fixed stars against which the normal sun moves, then "beyond that realm" could easily refer to the circumpolar (immortal, invincible) stars of the Northern Dipper and the Pole Star. Ulansey points out that some depictions of the god Mithra slaying the bull take place at a spot "above" the zodiacal belt, reinforcing the theory of this author that the cult of Mithra was focused on those stars that are not part of the zodiacal belt and that appear "above" it. If Ulansey is correct and the worship of the Mithra cult was directed at a hypercosmic sun, then the seven degrees of initiation may not refer to the seven Platonic planets but to some other entities. The ladder of Mithraic initiation would lead — as does the vision of Ezekiel, the Opening of the Mouth ceremony, the Shang Qing mystical practices — to the circumpolar stars of the Northern Dipper and Polaris.

The problem with Ulansey's thesis is that the Mithra cult is of relatively recent origin; its beginnings can safely be situated only in the first century BCE unless we accept Cumont's proposal that it represents a much older religion. Cumont's argument came under attack in the 1970s when it was admitted that there was no mythos corresponding to the slaying of the bull in the Persian religious corpus; it was eventually agreed by scholars that Mithraism was a more recent phenomenon. If that is so, then there would have been no particular point in sacralizing the ancient, premodern zodiac since the twelve signs as we know them were already in use by that time and phenomena relating to the precession of the equinoxes (the shift of the Pole Stars from Thuban to its successors) were already recognized even though the nature of the precession itself was not committed to study until the time of Hipparchus in 128 BCE.

Ulansey does relate the Mithraic mysteries to the concept of "astral immortality" and the ascent of the soul to the heavens. What he does not do, however, is provide the link between the celestial ascent of the Mithra cult and the celestial ascent of other religions and esoteric practices with which it had come into contact. It is possible, though by no means proven as yet, that the secret rites of Mithra were reflections of the celestial ascent practices that we have found in Egypt and Babylon, as well as with the *merkavah* mystics of ancient Israel. We can see that the common astrological focus on the ecliptic and the signs of the zodiac and the transits of the seven "planets" through them are related more to mundane life and affairs, whereas the circumpolar stars and the Pole Star itself are identified with transcendental concerns and the survival of the soul after death: two completely different preoccupations, the one earthbound and the other heavenly. There is much that is consistent between the seven-staged initiation of Mithra, its meeting place in underground chambers, its reverence for an "invincible sun," and its concentration on "astral immortality" and the practices of other mystics throughout the Middle and Near East. Cumont makes a case for the survival of much Mithraic imagery and doctrine in the Catholic Church, the main competitor of Mithra during the Roman period. If so, then it is ironic that the church, which had its origins as a Jewish sect, would find itself adopting Mithraic symbols and sacred sites as well, thus uniting two different (yet possibly complementary) approaches to the idea of celestial ascent.

The Mithras Liturgy

When first translated, there was an assumption that this Egyptian text represented a ritual of the cult of Mithra. However, critical attention to its contents have shown that Mithra is mentioned only once in the entire body of the text whereas references to Egyptian and Greco-Egyptian gods and concepts abound. As this text dates from the same general period as the heyday of the Mithra cult, from about the second century BCE to the fifth century CE, it is worthwhile investigating for the insight it may provide into the celestial mythology of the period and the region.

Part of a body of texts known as the Greek Magical Papyri, the bulk of which was discovered in the eighteenth century by one Jean d'Anastasi, a remarkable person of questionable ethnicity (some say he was Armenian, but he was the Swedish consul in Alexandria), the Mithras Liturgy is fascinating for the light it sheds on the themes we have been discussing. The texts acquired were from Thebes (the present-day Luxor) and were part of a collection of magical documents that somehow had survived the *autos-da-fe* of the church. There is, of course, some controversy over whether such documents should be considered "magical" as opposed to "religious," the former presumably indicating a bias on the part of the historian of religion. It is not the intention of the author to get involved in that argument, but to allow the sources to speak for themselves.

The Mithras Liturgy begins with a prayer to "Providence and Psyche" to be gracious to the adept, and to grant the gift of immortality using the herbs revealed to him by an archangel of the great god "Helios Mithras," so that "I alone may ascend into heaven as an inquirer and behold the universe."[12] Thus, the opening lines of the liturgy contain references to immortality and celestial ascent, as well as a prescription for "herbs and spices," all themes that would be familiar to a Chinese alchemist of the Shang Qing school.

There follows an invocation that refers to the transformation of the adept from an earthly body to one (if only momentarily) capable of ascent. After this invocation, according to the liturgy, one breathes in "drawing up 3 times as much as you can" and will soon see oneself rising so that it seems one is in midair. There follow various instructions on what should be said and done when finding oneself in the divine presence — with admonitions to "Silence! Silence" and the familiar gesture of putting one's finger to one's lips — and then we read that the "7 immortal gods of the world" are to be invoked.[13] This the biblical scholar Hans Dieter Betz interprets as a reference to the seven-staged initiatory schema of the cult of Mithra, consistent with his theory that this is, indeed, a Mithraic liturgy, but just as easily could refer to the Northern Dipper. This identification of the "7 immortal gods of the world" with the circumpolar stars becomes more obvious a little later on when Helios is asked to intercede for the adept with the "supreme lord, the one who has begotten and made you" who then comes "to the celestial pole" and who opens the seven gates of heaven from which appear the virginal seven Fates of heaven, who are followed in turn by seven gods with the "faces of black bulls" who are "the so-called Pole Lords of heaven."[14] A more obvious set of references to the Northern Dipper could hardly be imagined. The "supreme lord" who has "begotten and made" the sun god Helios could reasonably be interpreted as the Sol Invictus of the Mithraists if we accept Ulansey's interpretation of the hypercosmic sun of the cult.

The seven Pole Lords are then greeted individually by name, after which a curious personality makes his appearance. According to the translation given by Betz:

...a god descending, a god immensely great, having a bright appearance, youthful, golden-haired, with a white tunic and a golden crown and trousers, and holding in his right hand a golden shoulder of a young bull: this is the Bear which moves and turns heaven around, moving upward and downward in accordance with the hour.[15]

Betz argues that this description is consistent with images of Mithra. Another, more recent, translation defines the trousers as "Persian" and the Bear as Ursa Major,[16] thus emphasizing the possible Mithraic nature of the liturgy in the former case, and the absolute certainty that the Bull represents the Northern Dipper in the latter. If we argue that the Bull being slain by Mithra is really the Dipper and not Taurus, then we can reevaluate the Mithras Liturgy as a genuine Mithraic text and not merely a Greco-Roman or Egyptian "magical" text. Further, we can characterize the Mithras Liturgy as an example of ascent literature which would force us to look at the Mithra cult from a new perspective. Indeed, a Bear that "moves and turns heaven around, moving upward and downward in accordance with the hour" can only refer to the Dipper, which rotates about the Pole Star every twenty-four hours and which can thus be used as a celestial timekeeper. This would not be true of Taurus, or any other sign of the zodiac.

Further, considering the social organization of the Mithra cult, this would represent a profound shift taking place in ascent technologies. Heretofore, ascent has been either the solitary practice of the *merkavah* mystics and the Chinese alchemists or the ritualized ascent performed on the dead bodies of Egyptian pharaohs. With the Mithra cult, we have a series of ascent initiations in which individuals are brought up the seven-runged ladder by other initiates. In other words, the ascent has become the theme of a formalized ritual in which each rung of the ladder represents a level in the social hierarchy. The leaders of the Mithra cult, the "Fathers," have thus placed themselves between the individual aspirant and the upper heavens. While acting as facilitators they have become, in essence, gatekeepers. The formula of celestial ascent has become the focus of a guild that wishes to control access to the divine realms, while at the same time offering that access as a possibility with greater and greater initiations. This dynamic will recur with the formation of the esoteric orders and secret societies of more modern times as gradually the ability of the individual to ascend to the heavens becomes eroded or devalued in favor of the collective approval and facilitation of organized groups. With a strong state religion such as the Catholic Church in Europe, individual spiritual praxis outside the control or purview of the clergy becomes dangerous and forbidden. Individual spiritual practitioners will become identified as heretics, or worse.

Chapter 10

Christian Kabbalah
and the Esoteric Orders

In nearly all mythologies, we find that the gods assembled on some
high mountain to take counsel. The Olympus of the Greeks and Mount
Zion of the Hebrew Bible mean the same, the Pole-Star; and there, on
the pictured planisphere, sits Cephus, the mighty Jove, with one foot
on the Pole-Star and all the gods gathered below him. The Pole-Star is
the symbol of the highest heaven.
> —Thomas H. Burgoyne ("Zanoni")
> of the Hermetic Brotherhood of Light[1]

So far, we have discussed ancient scriptural and mystical references to celestial ascent. Although we have focused on the Abrahamic religions, we have
also considered non-Abrahamic, Asian, and African approaches to the same
theme. Some of these practices and beliefs have survived centuries and even
millennia, of course, even though their origins in most cases are at least two
thousand years old.

In part 4, however, we are examining more modern practices and concepts
concerning ascent. Some of these are represented by the flowering of Renaissance thought most beautifully typified by the speculations of the members
of the Florentine Academy of the fifteenth and sixteenth centuries; but the
rest are the special province of the secret societies and esoteric orders of
the nineteenth and twentieth centuries, most of which had a predominantly
Christian focus, even though this was mixed with Kabbalistic influences.
These latter, I will propose, came by way of the Sabbatean movement and
most notably its offshoot, the Frankists. The implication of this is that the
ascent ideas and practices encoded within the rituals and other documents of
the secret societies of the last 150 years are descendants of the Jewish mystical sects of the third and fourth centuries CE and thus retain knowledge
of the north celestial pole technology.

We will begin with a discussion of Gershom Scholem and his evaluation
of the apologists of the "Christian Kabbalah" school and then concentrate
on the development of some of the earliest German Masonic lodges and

146

their counterparts in France, Italy, and England. This will provide us with a context within which to approach the more famous lodges and groups of the nineteenth and twentieth centuries, particularly the Hermetic Brotherhood of Light, the Societas Rosicruciana in Anglia (the Rosicrucian Society in England), the Hermetic Order of the Golden Dawn, and the Ordo Templi Orientis (Order of the Temple of the East) and Argentum Astrum (Silver Star) of Theodor Reuss and Aleister Crowley, respectively. While these were controversial organizations in their time, and remain so today, they provide us with a rich vein of highly articulated ascent practices and ideas that form the substance of the rituals of their followers today. We will also look at the concept of initiation: a core concept for all of these groups, although one that is rarely defined or qualified. Initiation becomes inextricably linked with the ideas we have been discussing so far and implies a voyage or spiritual quest from the earth to the Pole.

Gershom Scholem and the Christian Kabbalists

The activities of French and English occultists contributed nothing and only served to create considerable confusion between the teachings of the Kabbalah and their own totally unrelated inventions, such as the alleged kabbalistic origin of the Tarot-cards. To this category of supreme charlatanism belong the many and widely read books of Eliphas Levi (actually Alphonse Louis Constant; 1810–75),[2] Papus (Gerard Encausse; 1868–1916),[3] and Frater Perdurabo (Aleister Crowley; 1875–1946) [sic],[4] all of whom had an infinitesimal knowledge of Kabbalah that did not prevent them from drawing freely on their imaginations instead. — Gershom Scholem[5]

Thus, the eminent scholar of Kabbalah has thrown down the gauntlet and dismissed three of the most famous authors of occult literature of the nineteenth and twentieth centuries, the godfathers of the New Age movement, as "supreme charlatans" in a single sentence. It is difficult to go up against someone as thoroughly iconized as Scholem, particularly as his scholarly integrity is beyond reproach even though, at times, his conclusions may be open to debate among his peers. However, we can take this statement of Scholem's as a challenge and as the foundation for an analytical approach toward an understanding of the relevance and possible importance of modern western esotericism represented by the above personalities and especially concerning what may be called the Christian Kabbalah of the nineteenth and twentieth centuries. This area has largely been ignored by Kabbalah scholars such as Scholem, Idel, Himmelfarb, Wolfson, Janowitz, Dan,[6] and others even as they open a space for discussions of the Christian Kabbalah of the fifteenth and sixteenth centuries, a phenomenon that grew out of the Florentine Academy and the neo-Platonic movement. The "infinitesimal knowledge" of the "charlatans" listed by Scholem was based on the works of the early Christian Kabbalists, as translated by the "French and English occultists" of the nineteenth century, such works as the *Kabbalah Denudata* of von Rosenroth, which was translated (in part) by MacGregor Mathers,[7] or the *Sepher Yetzirah* in translation by the above-mentioned Papus, Wynn Westcott, and others, all of whom were members of one secret society or another.

At the same time, it must be admitted that these societies appear to contribute nothing to Kabbalah studies per se since their access to the Kabbalah was mostly through secondary sources. Had these societies developed links or connections with active Kabbalists, however — such as with members of the Hasidic movement or with devotees of Sabbatai Sevi or Jacob Frank — then we might suspend our disbelief for a moment and ask whether or not some genuine Kabbalistic ideas made their way into the theories or practices of these western esoteric orders.

The challenges that present themselves in this type of research are the same that confronted Scholem in his lifetime when it came to identifying the age and pedigree of the *ma'aseh merkavah* literature, one of the earliest forms of Jewish mysticism, which predates what we know as the Kabbalah. Scholem had to rely upon textual evidence and thematic and linguistic clues to arrive at his dating of the *ma'aseh merkavah* practice even though original documents of the period in question have not been found. Indeed, we possess nothing earlier than the fragmentary texts discovered at the Cairo Genizah at the end of the nineteenth century (and some edited texts from the archives of the Ashkenazic Hasidim) which indicate the earliest paleographic sources date from the sixth to the ninth century CE. Based on a literary analysis of the texts, Scholem tended to believe that the *ma'aseh merkavah* practices dated to the second century CE if not earlier, and some recent scholars tend to agree with this early dating in spite of the fact that documentary proof is still wanting.[8]

In our case, we are confronted with similar obstacles since we are dealing with secret societies that did not commit everything they knew to paper. Still, we have a voluminous amount of published material of what they *did* reveal, and there are scattered references to other sources in their writings providing us with linear lines of succession between one society and another, and one "charlatan" and another, thereby giving us a timeline and an indication of philosophical influences. While many of these orders and secret societies were created or led by persons whose credibility or even mental stability has been called into question, the rank-and-file membership included some of the most important, influential, and creative members of their respective times.

What is offered here, then, is not a polemic in favor of loopy occult "charlatanism" but the results of research concerning the origins of the most influential of the nineteenth- and twentieth-century secret societies — the Hermetic Order of the Golden Dawn — and its relationship to (*a*) genuine Kabbalistic groups[9] and individual Jewish or "Christian" Kabbalists, and (*b*) the possible survival of some Kabbalistic concepts of the *ma'aseh merkavah* literature (the descent and ascent, the seven palaces) in the syncretistic rituals and beliefs that were embraced and developed by this secret society. It is hoped that this type of research will encourage more study of so-called Christian Kabbalah in the post-Renaissance, early modern period by specialists both in Jewish Kabbalah and in European religious history. This may contribute to the field of Kabbalah studies by enriching its associations with the cultures within which the Jews had found themselves at the time of tremendous revolutionary activity in Europe, an era when secret societies were both the bugaboo of conservative (i.e., monarchical) political forces and the hope of free-thinking intellectuals and revolutionary adventurers.

To do this, we will focus on specific examples of *ma'aseh merkavah* literature, including the *Re'iyyot Yehezkel,* and compare their structure to the initiation rituals of the Golden Dawn: the secret society that exerted such a tremendous influence over the growth of modern, non-Jewish "Kabbalistic" movements in the West. We will also look at possible historical antecedents to the Golden Dawn among the "Jewish Masonic" societies of the eighteenth and nineteenth centuries and their links to the Sabbatean movement.

Works of the Chariot

> No doubts are possible on this point: the earliest Jewish mysticism is throne-mysticism. Its essence is not absorbed contemplation of God's true nature, but perception of His appearance on the throne, as described by Ezekiel, and cognition of the mysteries of the celestial throne-world. — Gershom Scholem[10]

The scholar who reintroduced Kabbalah to the world and made a persuasive and still relevant case for its importance has identified the key issue around which this study revolves. There are two points to be considered here: the first, that "throne-mysticism," or what has been called the *ma'aseh merkavah* or "works of the Chariot," constitutes the earliest form of Jewish mysticism, going back, again according to Scholem, to the first century CE, the time of the Second Temple and its destruction; the second point is that the essence of this practice was not quiet contemplation of God but a direct perception of God and experience of the heavenly realms.

As we investigate the core works of the *merkavah* mystics — the *Re'iyyot Yehezkel* and others — we will discover that there is a heavy magical or theurgical element to the practice of the *merkavah*. Some scholars trace this to the Book of Enoch, with its detailed descriptions of the Throne and the heavenly choirs. When Scholem wrote the above words, in 1941, the Dead Sea Scrolls had not yet been discovered, nor the famous Gnostic library at Nag Hammadi. These later documents would tend to support Scholem's thesis that there was a continuity of understanding and practice from the Second Temple period in Palestine to the works of the *merkavah* mystics of Palestine, Babylonia, and Provence of the ninth and tenth centuries CE.

However, much of this material became lost in the centuries between the destruction of the Second Temple and the renaissance of Kabbalistic learning and publication that took place a thousand years later. Solid epigraphic evidence for the survival of the *ma'aseh merkavah* from the first century CE to the ninth century CE is mostly lacking; one can only analyze later editions of the texts to find traces of more ancient theories and practices. During the fifteenth to seventeenth centuries in Europe, Christian authors discovered many of these documents[11] — having been translated by Jews and Marranos (Jews who had converted to Christianity, usually under duress) — and were seduced by the possibility that the Kabbalah had a key that would enable the church to prove that Jesus was the Messiah. The texts that bore the brunt of this attention were the Zohar, the *Bahir*, and the *Sepher Yetzirah*, although these texts were known to the Christian authors only in poor translations, in excerpted and heavily edited form, and in Latin or vernacular editions and rarely in the original Hebrew or Aramaic.

While the term "Chariot" and its Hebrew original, *merkavah*, seem to have been known to the Renaissance authors of "Christian" Kabbalah, there was little or no understanding of the "descent to the Chariot" — the mystical *merkavah* practice — itself. Yet in the late nineteenth and early twentieth centuries, elements of what can only be considered *ma'aseh merkavah* found their way into the rituals and organizational structure of European, and largely Christian, secret societies, originating from some Masonic groups of the late eighteenth century to flower more blatantly in the occult orders of the twentieth. How did this happen? Was there an esoteric current running through European, Christian mysticism that had its source in a deeper understanding of this earliest form of Jewish mysticism, even though its central texts were unknown to its practitioners and, indeed, there was an assumption that no such texts actually existed?

Methodology

We must take a dual approach to this material, as reflected in the two types of documents we have at our disposal. The first involves the actual Kabbalistic texts themselves, principally those works denoted as *ma'aseh merkavah* by the authorities in the field; there exists considerable controversy, however, as to which texts deserve inclusion in that category as well as controversy concerning the dating of these texts. We will consider some of these issues insofar as they impact our overall study, but our concentration will be on those texts that deal specifically with the "descent to the Chariot" and the experience of seven heavens, palaces, or *hekhalot*. The second approach consists of analysis of the history, writings, and rituals of the secret societies of Europe and America of the last two centuries, principally the Hermetic Order of the Golden Dawn (which presents us with a large corpus of ritual material and published commentary by initiated members),[12] the Hermetic Brotherhood of Luxor (whose documents have been the subject of recent studies),[13] and the Ordo Templi Orientis (whose core ritual documents have been suppressed by that order, but a copy of which is in the author's possession).[14] We will seek in the latter traces of the former. This is an important area of research because, according to the initiates and commentators of the relevant secret societies, there was no published material available on the *ma'aseh merkavah* and, indeed, it was considered by them to be a purely oral tradition.

This study will be buttressed by an examination of the informed opinions of the leaders in the field of Kabbalistic research, beginning with Gershom Scholem and Moshe Idel. Attention will be paid to the phenomenon of what is known as "Christian Kabbalah," a movement begun in the fifteenth century CE, since it is the direct ancestor of the European esoteric societies; however, there will also be a visit to the late Sabbatean movement represented by Jacob Frank, as his disciples will be found joining and forming secret societies in western Europe in the eighteenth century.

Therefore, we will ask some questions concerning the nature of ritual initiation. The complex and extensive degree systems of the Masonic orders and those secret societies that flowed from them represent an unusual development in the history of occultism. Do these systems have their origin in the seven palaces of *merkavah* mysticism?

Forbidden Teachings

There are two fields of inquiry that were virtually forbidden to Jews according to Mishnaic injunction:[15] the study of Genesis 1 (*ma'aseh bereshit*, or "works of creation") and the study of Ezekiel 1 (*ma'aseh merkavah*, or "works of the Chariot"). This injunction served to conceal Jewish esoteric studies from the outside world for centuries since very little was committed to writing on these subjects save the nearly incomprehensible texts of the *hekhalot* and *merkavah* mystics, many of which are of a theurgic or magical nature. The earliest documents we have from either *ma'aseh bereshit* or *ma'aseh merkavah* are fragments that date from the ninth century CE, and these were from the Cairo Genizah. Later published works, such as the *Sepher Yetzirah* and the *Sepher ha-Bahir*, are considered part of an ancient tradition even though they appeared in manuscript or published form only in later centuries. According to Joseph Dan, between the day of creation and 1960, there were only three books published on the subjects of *hekhalot* and *merkavah* mysticism.[16] Thus, we are presented with something of a puzzle, for the structure of several European, Christian secret societies of the nineteenth and early twentieth centuries clearly owe a great deal to these subjects; even so, their most prominent authors and spokespersons have gone on the record as stating that the *ma'aseh merkavah* is an "oral tradition" that had not been preserved in writing.[17] If that is so, then where did the creators of these societies get their information?

Another area of study forbidden to the Jews was the Song of Songs, also known as the Song of Solomon. It is a frankly erotic text that is nonetheless part of the biblical canon, and its study was considered to be as dangerous as that of the *ma'aseh merkavah*. Yet it did attract the attention of numerous Christian commentators, including Bernard of Clairvaux, who wrote extensively on it in the twelfth century CE.[18] These three strains — the works of creation, the works of the Chariot, and the Song of Songs — would be woven into a complex tapestry of occult initiation, hermetic secrets, and scandalous accusations that characterize the rituals and the personalities of the Hermetic Order of the Golden Dawn and its associated cults, the Hermetic Brotherhood of Luxor and the Ordo Templi Orientis.

The key documents of this school of mysticism were circulated in manuscript form long before they were officially published. As mentioned above, dating of the documents is difficult and there are several points of view as to when *merkavah* and *hekhalot* mysticism first appeared. Internal evidence, augmented by the discovery of the Qumran scrolls, seems to support the idea that this school of mysticism existed at least as early as the Second Temple period or, at the latest, the second century CE. Texts such as the Songs of the Sabbath Sacrifice are thematically quite reminiscent of *merkavah* literature, and may provide a clue to the origins of this practice.[19]

As we investigate the structure of one of the oldest of all the *merkavah* texts, the *Re'iyyot Yehezkel*, or "Vision of Ezekiel," which is in the form of a midrash (or commentary) on the Book of Ezekiel but which expands the biblical text in interesting and provocative ways, we will notice similarities between this classic example of *merkavah* mysticism and the initiatory structure of the Golden Dawn, and in the process learn something about the colorful cults and personalities that contributed to the creation of the Golden Dawn's idea of spiritual advancement along the vertical axis of the *Etz Chaim,* the Sephirotic Tree of Life, at a time when none of the *merkavah* texts had yet been translated into English or indeed any European language and were scarcely available in Hebrew or Aramaic outside the small circles that still preserved these practices.[20]

Interest in the *merkavah* and *hekhalot* literature exploded once Scholem had introduced the relevant documents and their importance to the world. Prior to 1941 and the publication of his *Major Trends,* scholarly interpretation of this field was the province of a very few individuals, notably among them Graetz, who was noticeably hostile to the content of the *merkavah* texts. But it was Scholem who provided a cultural and religious context for these texts, on the basis of which he identified a continuum of Jewish mystical belief and practice that extended from at least the sixth century CE to the medieval period, showing the texts were influential in the development of the German Pietist (Hasidic) movement.

Scholem had identified the *merkavah* texts — and the Kabbalistic literature generally (including the *Sepher ha-Zohar,* the *Sepher Yetzirah,* and many others less well known) — with Gnosticism, a claim that has been contested by many scholars since then, including Ioan Couliano, who prefers a Hellenistic influence rather than a Gnostic one. Even more importantly, perhaps, was the discovery of the Qumran scrolls in 1947 and their implications for the *merkavah* practices. Yet a search through the indices of all the sources used in this study demonstrates that the idea of "initiation," particularly as that term is understood in Masonic circles, is foreign to Judaism and foreign to Kabbalah. However, this very "Hellenistic" concept finds its way into the European secret societies under consideration. Indeed, the very formal structure of Masonic-type initiation with its multiplicity of degrees bestowed in theurgic rituals by other human beings (rather than through direct contemplation of the Divine, as we find in *merkavah* practice) can be thought of as unique to Masonic societies[21] and their imitators. How, then, did this idea come to be associated with the occult lodges and esoteric groups which based their degree structure on the Kabbalistic Tree of Life?

Initiation

One of the most important backgrounds of the system, the fundamental philosophy underlying the same, is the scheme of the Qabalah. An understanding of this mysticism is an absolute necessity if the function of the Rituals is to be understood. For the grades of the Order are referred to the Ten Sephiroth of the Tree of Life, and the passage from one grade to another is accomplished by way of the several connecting paths.   — Israel Regardie[22]

The theme of initiation occurs again and again in the texts of the secret societies under discussion, whereas there is virtually no mention of this concept in the *merkavah* texts. For that reason, it is considered best to address what is meant by initiation in the rituals and knowledge lectures of the Golden Dawn and its associated groups since it impacts directly on how certain concepts of *merkavah* were encoded in them. The term "encoded" is carefully selected, since the initiation rituals themselves were actually provided to the founders of the British Golden Dawn in the so-called Cypher Manuscripts, i.e., in actual code.

Initiation itself is a problematic concept. As addressed by Van Gennep (1960) and modified by Turner (1969), initiation has been viewed by a generation of anthropologists as the move from one social or psychological state to another, a process involving the eradication or sublimation of certain aspects of one's secular identity, at least temporarily, so that the initiand may join a new community (Turner's *communitas*) and identify with that community rather than with his or her previous existence. This often involves taking a new name, learning an arcane language or set of coded phrases and words, and experiencing a kind of rebirth. Typically, the initiand will have secular clothing removed and will enter the ritual area with bare skin, after which new clothing in the form of ritual garments will be provided. The ritual area itself becomes a cosmological system, with various officers of the ritual standing or sitting in appropriate places, holding symbols or implements of their respective offices. The new world that the initiand enters is complete; it is a lens through which the initiand views and understands the world in a new and different way. The new initiate then returns to society in a modified state — "reaggregated" or "incorporated" — empowered in a new role or a new consciousness, but nevertheless still part of society and united to it even more strongly through the bonds of the secret society just joined.

Lesley Northup (1993) describes religious ritual from a gender perspective, equating male/patriarchal religion and discourse with a (chromosomal?) "Y-Axis" or vertical direction, i.e., above the earth, transcendent, reaching heavenward while a female/matriarchal perspective would be "X-Axis" and horizontal, a religion of community, relationship, and the earth. This is nowhere as evident (or as blatant, perhaps) as in the ascent literature of the Jewish mystics, which was strictly Y-Axis in orientation: there are seven levels reaching from the earth to the heavens, and the mystic would rise on these levels, ever higher, to find himself — always *him*self — in the presence of God.[23] The ascent literature is the apotheosis of the Semitic religious ideal to which Northup refers and is an individual quest that involves separation from society, physical deprivation, solitude, and an interior, internal approach to a transcendent divinity. It is perhaps no surprise to learn that women were not permitted to become involved in this type of mystical activity; one had to be male, Jewish, of a certain age, and married.

Yet where was the *communitas* in this form of initiation? Were there secret societies, occult orders, associated with the ascent to the Chariot? If so, did they serve the same purpose as the types of religious initiation discussed by Turner and others? While there is evidence to suggest that there were communities of Jewish mystics, all engaged in the pursuit of kabbalistic knowledge and experience,[24] when it comes to the ascent literature itself (the *ma'aseh merkavah*) we do not find strong proof of the existence of a cult of men gathering together to pursue this quest. Indeed, Jewish tradition as we have seen specifically forbids it.

How, then, to apply Turnerian structure to the initiatory framework of the secret society of post-Renaissance western Europe? Is there a reaggregation phase, a postliminal cigarette in the afterglow of the *hieros gamos?* While the Masons eventually devolved to a kind of businessmen's club in many communities — a way to forge links with potential business partners and thus to become "incorporated" into capitalist society — the more ambitious and serious occult orders split off from this approach and had much more in common with the descenders to the Chariot than they did with the Elks Club, the Odd Fellows, or even the Freemasons themselves. For them, the liminal phase never ended; to succeed in the scheme of initiations was to find oneself not only in constant contact with the Divine but also to become divine in the process.

What is problematic for us is the fact that the secret societies under discussion did not see initiation in quite the way Turner and Van Gennep saw it. Initiation — for the Golden Dawn, its forerunner the Societas Rosicruciana in Anglia (SRIA), and other occult orders — was an ongoing process up a system of degrees that would culminate in a more or less total transformation of consciousness that reflected the rarified atmosphere of esoteric knowledge and supernatural power. This was not a validation or even an extension of one's social identity or role in the community in general; it was not a rite of passage or a means of cementing social ties or reinforcing one's standing in the community. Rather, it was designed to provide a mechanism for evolution: evolution beyond the understanding of the rest of society. It was, in short, an elitist program where the code words and phrases no longer served merely to separate ritual life from mundane life, or secret society from quotidian society, but actually caused change in the world around the initiate: caused change in reality itself.[25] As the foremost apologist for the Golden Dawn, Israel Regardie, has written:

> The primary and direct effect of a successful initiation — or the real progress through the grades, which progress consists in the gradual bringing into operation of the Higher Genius, the real Self — is the stimulation or production of creativity, some form or other of genius.[26]

As for the goals of the Golden Dawn itself, he goes on to say:

> The system and technique of spiritual training which it affords to initiates unquestionably could have been a mighty cultural and integrating factor in the enhancement of the race consciousness. The whole mass of people could have been automatically exalted to a higher level of integration and spiritual awareness.[27]

Thus it is clear that there are at least two different ways of looking at the theme of initiation. The prevalent view among anthropologists has been formed by the ideas of Van Gennep and Turner and involve an examination of rituals that are employed by societies to sacralize life events, such as birth, death, marriage, and puberty. This can be expanded to include the ideas of shamanic initiation represented by the works of Eliade, among others; in this view, initiation is a process involving frightening experiences of death, torture, and dismemberment undergone by the initiand with the goal of attaining communion with spiritual forces and the resulting magical empowerment.[28] In both these cases, however, those of Van Gennep/Turner and those of Eliade, the initiand returns to society and becomes a valuable member of his or her community. One may say that the *merkavah* mystic is such an initiate; his ascent to the *merkavah* results in greater spiritual awareness, theological insight, and other gifts that can be shared with the community once they have been properly "decoded" and made comprehensible.

Another way of looking at initiation, however, reflects a concern with perfectibility. While this is also a preoccupation of some Jewish Kabbalists[29] it is more common — indeed, commonplace — among the *Christian* Kabbalists under discussion. The specific technology of ascending to the Chariot to come into the divine presence is noticeably lacking, even though there are scattered references to the *ma'aseh merkavah* and the *ma'aseh bereshit*. Rather, the organizing principle of the secret societies of the nineteenth and twentieth centuries is nothing less than the total transformation of the initiate.

> The Mysteries taught man how to enfeeble the action of matter on the soul, and to restore to the latter its natural dominion. And lest

the stains so contracted should continue after death, lustrations were used, fastings, expiations, macerations, continence, and, above all, initiations. Many of these practices were at first merely symbolical, material signs indicating the moral purity required of the initiates; but they afterward came to be regarded as actual productive causes of that purity.

The effect of initiation was meant to be the same as that of philosophy, to purify the soul of its passions, to weaken the empire of the body over the divine portion of man, and to give him here below a happiness anticipatory of the felicity to be one day enjoyed by him, and of the future vision by him of the Divine Beings.[30]

Thus initiation is the "actual productive cause" of the spiritual transformation of the initiate, according to the words of one of the major figures in American Freemasonry, Albert Pike. This may be due in part to the influence of ideas of resurrection inherent in Christian theology and in certain Gnostic ideas about the impurity of matter as a prison for the soul. Judaism concentrates on the world and on life in the world; Christianity placed the emphasis and focus on life after death: heaven, hell, purgatory, limbo, and the possibility of the resurrection of the body for those who had lived exemplary lives.

Along these lines the historian of religion Mircea Eliade has defined initiation as follows:

The term initiation in the most general sense denotes a body of rites and oral teachings whose purpose is to produce a radical modification of the religious and social status of the person to be initiated. In philosophical terms, initiation is equivalent to an ontological mutation of the existential condition.[31]

Eliade identifies three types or categories of initiation: rites symbolizing the transition from childhood to adolescence (puberty rites); the shamanic or ecstatic initiation (usually a highly individual event); and the initiation into a secret society.[32] While elsewhere he is highly critical, even contemptuous, of the initiation rites of modern secret societies (with a possible exception for those of Freemasonry, which, at least, seem to have something of a pedigree in Eliade's eyes),[33] he admits that there is a basic human need or desire for this type of experience. Without spending too much time analyzing this need, let us keep in mind that the shamanic initiation and the secret society initiation are the two with which we are most concerned here, for the former may be thought of as an example of the *ma'aseh merkavah* literature of ecstatic flight and the latter as a reference to the rituals and practices of a particular society that is our focus here.

Eliade has been criticized for making generalized assumptions about the universality of beliefs and practices, and for extrapolating from isolated examples of what is known of Siberian shamanism a kind of ancient racial memory (to use a Jungian term with which Eliade would have been comfortable) common to all humans. This universalizing instinct has been identified with colonialism and, indeed, the "mystification" of the religious and cultural practices of "third world" populations has been seen as more of a reflection of colonial ideas about "the primitive" than an objective evaluation of the data.[34]

One of Eliade's mystifications concerns the concept of ecstatic flight and ascent, a theme that is central to this study. Nevertheless, by associating ecstatic flight and ascent with shamanism, Eliade has raised an important question. Is the ecstatic flight of the Jewish *merkavah* mystics a form of "Eliadean" shamanism?

While Eliade himself does not raise this issue in his work on shamanism and tends to ignore Jewish mysticism altogether — the *merkavah* texts being largely unknown at the time his *Shamanism* was published — even though he does reference Christian and Gnostic forms of "ecstatic flight," it is a question worth asking for what it will tell us about the power of the text. The Jewish form of ecstatic flight was primarily textual in that its practitioners left written instructions as to how it was to be performed and, indeed, the practice was based on another text, the Book of Ezekiel. This literary "line of succession" implies a different category of experience from that of the Siberian shamans who do not commit their rites and beliefs to writing and who do not reference a written text. Does that mean that the *merkavah* mystics are not shamans?[35]

The relationship between oral text and written text is one that has occupied other observers. The priority given to the written text as an indicator of civilization or of religious sophistication has been criticized as racist and colonialist.[36] In a weird kind of reverse prioritization, however, tremendous importance has been assigned to the oral traditions of nonwestern cultures. Yet in our examination of the texts of the western secret societies under discussion we can see that both forms of text, oral and written, are employed. The written text can be accessed in the rituals and knowledge lectures of the Golden Dawn; but there is an implied oral text in the idea of "secrets" and "secret chiefs" and "secret doctrines": i.e., knowledge that cannot be had from written texts but from direct experience and oral transmission during initiation. This is true for all of the organizations we have referenced, and is especially true of the O.T.O. (Ordo Templi Orientis), the British and American branches of which were run and essentially reinvented by a Golden Dawn initiate, Aleister Crowley, one of the men characterized by Scholem, above, as a supreme charlatan.

In the latter case, the rituals of the O.T.O. were published and then pulled from circulation because the rituals were supposed to be "secret." Thus, we have the example of a text that is written but immediately concealed. Although the ritual initiations for the first seven grades are Masonic in character — employing a lodge, officers, lengthy speeches intended to convey knowledge, and grips, gestures, etc. — the initiatory phases of the eighth and ninth degrees are not. The secrets of these initiations are transmitted orally, thus demonstrating a vertical succession from written text to oral text within the same organization. That these secrets are of a sexual nature (in a Tantric sense, as the O.T.O. claims to have received its secrets from the Middle East and India) reminds us of the esoteric fence that was built around the Song of Solomon by the rabbis.

Somehow these strands of Kabbalistic interest — the *merkavah,* the *bereshit,* and the Song of Solomon — became united in a single initiatory framework in the secret societies of western Europe and England. The higher one progressed in the degree system, the more the "secrets" had to do with the purification of the personality and the "initiated" understanding of sexuality, and the secrets became less a matter of text and formal ritual and more a matter of oral teaching and individual practice.

The Golden Dawn and Christian Kabbalah

The Qabalah, to recapitulate the whole situation, emphasizes the attainment of a transcendental state of consciousness as the next step for every man, and I have endeavoured to make clear what is the essential nature of this mystical experience, without which there is neither peace nor accomplishment, the steps leading up to its consummation, and an account of the spiritual formulae by means of which the significance of its revelation may be grasped.   — Israel Regardie[37]

One of the most disconcerting and frustrating things confronting any historian of the secret societies of the last two centuries is not the lack of documentation but the lack of *credible* documentation. Virtually all of the major figures of the occult renaissance that can be said to have begun in the late nineteenth century have been denounced as either frauds or criminals or both by various observers and chroniclers of the phenomenon. This is certainly due, at least in part, to the proclivity of these spiritual innovators to "innovate" their own identities and lineages. During the Renaissance and the Reformation, there was ample reason to disguise one's allegiance due to the various religious and secular powers in force at different times, from the Roman Catholic Church and its dreaded Inquisition to the holy wars that raged across Europe from the time of Luther. Creative thinkers such as Galileo and Giordano Bruno ran afoul of the church and wound up in prison for their beliefs; in Bruno's case, he was burned at the stake as a heretic.

Later, during the time of great upheaval in Europe in the eighteenth century, Masonic societies and their offspring — such as that notorious bugaboo of conspiracy theorists, the *Illuminaten Orden*, or Illuminati — were suspected (and usually rightly so) of political intrigues against the state and monarchy. The secret names and code words of these societies served not only to unite their members in an esoteric brotherhood but also to protect their identities and activities from inquisitive police investigators.

By the nineteenth century, however, these stratagems were no longer as necessary as they had been. Revolutions, both political and industrial, had taken place in Europe and the Americas; indeed, the American Revolution had been championed, at least in part, by the Masonic societies themselves. George Washington, famously, was a Mason, and there was nothing covert about his membership in that order.

Why, then, did the European and American secret societies of the nineteenth and twentieth centuries witness such a resurgence of multiple identities and aliases among its founders and members while, at the same time, these same individuals were such assiduous seekers of fame in the "mundane" world? In several cases, it was to increase the amount of mystification considered so necessary in attracting recruits. In other cases, it was to disguise more nefarious activities.

It is not the intention of the author to try to disentangle the various lineages, identities, and confidence tricks of the societies under investigation. That would require much more space than can be afforded here and even then one would not be certain of having achieved the desired goal. Scholarship in this area is sparse; aside from two specialists — Joscelyn Godwin[38] and the late Ellic Howe,[39] the first sympathetic and the second unsympathetic — most of what has been written about the societies has been by partisan members and is therefore suspect. There is a further difficulty in the form of a general bias against the subject matter itself: occultism, magic, witchcraft, and the like traditionally have been dangerous areas for career academics to pursue. In addition, so many of the occult personalities themselves have at one time or another been accused of espionage, criminal activities, and fraud that much of the documentation concerning them has been in the form of indictments and arrest warrants!

And yet these are the same individuals who created the occult renaissance. It would be easy to dismiss the entire phenomenon as charlatanism writ large, the sanctuary of the credulous and feeble-minded, if it were not for the fact that the influence of occult ideas has been profound in Europe, America, and Asia. Joseph Smith Jr., the founder of the Church of Jesus

Christ of Latter-Day Saints, or the Mormons, began his career as a magician in the woods of New York State, conjuring spirits in an effort to find buried treasure, and ended his career as a Freemason.[40] In 2008, a Mormon former governor from Massachusetts, Mitt Romney, was running for the office of president of the United States as a Republican. Madame Helena Blavatsky, who founded the Theosophical Society in New York City in 1875, is another personality who has been accused of fraudulent practices, deception, and charlatanism, yet members of her society were influential in the Indian Nationalist Movement[41] and, as recent research suggests, in the Indonesian independence movement as well.[42] The Theosophical Society boasted of its connections to the Hermetic Brotherhood of Luxor (HBL), which itself seems to have been run by fugitives from justice posing as spiritual masters. The HBL was also influential in the spiritual movement around Sri Aurobindo, and the Theosophical Society also gave birth to the movement around the late Krishnamurti, who distanced himself from the Society and its pedophilic "master," Rev. Charles Leadbeater.[43] L. Ron Hubbard, the founder of Scientology and the author of many works of fiction and nonfiction, began his career as a ritual occultist and follower of the notorious magician Aleister Crowley,[44] himself accused of all sorts of criminal and immoral activities.

So we are faced with a conundrum. Accustomed as we are to investigating religion and religious organizations within a framework of the ethical and moral ideals that these religions represent, when we approach the occult orders and secret societies we are confronted with voluminous evidence, some of it circumstantial, some of it well documented, of criminal activity and fraud. If, on the other hand, we are accustomed to investigate religion and religious experience after the manner of anthropologists who interview informants and build databases of creation myths, trickster legends, symbol systems, etc., optimistically expecting that the informants will be honest in their accounts, when we approach the occult orders we are faced with an almost surreal tableau of legends and myths that are themselves couched in enigmatic phrases, codes, and other instruments of obfuscation designed to "protect the secrets." The deliberate and stated intention of the occultists is to deceive or at least to conceal, except perhaps from their own initiates; when it comes to their spiritual lineages, however, they may be concealing the truth from everyone. How, then, to approach the documents these groups themselves generate, particularly when it comes to their alleged spiritual pedigrees and the rituals and initiatory practices that they represent?

Freemasonry for centuries has insisted that its roots run as deep as the building of King Solomon's Temple and, even before that, to ancient Egypt and secrets brought out of Egypt by Moses. While there is virtually no evidence — paleographic, archaeologic, or otherwise — to support this claim, what is important is the context in which the claim is made, for it reveals a

narrative with specific characteristics and it is this narrative that can be investigated safely. If the history we have presented to us is a lie, then perhaps
the lie itself can be examined in an effort to determine what truth is being
obscured. Freemasonry does not claim origins in Asian religions or those
of Eliade's Siberian shamans, for instance. It places itself within a distinctly
European framework and selects those elements of the European religious
experience that are rooted in a particular worldview: one that is neither
Roman Catholic nor pagan, but originally anti-Catholic in that it claims
lineage through the Knights Templar. It may be recalled that the Templars,
while originally champions of the church, came under suspicion of heresy
and blasphemy in the fourteenth century and were suppressed by both the
Catholic Church and the king of France. The charges of heresy were based
on the idea that the Templars had been exposed to Islam during their sojourn as crusader knights in Palestine and that this exposure had somehow
corrupted them. While the charges were almost certainly fabricated and the
order suppressed in order to erase the massive debt owed to the order by
both king and pope, there is no doubt that the Crusades in general were
instrumental in exposing Europe to a new world of philosophy and science.

   Thus, while we acknowledge a certain level of difficulty in the evaluation of the texts of the secret societies, we would be well served if we
employ a multi-disciplinary approach incorporating history, a little inves-
tigative journalism, and the anthropology of religion toward unraveling
what these societies represented and still represent.[45] The importance of this
may lie in the idea that today's heretical organizations can be tomorrow's religious movements. After all, the movement that grew up around the Jewish
prophet Jesus was considered heretical by the Jewish religious authorities.
Joseph Smith Jr. was certainly a career occultist. The movement spawned by
L. Ron Hubbard is now incorporated as a religion in the United States, even
though its origins can be reliably traced back to the same occult themes and
rituals that we will study here and to the secret society that spawned them:
the Golden Dawn.

   The secret society that has captured the attention (and the imagination) of
the occult movement of the late twentieth century is the Hermetic Order of
the Golden Dawn, known simply as the "Golden Dawn." Formally organized in 1887 and formally opened in 1888 by a group of three English
occultists in London, it claimed to have an older, Continental, pedigree. According to the official history of the order,[46] this was a German occult lodge
based in Frankfurt;[47] according to other documentation,[48] there was a link,
however tenuous, with a Jewish Masonic society and, ultimately, with the
infamous Dr. Samuel Falk and from there to the apostate Jacob Frank and
his dissenting Sabbatean sect from Podolia (Ukraine). As we shall see, these
two stories are not mutually exclusive.

While this history is certainly suggestive, and while the Jewish Masonic lodge did, in fact, exist, as we shall see, the connection has not been proven in its entirety. As in the case of alleged political conspiracies, secret societies ("religious conspiracies," if you will) are notoriously difficult to pin down, verify, or document. This is as true of tracing the origins of Kabbalistic groups and texts as it is with more modern groups like the Golden Dawn. The tradition of pseudepigrapha in both cases does not help matters and only serves to increase the confusion.

The western, European secret societies of the late modern period, dating from roughly 1875 to 1941, were based, at least in part, on Masonic ideas and structures. Freemasonry itself came into existence about 1590 in Scotland and 1700 in England, according to modern scholarship,[49] and has continued to wield an influence over esoteric organizations and ideologies to the present day: the furor over the fictional *Da Vinci Code* and its nonfiction but speculative source, *Holy Blood, Holy Grail,* is certainly evidence of the extent to which Freemasonry (and its putative origins in the Order of the Knights Templar) influences popular conceptions regarding secret societies and hidden knowledge.

The rituals of the Freemasons — especially the first three degrees, which are the most important and critical — are centered around myths concerning the building of the Temple of Solomon. These myths are extended to include the Great Pyramid at Gizeh and other ancient sacred sites to provide an ideological and historical continuum for the order by alleging that the Masonic society has its origins first in the design of the Egyptian pyramids, then in the building of Solomon's Temple, and eventually, in the later degrees of the order, the Knights Templar themselves who were based, of course, at the site of the Second Temple in Jerusalem during the time of the Crusades.

The publication, in 1614 CE, of a document known as the *Fama Fraternitatis* gave further impetus to the idea of secret societies in Europe whose members were unidentified but who possessed tremendous occult power. The *Fama* was the first public announcement of the existence of the Rosicrucian Society, an order supposedly founded by the pseudonymous "Christian Rosenkreutz," who had sojourned in Arab lands — including the cities of Damascus and Fez, the latter especially a hotbed of Kabbalistic learning according to Moshe Idel[50] — and studied ancient mysteries. While it is generally understood that this Society did not actually exist but was invented, stories and legends about the Rosicrucians continued to excite the popular imagination for centuries to come, for they found fertile ground in what is known as "Christian Kabbalah" and the occult orders that derived from its study.

The Golden Dawn is just such an order, founded by three modern-day Rosicrucians[51] (members or associates of a Masonic society known as the Rosicrucian Society of England, the Societas Rosicruciana in Anglia, or SRIA), and its rituals are replete with Kabbalistic references including, most importantly, that of the Sephirotic Tree upon which their entire initiatory structure is based, and also including Christological references as well as Egyptian mythology, Greek Hermeticism, alchemy, and eclectic *nomina sacra* and *termini technici*. It is as if a Kabbalist of the Provence or Gerona school had gone berserk and applied the methodology and scriptural references of the Zohar to ... well, the Egyptian *Book of the Dead*.

So what is "Christian Kabbalah"? According to Scholem:

> The Christian Kabbalah can be defined as the interpretation of kabbalistic texts in the interests of Christianity (or, to be more precise, Catholicism); or the use of kabbalistic concepts and methodology in support of Christian dogma.[52]

While that definition suffices for understanding mainstream Renaissance philosophers such as Marsilio Ficino (1433–99) and Giovanni Pico della Mirandola (1463–94), who are referenced by Scholem, the situation changes when we get to the realm of the secret societies by the time of the eighteenth and nineteenth centuries. In these groups — among which the most famous would be the Freemasons (1590), but also including the Illuminati (1776), the Asiatic Brethren (1780), the Societas Rosicruciana in Anglia (1866), and their offshoots the Golden Dawn (1887) and the Argentum Astrum, or A∴A∴ (1907) — orthodox Christian (or, to be more precise, Catholic) dogma has been either ignored, so mutilated as to be unrecognizable or, in some cases, abrogated completely. Indeed, Freemasonry was quite specifically banned by the Roman Catholic Church and membership in that society was punishable by excommunication. There is therefore no margin in using a Jewish tradition to "prove" the truth of Christianity if the effort has to remain secret, especially from other Christians. In fact, initially Freemasonry was hostile to Judaism and Jews were forbidden to join. While the interests of Christian philosophers in the Kabbalah may have originally stemmed from a desire to prove Christian dogma — Pico della Mirandola himself famously observed that the study of magic and the Kabbalah would demonstrate the truth of Christianity[53] and was censured for stating this so baldly — there was another element to the popularity of this literature among the Christian elite, an element that becomes clear only in the writings of later Christian Kabbalists, such as Johannes Reuchlin (1455–1522), Athanasius Kircher (1602–80), Robert Fludd (1574–1637), etc.

Joseph Dan, in his article on the Christian Kabbalist Johannes Reuchlin, clarifies this point of view when he states:

The Christian Kabbalist rejects, knowingly or unknowingly, the concept that Christianity is right exactly in as much as Judaism is wrong, and any diminishing in the rightness or wrongness of the one immediately is transferred to the rightness or wrongness of the other. For him, the statement that there is more truth in Jewish traditions than was supposed before, does not diminish Christian truth but ENHANCES it.[54]

Dan, in fact, is impressed with the degree to which Christian Kabbalists were open-minded and accepting of Jewish religious and mystical sources as factors that could be used to enhance their own faith. He does not find similar attitudes where Jewish appreciation of Christian or Islamic mysticism or religion is concerned, of course, nor in Islamic attitudes toward Jewish or Christian mystical sources.[55] This eagerness among the Christian Kabbalists since the time of the Renaissance to explore the depths of Jewish mysticism (as much as they were able to do, in light of a paucity of genuine Kabbalistic documents in translation or available in *any* form) would find its greatest manifestation in the hundred years from roughly 1775 to 1875, when the revolutionary movements in the Americas and Europe were accompanied by a surge in the activities of the secret societies and the publication of hundreds of volumes on Kabbalah, magic, apocrypha, and apocalyptica.[56]

Instead, Christian Kabbalah, especially in its later manifestations in the Golden Dawn and the other schools of the nineteenth century, formed an aggressive syncretism that tried to show the universality of Kabbalistic doctrine in its application to areas of study as diverse as Egyptian religion, Babylonian ritual, Pythagorean mathematics and philosophy, and other neo-Platonic pursuits, as well as to medieval ceremonial magic. Kabbalah, indeed, was used as a tool to unite these various forms of religious and mystical doctrines into a coherent whole for the purpose of understanding the underlying matrix of reality. As Dame Frances Yates has suggested, the installation of Kabbalah as the "system" for interpreting religious and natural phenomena eventually became the basis for the modern scientific method.[57]

Yet there was another aspect to this "Christianizing" of the Kabbalah that concealed a germ of anti-Semitism at its core: the idea that the Kabbalah was not a purely Jewish phenomenon but that it had its roots in ancient Egypt and was a secret doctrine transmitted by Moses — allegedly a high priest of the Egyptian mysteries — orally to his followers, presumably after receiving the Law on Mount Sinai. This belief has uneasy resonance with the ideas of twentieth-century scholars of the Kabbalah, such as Scholem, who see in Kabbalistic literature the distinct traces of Gnostic (i.e., dualist, neo-Platonic, and crypto-pagan) influence. Of course, Judaism did not develop in a vacuum, and the efforts of Scholem — and later scholars of the

Kabbalah, such as Moshe Idel and Ronit Meroz — to show Arab, Greek, possibly Persian, and certainly Islamic and other influences at work in the development of Kabbalistic ideas has been generally accepted by some, but not all, authorities on the literature.

Without delving too deeply into this controversy, we may simply cite one of Scholem's critics, Ioan Couliano, a disciple of Mircea Eliade, who states:

> It was one of Gershom Scholem's favorite ideas that early Jewish mysticism was a form of Gnosticism. It is easy to see that this is not so: multiplication of heavenly angels, watchwords, and seals is something some gnostic texts have in common with Merkabah mysticism, yet it is neither gnostic nor Jewish. It is common Hellenistic currency that circulates among the magical papyri as well. If we were inclined to search for "origins," the late Egyptian derivate of the Pyramid and Coffin texts known as "The Book of the Dead" is probably the closest we could get.[58]

This is precisely what the secret societies believed, from the Freemasons of the seventeenth century to their later, twentieth-century counterparts in the Golden Dawn. In fact, it is also what this author has been attempting to prove, at least insofar as *merkavah* mysticism is concerned. The emphasis by the secret societies on "Hermeticism" was a clear reference to a tradition that was believed to be a survival of ancient Egyptian mysteries, represented by the god Thoth, the inventor of writing, calculation, and magic, and his Hellenistic counterpart, Hermes, and based on the discovery of the *Corpus Hermeticum*, which was widely distributed among the members of the fifteenth-century Florentine Academy. The fact that Moses, as related in the Torah, was in Egyptian captivity until the parting of the Red Sea, and that the Jews, waiting for Moses to descend from Mount Sinai, reverted to the worship of a golden calf, a form of Egyptian religion, was seen as proof that Egyptian beliefs and practices found their way into Judaism, albeit secretly: in the form of Jewish mysticism and esotericism, which we call today by the name "Kabbalah."[59]

That this may not be true, of course, is the focus of much research concerning the relationship between Kabbalah and other esoteric movements, such as Gnosticism (as represented by the Nag Hammadi texts, among others) and Essenism (possibly represented by the Qumran scrolls). The arguments for and against Gnostic influences on the Kabbalah (or vice versa) may be a diversion from a potentially more important argument: that the Kabbalah, particularly the pre-Zoharic Kabbalah, contains within itself elements of an ancient shamanistic practice that can be traced to both dynastic Egypt and Babylon, and that these elements erupted to the surface in the esoteric practices of the secret societies of the late nineteenth century, thus raising the question: was the *ma'aseh merkavah* technology already known to these "charlatans" and, if so, through what channels?

> The MAASEH BERESHITH and the MAASEH MERKABAH there referred to are not a written tradition, nor does that of the written Kabbalah necessarily represent it. The ZOHAR identifies MERCABAH with the SEPHIROTH or Ten Emanations.[60]

Thus as late as 1924, A. E. Waite, understandably dismissed by Scholem as "confused,"[61] understood the *ma'aseh merkavah* to be an oral tradition not represented by the written Kabbalah, yet he states that the *merkavah* is identical to the ten *sephiroth*. This is important because Waite was an initiate of the Golden Dawn, although he eventually left to form his own, distinctly Christian, version. The Golden Dawn initiatory system, which consists of ten levels or degrees based specifically on the ten *sephiroth*, assumes that one "attains" each level or *sephira* in turn, from *Malkuth* to the higher degrees. It was expressly understood that the top three degrees — corresponding to *Kether, Chokmah,* and *Binah* and usually referred to as the "three Supernals" — were not attainable by humans but were the domain of the disembodied "secret chiefs" who guided the order from one of the higher heavens.[62] For the bottom seven degrees there were appropriate rituals of initiation that would only be conferred after the candidate had passed the requisite tests and demonstrated a mastery of increasingly difficult occult material and texts. Thus, the ten *sephiroth* — which first come to us in written form in the *Sepher Yetzirah* (possibly the earliest representative text of the *ma'aseh bereshith*) — become the template for initiation into a secret society, an initiation that is bestowed by human beings on other human beings and that approximates the idea of a celestial ladder leading to heaven. In the Golden Dawn, one "climbs" from one level to the next, a journey that in most cases takes years, particularly as the paths between the *sephiroth* must be mastered as well, each path corresponding to one of the letters of the Hebrew alphabet but, even more strangely (from the point of view of a traditional Kabbalist), a series of correspondences that range from Tarot card trumps (the "major arcana," or twenty-two picture cards, as opposed to the "minor arcana," which contains fifty-six cards divided into four suits, each suit representing one of the four platonic elements: earth, air, water, fire) to planets, precious stones, specific colors, divine names, angels and archangels, etc. In other words, the Sephirotic Tree was simultaneously viewed as a symbol of creation and everything within it, a database of existence (and thus of the *ma'aseh bereshit*) *and* as a means of spiritual initiation, or *ma'aseh merkavah*. This was represented in the tables of correspondences for each of the ten *sephiroth* and the twenty-two paths, carefully constructed to show not only the traditional Kabbalistic attributes but contributions from virtually every other — non-Jewish, non-Kabbalistic — religious and occult source. These sources included Egyptian, Roman, Greek, and eventually even Hindu and Buddhist concepts, deities, practices (such as various forms of yoga and meditation), etc. One measured one's progress in terms of the symbols that presented themselves during various rituals and other practices. This was an intriguing synthesis of *ma'aseh bereshit* with *ma'aseh merkavah,* with the seven heavens of the latter identified with the *sephiroth* from *Malkuth* to *Chesed* or, alternatively, from *Yesod* to *Binah.*

This application of the "form" of *ma'aseh bereshit* to ritual "function" seems at first glance what the Talmudists warned against: the practical, mundane use of sacred information. Yet the purpose behind the Golden Dawn's version of the Sephirotic Tree was not mere "practical Kabbalah" in the sense of casting spells for money or love or finding treasure, etc., but was instead the attainment of spiritual enlightenment. The initiates of the Golden Dawn wanted to "see" the spiritual realm; they wanted to catch a glimpse of the Divine, and in this they were no different from other seekers after the Divine, whether "descenders to the Chariot" or the contemporary groupies who swirl around the Indian masters of Hinduism and Buddhism. The difference was not one of intention but of seriousness and personal commitment. The descenders to the Chariot were enjoined to lead pure lives of spiritual devotion — lives of sinlessness and adherence to the Law — and comprehensive and exhaustive sacred learning, as represented by the Torah and its commentaries and exegetical literature. This was not necessarily the case with the Golden Dawn, which placed its faith in the correct performance of the initiatory rituals in combination with the commitment of its initiates to the intellectual study of occult topics. One could be relatively certain that there were no Talmudic scholars among the effete English drawing-room membership of the Golden Dawn; if there were, they have yet to surface. Instead, the occultism studied by the members was pure occultism: alchemy, ceremonial magic, and the like. Since the Golden Dawn accepted members from all religions, there could be no adherence to any set of doctrines or teachings specific to any organized faith. Rather, the appropriate study of the Golden Dawn was occultism and mysticism itself, with an end to attaining the "Great Work": the elevation of one's consciousness to the contemplation of the Divine and the uniting of one's soul to God through the medium of "The Holy Guardian Angel," a being roughly identical to that of one's "Higher Self":

> ...if one may speak of the Order as having a specific purpose, then
> that sublime motive is to bring each man to the perfection of his own
> Kether, to the glory of his own Higher Genius, to the splendour of the

Golden Dawn arising within the heart of his soul. And its technique is always encompassed through the uplifting of the heart and mind by a theurgic invocation to Isis-Urania, the symbolic personification of the Sephiroth of the Supernal Light.[63]

The ultimate ritual initiation that would set the initiand off to the fulfillment of this goal was the Adeptus Minor ritual, which "took place" at the sphere of *Tiphareth* and which involved a ritual crucifixion. This ceremony was conducted within a reconstruction of the seven-sided tomb of Christian Rosenkreutz and thus cemented the idea of crucifixion and resurrection within a Kabbalistic framework of the seven palaces of the *merkavah*.[64] Beyond this stage of initiation were found only the leaders of the order or the specific lodge at the levels of *Hesed* and *Gevurah*; the *sephiroth Binah*, *Chokmah,* and *Kether* had no initiations assigned to them (and no human representatives) and it was expected that the initiand make the spiritual journey the rest of the way based on his or her own energy and commitment. It would take an occult adventurer like Aleister Crowley to challenge all that and to employ sense-gratification as a channel to God.

The idea that one attained spiritual perfection through strict adherence to the Law began to change in the post-Lurianic period with the arrival of a series of false Messiahs and the threatening ideas they represented: that one could be "redeemed through sin."[65] The effect of *some* Kabbalistic teaching and practice among eastern European Jews led to the fantastic phenomenon of Sabbateanism and its offshoots, such as the Doenmeh in Turkey and the radical movement begun by Jacob Frank. These "Kabbalistic" messianic movements were identified by the willingness of their leaders to turn apostate — Sabbatei Zevi to Islam, Frank to Islam and Catholicism — and by a determinedly hostile approach to certain aspects of Jewish Law, in particular those regulations concerning sexuality. Eventually, these teachings would make their way into western Europe as well, and with interesting results.

Until that time, however, Christian Kabbalah was dominated by a general knowledge of the ten *sephiroth,* the concept of the *Ein Sof* (or "negative existence" as described by Mathers[66]), and the existence of the *Sepher ha-Zohar,* the seminal text of what was popularly understood to be Kabbalism. This came about in Florence in the fifteenth century as a result of some translations of selected Zoharic texts for Pico della Mirandola by his partner (and sometime teacher) the enigmatic Flavius Mithridates, whom Scholem[67] identifies as Samuel ben Nissim Abu'l-Faradj, a Sicilian Jew of the Agrigento who also went by the name Guglielmo Raimondo Moncada, and who was the source for della Mirandola's knowledge of genuine Kabbalistic texts, such as the *Bahir* and the Zohar.

Giovanni Pico della Mirandola was a young genius who raced enthusi-astically through the available ancient Jewish sources and found enough evidence to support his idea that Jewish mysticism contained proofs of Christian claims concerning the divinity of Jesus, an idea that had a certain attraction in those early days of the Renaissance, which was itself largely influenced by Jewish ideas, as Frances Yates has shown.[68] It is in the pages of Pico della Mirandola's *Opera Omnia*[69] that we first encounter the idea that one could "ascend" up the spheres of the Tree of Life. (However, it should be noted that this work has not appeared in English or in any mod-ern translation and was available only in Latin and in the rare book rooms of museums and libraries at the time the secret societies were flourishing in Europe. A. E. Waite, one of the initiates of the Golden Dawn, had translated some of the "Cabalist Conclusions"[70] but from an abridged form which he collated with a very bad translation into French by Eliphas Levi. It could be said that neither of these gentlemen's work was improved by the other.) While his theories were condemned by the church, they influenced a number of his contemporaries and continued to exert a fascination for generations of "free thinkers" thereafter. These ideas would lose some of their luster at the dawn of the Industrial Age, when opposition to the Catholic Church and its teachings among European intellectuals resulted in a different kind of esoteric movement, one that blended Jewish Kabbalah with more an-cient sources, such as Egyptian, to create an order that was less purely Judeo-Christian and more syncretistic: the Freemasons.

While modern scholarship has traced the origins of the Masonic order to the late sixteenth century, it did not reach its heyday until the mid-eighteenth century, a time of tremendous upheaval in Europe and the Americas. The ephemeral Rosicrucian order had already been announced at the beginning of the seventeenth century and was believed to be an underground Protes-tant movement composed of scientists and other intellectuals who valued esoteric knowledge, in particular, alchemy, as a means of resistance to the monopolization of information by church and state. While the Rosicrucians were invisible — there were no monthly meetings, no temples, no visible manifestation at all aside from the infamous *Manifestos* — the Freemasons were quite visible and at times its membership was well-known in artistic, scientific, and cultural circles.

An important philosophical difference between the esoteric movements of the eighteenth century and those of the Renaissance, however, can be found in their relationship to organized religion. The Renaissance philosophers sought a deeper communion with what they saw as the central truths of Christianity: the divinity of Jesus, the resurrection, the promise of life in the world to come. By the time of the American and French revolutions, however, the emphasis had shifted from acceptance of Christian dogma and church authority to one of independence from authority and the belief that there existed hidden truths that were universal and not the property of any one religion or cult. What had changed was the idea of the *perfectibility of the human being,* a perfectibility that could be realized through esoteric knowledge and passed on, from one human to another, rather than wait for God to intervene directly.

That this owed something to the practice of alchemy — the core of which is the gradual transmutation of metals from base or lower forms, such as lead, to more "perfect" forms, such as gold — cannot be doubted. Connections were alleged between Kabbalah and alchemy as early as the fifteenth century in the writings of the medieval occultist Cornelius Agrippa and later in the ambitious volumes of Heinrich Khunrath (1560–1605), which were followed by the experiments of Thomas Vaughan (1641–66)[71] and Robert Fludd (1574–1637):[72] two English alchemists with a fascination for the Kabbalah. The first published translation of the *Sepher ha-Zohar* into a European language was Knorr von Rosenroth's Latin version *Kabbalah Denudata,* or "Kabbalah Unveiled" (1677), which contained among its volumes the important alchemical work mentioned above, the *Aesch Mezareph,* thus uniting the concepts of Kabbalah and alchemy in the European mind, something that had already begun with the Rosicrucian literature and that would continue in somewhat more altered form in Freemasonry.

It was Heinrich Khunrath, whoever, who wrote that "Kabbalah, magic and alchemy shall and must be combined and used together."[73] This would be accomplished with considerable élan by the creators of the Golden Dawn in 1887. We have noted that alchemy was used as a metaphor for the perfectibility of human beings. Was there a precedent for this same concept in Kabbalah? And how was magic related to both of these?

Probably the earliest example of the "perfectibility" of a human being in Jewish mystical literature is that of Enoch, a biblical figure whose hagiography has elicited much fascination with occultists and Kabbalists alike. Although he made only a brief appearance in Genesis (5:18–23), the fact that Enoch is described as "walking with God" after which "he is seen no more" indicated to Jewish mystics that Enoch, while alive, ascended to heaven, becoming in the process the archetypal model of the initiated or illuminated human being.

The mysticism associated with Enoch appears in the literature as early as the third century BCE with the *Astronomical Book of Enoch* and the *Book of the Watchers,* and thus centuries before the earliest known *ma'aseh merkavah* texts. In later *hekhalot* writings, Enoch is associated with the angel Metatron, a figure central to many visions of those who descend to the Chariot as the Angel on the Throne whom one must not confuse with

God.[74] That Enoch ascended to heaven and became an angel, specifically Metatron, is an idea that persists through Kabbalistic works and in those of Christian Kabbalah as well and became a central issue for the founders of the Golden Dawn.

As the core document of the Golden Dawn, the "Cypher Manuscripts," demonstrate, the magical system known as "Enochian" formed the basic "operating system" for the order. While the initiatory degree system was based on the ten *sephiroth,* the language and complicated matrix of correspondences was purely Enochian. What was Enochian?

In the period 1583–89, the Elizabethan philosopher, mathematician, and magician John Dee was in eastern Europe on what has since been described as a political mission to the courts of Cracow and Prague.[75] While in Prague, he was engaged in a series of occult operations that involved communication with angels, principally Uriel and Gabriel. It was during the course of these lengthy séances that he obtained a variety of complicated figures and tables, a strange alphabet, and a stranger language that was written in it. This language Dee called "Angelic," and the tables and figures represented combinations and other arrays of the letters of this language in powerful symbols that were believed by Dee to be capable of summoning tremendous occult forces. The language, alphabet, and some of the tables and figures were eventually published in 1659 by Meric Casaubon as *A True and Faithful Relation of What Passed for Many Years between John Dee and Some Spirits.*

The text of this book would not be republished until the late twentieth century, but it had been copied by hand from an original version at the British Museum by S. L. MacGregor Mathers in the late nineteenth century. By that time, the system Dee had received during his angelic séances had come to be known as "Enochian" after the biblical Enoch. Mathers used the Angelic, now called "Enochian", alphabet, language, and system of magic squares as the basis for the teachings and rituals of the Golden Dawn, an order that was being formed by members of the Societas Rosicruciana in Anglia, or SRIA, and based on the acquisition of a manuscript, in code, from one "Fräulein Sprengel" of Germany, who was allegedly a member of the German mother lodge of the Golden Dawn. This was known as the Cypher Manuscript, and while its provenance has been hotly debated by scholars, there is no doubt that what the manuscript provided was a unique contribution to the development of Christian Kabbalah in the nineteenth century.

That the Golden Dawn was really a branch of an older, German order based in Frankfurt was believed for many years to be an invention of either one or two or all three of the British founders, Westcott, Woodman, and/or Mathers. Recent scholarship has come to light, however, suggesting that there was, indeed, a German "mother lodge."[76] The Cypher Manuscripts themselves contained instructions for establishing a British lodge contained in a series of roughly drawn pages showing the symbols and basic rituals of the order in a cypher, or secret key. Once decoded, the result was the tremendously complex and wholly syncretistic system of initiation with which the Golden Dawn became synonymous: a series of ten degrees based on the ten *sephiroth* of the Jewish Kabbalah and the rituals appropriate to the first seven of these (the last three, that of the supernal triad of *Kether, Chokmah,* and *Binah* being beyond human comprehension). Closely associated with this Kabbalistic system was that of the Enochian method of John Dee. What Mathers — or the above-mentioned "Fräulein Sprengel" of the alleged mother lodge in Frankfurt, Germany, or her superiors — had done was to form a symbiotic pairing of the Sephirotic Tree and the Enochian system.

The result was a brilliant, if sometimes confusing, amalgam of traditional Jewish Kabbalah with the arcane matrices of Dee's magical squares. This provided the Golden Dawn with a system of initiation that could not be found in other fraternities, one that seemed to extend the associations of the original Sephirotic Tree into other disciplines and philosophies and using the precedent of the angelized Enoch as their "role model."

This had been tried before, most notably in France by Scholem's charlatans: Eliphas Levi (Alphonse Louis Constant) and Papus (Gerard Encausse), both of whom wrote lengthy treatises on the Kabbalah armed with not much more than von Rosenroth's *Kabbalah Denudata* and scattered references to the writings of Christian Kabbalists such as Pico della Mirandola, Athanasius Kircher, Robert Fludd, et al. What the Golden Dawn had done was to strip much of the Christian imagery and dogma from the system and incorporate instead the "practical Kabbalah" aspects of Dee's work: the rituals, angelic language, and magic squares and complex matrices. Indeed, it was Golden Dawn co-founder Mathers who translated portions of von Rosenroth's translation of the Zohar and other Kabbalistic texts into English, so his understanding of Jewish Kabbalah was perhaps deeper than some of his colleagues though by no means expert. New initiates to the order were expected to learn the Hebrew alphabet, including the numerical values of the letters, the numerological and combinatorial arts of *gematria* and *notarikon,* and to have a thorough grounding in what was then understood to be basic Kabbalistic learning: the Tree of Life, the divisions of the soul, the four worlds, the *Sepher Yetzirah* (in translation by one of the founders of the Golden Dawn, Dr. Wynn Westcott), and what of the *Sepher ha-Zohar* was available to English-speaking readers.

The Golden Dawn was unique in another way, as well. It was the first Masonic-type order, run by Freemasons, that admitted women (and Jews) into its ranks as equals. That this might have been a reflection of Zoharic influence concerning the importance of the feminine and of *Shekhinah* is only conjecture at this point, although one can see in their initiation rituals a focus on the feminine by way of the invocations of Egyptian goddesses such as Isis and the identification of their order with the figure Isis-Urania, an icon of Venus.[77] What compels us to study the Golden Dawn even further, however, is the design of the rituals around the concept of human perfectibility in the process of a heavenly ascent.

The Abyss

> In the Talmud, too, there are dark hints as to the existence of a devel-
> oped tradition of the "Mercavah" [sic], or the Divine Chariot seen in
> vision by Ezekiel. Since the world is a process of Emanation, an out-
> going of Reality into Otherness (to use an Hegelian expression), there
> must be a corresponding way up for man by way of this "chariot" —
> the vehicle of means by which he could be transported into the realms
> of the unseen.   —Israel Regardie, initiate of the Golden Dawn[78]

Once again, an initiate of the Golden Dawn goes on the record to suggest that there was no knowledge of the *merkavah* technique in his organiza-tion — in this case nothing beyond "dark hints" — but that there exists a similarity between the *merkavah* and the ascent (the "corresponding way up") as depicted in the Tree of Life (the "process of Emanation," which is a "vehicle" to the "realms of the unseen").

For the Golden Dawn, there was an intimate connection between the ini-tiatory system of ascent up the *sephiroth* and practices of a more frankly theurgic nature. Published rituals show that the order was involved in train-ing their initiates in making and using talismans,[79] attaining invisibility,[80] and summoning spiritual forces[81] in addition to complicated instruction in divination[82] and in the Enochian or "Angelic" system of spiritual evoca-tions.[83] For the Golden Dawn, ascent and magic were inextricably linked in a manner reminiscent of the *merkavah* texts themselves.

One of the oldest,[84] and therefore most interesting, of *merkavah* writings is the *Re'iyyot Yehezkel*[85] or "Ezekiel's Vision," which we have already looked at in previous chapters.

Re'iyyot Yehezkel discusses the seven "compartments down below": the layers of the Underworld. As we have seen, these bear an uncanny similar-ity to the basic structure of the Sumero-Babylonian Underworld of Queen Ereshkigal.[86] As we have noted many times in this study, the idea of an as-cent up seven levels to a Throne at the top level, and consequent communion with God, was actually basic to the ancient religion of the country where Ezekiel found himself: Babylon.

To recapitulate: the famous ziggurats of Babylon were stepped pyramids up which the king would ascend on certain days of the year and commune, privately, with the gods in a special throne room at the top. The number of these steps varied, sometimes with the city and with the deity being invoked. Some of the older ziggurats unearthed by Rawlinson[87] were of seven levels and each level was painted a different color representing a different stage of the ascent. The king would ascend the ziggurat with much ceremony and, according to some reports, engage in a kind of *hieros gamos* with a priestess at the top level. This ceremony was usually performed on the New Year and has an uncanny correspondence to the practice of some Kabbalists who saw *Rosh Ha-Shonah*, the Jewish New Year, as an auspicious day for the descent to the Chariot.[88]

So far we have been suggesting that there exists a relationship between Ezekiel's vision in Babylon and the Babylonian ziggurats, temple practices, etc., and the similarities are compelling. However, the Golden Dawn initiates would not have known of these similarities as the discoveries relative to Ur and Sumer did not take place until the late nineteenth and early twentieth centuries CE. In fact, the discoveries of the Nag Hammadi and Qumran scrolls did not take place until 1945 and 1947, respectively, and Scholem's own research on Jewish mysticism was not published until 1941. That means that there had to be another channel of communication between the Golden Dawn initiates and the "descenders to the Chariot."

We may find a hint of this in an aspect of the ascent literature that remains quite consistent from text to text and that is found in the penultimate stage of the ascent process: the sixth level, the most dangerous and potentially fatal of all. At this stage danger is present and the mystic may find that passage to the seventh heaven is impossible. In the *merkavah* texts *Hekhalot Zutarti* as well as the *Hekhalot Rabbati*,[89] this is the sixth heaven. In the *Re'iyyot Yehezkel,* this dangerous sphere is *Makhon,* which is found between the fifth and sixth heavens.

In the Golden Dawn scenario, this stage, as mentioned above, is called the Abyss. It separates humanity from divinity; beyond it is the realm of the "secret chiefs," who mysteriously guide both the order and the affairs of humanity in general. The founders of the Golden Dawn believed it was not possible for a human being to cross that Abyss; that the level of *Chesed* on the Tree of Life was the highest possible attainment for any mortal, at least at the hands of other mortals, the *modus operandi* of the order.

One of the "supreme charlatans" mentioned by Scholem, however, considered that proposition to be inherently illogical and he determined to cross the Abyss and prove it to the world. Called by Scholem "Frater Perdurabo,"

this outlandish character's real name was Aleister Crowley or, more correctly, Edward Alexander Crowley (1875–1947). According to Crowley's
writings, it was possible to cross the Abyss only if one had completely dissolved one's ego so that there was no shred of ego, personality, or any other
"identifying characteristic" left to hinder one's progress.[90] That this forms
a close parallel to the teachings of Jacob Frank with his similar exhortation
to his followers to plunge into the Abyss and its *sephira Da'ath* may not be
coincidental.

Crowley was a member of the Golden Dawn and advanced rapidly
through all the degrees before leaving to form his own secret society, the
Argentum Astrum ("Silver Star") or A∴A∴ in 1907. The degree structure of
the A∴A∴ mimicked exactly that of the Golden Dawn, but with the addition
of three more degrees, representing the *sephiroth* of *Binah, Chokmah,* and
Kether. According to Crowley, it was possible to cross the Abyss and achieve
the rank of a Master of the Temple at *Binah,* then Magus at *Chokmah,* and
finally Ipsissimus at *Kether.* Crowley's legendary venality and licentiousness
were a carbon-copy of that associated with Jacob Frank. Both men cultivated
titles of nobility and assumed superhuman levels of spiritual cognomen and
awareness. Both men were, to an extent, religious charlatans; the difference
between them being that Crowley was well educated and his literary out-
put was prolific, whereas Frank by all accounts was not literary. Most of
what we know about Frank are sayings of his that were written down by
his devotees.

The obvious psychological parallels between Frank and Crowley aside,
there is another possibility for the Kabbalistic grade system of the Golden
Dawn and the A∴A∴, and that is the existence of a Jewish Masonic lodge
that owed its existence to the efforts of Frank and his followers, known as
the "Asiatic Brethren," which was active in Germany and Austria in the late
eighteenth century.

Scholem mentions the Asiatic Brethren — or "the Knights of St. John
the Evangelist for Asia in Europe" to give it its full name — in his treatise
on alchemy and the Kabbalah, where he refers to it as "a secret society of
freemasons that was much talked about in Germany and Austria between
1783 and 1790"[91] and that was founded by the Frankist Moses Dobruschka;
and in his autobiographical work *From Berlin to Jerusalem*[92] Scholem refers
to a Jewish Masonic lodge operating in Frankfurt under the name *Chabrat
Zereh Aur Bocher,* which was the Hebrew name for the Order of the Golden
Dawn, founded in 1807 by Freemasons. Thus, we have a trail of western
secret societies, founded by Jews with a working knowledge of the Kabbalah,
that leads us to the London-based Golden Dawn in 1887/88.

In several of his writings,[93] Scholem mentions both Frank and another
neo-Sabbatean, the London "Baal Shem Tov," Dr. Samuel Falk. While he

dismisses their importance from the point of view of Jewish Kabbalah, they were actually influential in the development of western secret societies due to their amalgamation of alchemy, Kabbalah, and magic — that is to say, practical Kabbalah — and the appearance they gave of possessing the secrets of all three. While it is obvious from Waite's work on the Kabbalah, mentioned above, that there was no direct knowledge among the Christian Kabbalists of the *ma'aseh merkavah* literature — which Waite presumes to be a purely oral tradition — the secret society of which Waite was a member understood that there was an ascent aspect to the Kabbalah and they superimposed ideas of the seven palaces over the first seven *sephiroth* on the Tree of Life.[94] They combined this with the idea of human perfectibility after the manner of Enoch/Metatron. They equated these concepts with that of alchemy, which is concerned with the perfectibility of metals and, possibly, as an analogue to the perfectibility of human beings (as per the writings of C. G. Jung, for instance, a thinker mentioned in passing by Scholem but considered more carefully by Idel). The whole endeavor — the rising up the Tree of Life to greater and greater degrees of spiritual illumination, mixed with the idea of human perfection obtained from alchemical sources — was undertaken with magical ritual, a system of magic that had at its core the image of Enoch: the human being who became an angel.

There is a telltale piece of evidence in the Golden Dawn rituals themselves which suggests that someone in the organization knew and understood the importance of the "seven *hekhalot*," or seven palaces, for the term "seven palaces" occurs several times in the initiation rituals but *without any further explanation*. While virtually every scrap of Kabbalistic terminology is carefully described at length and expanded to include other ideas, this concept of the seven palaces is nowhere explicated.

For instance, during the initiation ritual of the Theoricus Grade, which is assigned to the *sephira Yesod* on the Tree of Life, we read an interpretation of the twenty-first trump card of the Tarot, commonly referred to as "The World":

These ideas are symbolically resumed in the representation of the Twenty First Key of the TAROT, in front of you. Within the oval formed of the 72 circles, is a female form, nude save for a scarf that floats round her. She is crowned with the Lunar Crescent of ISIS, and holds in her hands, two wands. Her legs form a cross. She is the Bride of the Apocalypse, the Kabbalistic Queen of the Canticles, the Egyptian ISIS or Great Feminine Kerubic Angel SANDALPHON on the left hand of the Mercy Seat of the Ark. The Wands are the directing forces of the positive and negative currents. The Seven Pointed Hexagram or Star alludes to the Seven Palaces of Assiah; the crossed legs to the symbol of the Four Letters of the Name. The surmounting crescent receives alike the influences of Geburah and Gedulah. She is the synthesis of the 32nd Path, uniting Malkuth to Yesod.[95]

For the Adeptus Minor ritual, assigned to the *sephira Tiphereth*, we find the following intriguing reference:

> The shape of the Tomb [of Christian Rosenkreutz] is that of an equilateral Heptagon, a figure of Seven Sides.
> The Seven Sides allude to the Seven Lower Sephiroth, the Seven Palaces, and the Seven Days of Creation. Seven is the height above. Seven is the depth beneath.[96]

The one possible precedent for this mysterious statement in the rituals may be Mathers's own commentary on the *Sifra de-Zeni'uta* or "The Book of Concealed Mystery" in his translation of the Zohar:

> The seven palaces answer to the 3rd, 4th, 5th, 6th, 7th, 8th, and 9th Sephiroth, operating through the respective orders of the angels into the spheres of the seven planets, Saturn, Jupiter, Mars, Sol, Venus, Mercury, and Luna.[97]

It is obvious that this identification of the seven palaces with the *sephiroth* from *Binah* to *Yesod* is not identical to the ritual statement that the "Seven Sides allude to the Seven Lower *Sephiroth*" etc. since the seven lower *sephiroth* are *Chesed* to *Malkuth*, or the 4th to the 10th. Yet the ritual's identification of the seven palaces with the seven lower *sephiroth* is very suggestive of a link with *merkavah* and *hekhalot* literature, albeit in a somewhat cryptic manner. And the gnomic phrases "Seven is the height above. Seven is the depth beneath" are suggestive of the *Re'iyyot Yehezkel* description of Ezekiel first being shown the seven levels of the Underworld (the "depth beneath") before being shown the seven palaces of the heavens (the "height above"). The Golden Dawn initiation rituals were restricted to these seven *sephiroth*, and they represented for their members the theoretical and practical limits of an ascent up the Tree of Life to a state of perfection and spiritual refinement (in the chemical sense of the term). These seven palaces are the seven *hekhalot*, there can be no other interpretation; and the initiation structure of the Golden Dawn was designed to purify the human being and elevate him or her to higher states of spiritual attainment. To again quote former Golden Dawn member and apologist Israel Regardie on the subject of initiation:

> The root of the word [initiation] itself means "to begin," "to commence anew." Initiation is thus the beginning of a new phase or attitude to life, the entry, moreover, into an entirely new type of existence. Its

characteristic is the opening of the mind to an awareness of other levels of consciousness, both within and without. Initiation means above all spiritual growth — a definite mark in the span of human life.

Now one of the best methods for bringing about this stimulus of the inner life, so that one does really begin or enter upon an entirely new existence characterised by an awareness of higher principles within, is the Ceremonial technique. By this we mean that a Ceremony is arranged in which certain ideas, teaching, and admonitions are communicated to the candidate in dramatic form in a formally prepared Temple or Lodge room. Nor is this all — otherwise, no claim could be made on behalf of Magic that it really and not merely figuratively initiates.... The efficacy of an initiation ceremony depends almost exclusively on the initiator. What is it that bestows the power of successful initiation? This power comes from either having had it awakened interiorly at the hands of some other competent initiator, or that a very great deal of magical and meditation work has successfully been performed.... The entire object of all magical and alchemical processes is the purification of the natural man, and by working upon his nature to extract the pure gold of spiritual attainment. This is initiation.[98]

There does not seem to be a precedent for this in Jewish Kabbalistic lore. From the author's assiduous search through the available works of Scholem and Idel there seems to be no evidence of secret societies with degree systems, degrees that can be imposed on humans by other humans.[99] Instead, one sees that Regardie recognizes the possibility of initiation taking place when "a very great deal of magical and meditation work has successfully been performed," an allusion to the same techniques employed by the descenders to the Chariot. However, the reason for the existence of the Golden Dawn was to bestow this initiation at the hands of persons who were already initiated, who had already attained high levels of spiritual attainment, who had, in a word, already "descended to the Chariot." This seems to be a purely non-Jewish method, but one that was embraced by the descendants of the false messiah Jacob Frank, most notably by his nephew Moses Dobruschka and the Asiatic Brethren, when they became involved with Freemasonry.

Chapter 11

Frankist Influences on Western Esotericism

The history of the Asiatic Brethren cannot be told without reference to the Frankist movement of the eighteenth century. Jacob Frank (1726–91) was born Jacob ben Judah Lieb in a small town in the province of Podolia in what is now Ukraine but what was then considered Poland. He changed his name to "Frank" after his conversion to Sabbateanism, in imitation of the Yiddish word *frenk,* which meant a Sephardic Jew (something Frank was not, but seemed to be due to his long sojourn in Turkey and Salonika).

The phenomenon of Sabbateanism has been fully documented in Scholem's magnum opus, *Sabbatai Sevi: The Mystical Messiah.* It was a movement heavily influenced by the Kabbalah and by various antinomian doctrines such as abrogations of Talmudic teachings regarding sexuality and observance of *halakkah,* etc. Its founder, Sabbatai Sevi (1626–76) was born in Smyrna and studied Torah and Talmud from a young age, becoming a rabbi at the age of eighteen. During the following years he studied Kabbalah with a number of teachers, becoming in the process increasingly obsessed with mysticism and ecstatic practices. In May of the year 1665, at a time of intense chiliastic hysteria among the Christian communities of Europe, he declared himself to be the long-awaited Messiah after first having been identified as such by Nathan of Gaza. Nathan saw Sabbatai Sevi revealed to him as the Redeemer in an ecstatic vision that occurred during a descent to the Chariot.[1]

There was general excitement at the possibility that the true Messiah had incarnated and, as Scholem describes, many Jewish communities in Europe prepared to travel to Jerusalem in anticipation that the Messiah would be enthroned there, ushering in a Golden Age. Sevi traveled extensively throughout this period and found himself in Turkey, where finally he was either forced to convert to Islam to save his life or had already determined he would convert in order to bring about a reunification of all religions in a process known to Kabbalists as *tikkun:* the gathering-together of the shards of creation, in this case represented by different religious faiths. Whatever the actual motivation for the act, his conversion brought general despair to the Jewish communities, who considered it nothing less than apostasy. Even though he seemed to have converted to Islam, however, he did maintain ties with Jewish communities and even preached in their synagogues; the impression was that his conversion was not genuine, but a matter either of convenience (to save his life) or of deliberate calculation. Some of his followers remained loyal to him and to his teachings, even after his death in exile in Montenegro ten years after he declared himself the Messiah. These formed what is known as the Doenmeh in Turkey: a group of Sabbateans who outwardly profess Islam while secretly practicing Judaism, albeit from a Sabbatean perspective. This has given rise to speculation that the Doenmeh have ties to a Sufi sect known as the Bektashi and have combined elements of Sabbatean Kabbalah with Islamic mystical practices. The Bektashi Dervishes, considered heretical by both Sunnis and Shi'ites, have also been accused of antinomian practices and are an initiatory sect, with ascending levels of increasingly spiritualized teaching and praxis.[2]

Jacob Frank was believed to have descended from one such group of crypto-Sabbateans. Born in 1726 and thus forty-nine years after the death of Sevi, "there is no doubt" according to Scholem that his contacts with Sabbateans go back to his youth.[3] He began to study the Zohar and came to the attention of one of the leaders of the Sabbatean Doenmeh. By 1755 he had made a name for himself as an important Sabbatean prophet, even though he was not yet thirty years old. In Turkey in 1757, like Sabbatai Sevi before him, he converted to Islam.

His career was considered quite scandalous for his time, particularly due to the sexual excesses to which he and his followers seemed addicted, all in the name of the doctrine of "redemption through sin." Scholem notes orgies taking place behind locked doors,[4] and what dicta we have from Frank, as copied by Frank's followers, depicts an aggressive attitude toward religious law and even a rejection of the traditional Sabbatean theology in favor of a new dispensation. This development can be traced to the year 1759, when Frank left Turkey for the town of Iwanie in Poland (Ivano Zolot, now in Ukraine) under the protection of King Augustus III, who declared the Frankists to be "almost" Christians.[5] Indeed, on September 17, 1759, Jacob Frank was himself baptized a Catholic at the cathedral of Lvov, and he and his wife were baptized a second time, on November 18, 1759, during a royal ceremony attended by the king of Poland. His career after that time was a roller-coaster of fame and fortune on the one hand, and arrest and imprisonment on the other. He seemed to have an enormous appetite for self-promotion and to have a keen eye for cultivating friendships and support among the rich and famous and influential. His cavalier attitude toward organized religion is legendary, for he was a communicant of three monotheist faiths in his lifetime (Judaism, Islam, and Catholicism) and assiduously broke most, if not all, of their laws while preaching a doctrine of freedom and liberation. At the same time, he convinced his followers that he was the successor to Sabbatai Sevi and possessed a knowledge of Kabbalah that was deeper than any of his predecessors.

The degree to which Kabbalistic ideas informed his views can be deduced from the published dicta that have come down to us, and that are available in at least two separate editions.[6] Frank's most blatant statements seem to revolve around a focus on the so-called "eleventh" or "missing" *sephira* of the Tree of Life: *Da'ath*. Indeed, *Da'ath* (in his collected sayings spelled variously as *Daas, Dass,* and *Das*) is mentioned more often by far in the dicta than any of the other *sephiroth*. A few examples of this peculiar emphasis will suffice:

> You were prepared for that degree for a long time so that you could rapidly enter that secret *Das*. If you entered there then even if all the gods, wherever they are in this world, stood against you, they could not touch you there. We could [have] attain[ed] everything, only at that time you turned away to the left, and now we must enter a single step and only in several years will we come to this *Das* which is hidden.[7]

and

> We must strip off all the laws, just like the High Priest. When he enters the most holy place, he bathes first and also bathes again after having come out. Likewise here: when we enter that estate, we must strip off all laws and speculations. I wanted to give you *Das*, so you might do and not talk, only be silent, as it stands.[8]

and

> Indeed *Daas* is hidden among the Sephiroth and stands to the side; that shows that when the time comes when you enter *Dass* one must descend and go out from all the 10 Sephiroth and come to that *Daas* itself from which all the chambers are filled.[9]

Da'ath is located between the *sephiroth* of *Binah* and *Chokmah* on the traditional Tree of Life diagram; in other words, in what the Golden Dawn and later occult societies would refer to as the "Abyss." It represents Knowledge, but is not a *sephira* equal to the others; rather it occupies a different category. It is called "hidden," and when it is depicted as a circle or sphere the secret societies would normally draw it with broken lines to emphasize its different character. *Da'ath* did not make an appearance in Kabbalistic writings until the thirteenth century, when it was considered desirable to demonstrate a *conjunctio oppositorum* between the *sephiroth Binah* and *Chokmah* as there was between *Chesed* and *Gevurah* in *Tiphereth*, and between *Hod* and *Netzach* in *Yesod*.[10] This philosophical consideration does

not seem to require the kind of near-idolatry Frank expresses for *Da'ath* —
above and beyond all other *sephiroth* on the Tree — so it is curious, to say
the least. In modern times, however, *Da'ath* has preoccupied many spokespersons for the secret societies that have come out of the Golden Dawn
and its associated orders, and it has acquired a reputation as a gateway to
another reality.

Frank spent some thirteen years in a special "prison" in Poland, where
he lived after the death of his wife. His daughter, whom he called Eva but
who was born Rachel, became the embodiment of the feminine aspect of
his theology, referred to at various times with titles ranging from Eva (as
the first woman) to the Virgin or even the *Shekhinah*. He attracted wealthy
patrons and lived to the end of his days in regal splendor, dying in December
1791 at a time when Europe was being shaken by revolutionary movements.

One of his relatives, Moses Dobruschka (1753–94), the son of his cousin
Schoendel Dobruschka, had also converted to Catholicism, and was elevated to the nobility, taking the name Franz Thomas von Schoenfeld in the
process. Dobruschka would also become known as Junius Frey, a French
revolutionary and member of the Jacobins. It is to Dobruschka that we now
turn, for he is the connection between the Kabbalists of the Sabbatean and
Frankist movements and the Christian Kabbalists of the Golden Dawn.

Dobruschka was a member of the Austrian Frankists who sent their children to Frank's "court" at Offenbach. He converted to Catholicism in 1773
and became integrated with the Austrian hierarchy, becoming a noble in
1778 in Vienna. This was at a time when Frank was speaking openly about
revolution and intriguing with the Doenmeh in Turkey, predicting that the
Catholic Church and other power centers in Europe would be overthrown
and a Frankist kingdom established in their place. Dobruschka was considered as the person best able to take the reigns of the Frankist movement upon
the death of its founder, but for some reason he declined and instead wound
up in Europe conspiring with French revolutionaries. He was eventually
executed at the guillotine, as "Junius Frey," with Danton in 1794.

A few years prior to these events, however, Dobruschka with another
Frankist, Ephraim Joseph Hirschfeld, was instrumental in the creation of
a Masonic order, the aforementioned Knights of St. John the Evangelist
for Asia in Europe, commonly known as the Asiatic Brethren or *Asiatische
Brueder*. The official date of the creation of this group is somewhat open
to debate but its existence was known as early as 1783. It was well-known
in German-speaking Europe, headquartered in Berlin, as the first Masonic
society to accept Jews.[11] One of the co-founders was a member of Haps-
burg aristocracy, Baron von Ecker und Eckhoffen, who had been a member
of another Masonic order, the Gold and Rosy Cross — the *Guelden und*

Rosenkreuzer founded in 1777 — but who left (or was expelled) to help organize the Asiatic Brethren.

That there was a Frankist or Sabbatean connection to these secret societies receives further support from an unexpected source: an attack on Rosicrucianism by a disaffected member, one Magister Pianco (believed to be a pseudonym for the aforementioned baron), who wrote *Der Rosenkreuzer in seine Bloesse* (1781), a title that could charitably be translated as "The Rosicrucian Unveiled." It is referenced in a standard work on Freemasonry, *The Royal Masonic Cyclopaedia* by Kenneth MacKenzie (1877), and contains a curious table of initiatory degrees of what might have been the *Guelden und Rosenkreuzer* society to which Baron von Ecker und Eckhoffen belonged.[12]

The degrees are nine in number but bear surprising similarities to those of the Golden Dawn and the Societas Rosicruciana in Anglia, including many Kabbalistic references and the odd pairing of degree numbers, such as 1,9 for Magus, 2,8 for Magister, etc. (The Golden Dawn and SRIA used 10=1 for Ipsissimus, 9=2 for Magus, 8=3 for Magister Templi, etc.) Beyond the structural similarities, however, there is another startling reference. Each degree has a set of correspondences that relate to it, including colors, numbers, etc., as well as geographical locales where the initiates of the various degrees would meet, and how often. Most of these locations are in Germany or Austria, many in Poland, with a few in other countries, but the highest degree, that of Magus, meets every ten years in Smyrna.[13]

Smyrna is an odd choice for the meeting place of the highest-ranking members of a Rosicrucian order, but it makes excellent sense for members of the Sabbateans, since it is the birthplace of Sabbatai Sevi.

As mentioned above, Scholem himself would refer in his autobiography[14] to the existence of a Jewish Masonic lodge in Frankfurt with the title *Chabrat Zereh Aur Bocher,* which could reasonably be translated as Society of the Shining Light of the Dawn — or Golden Dawn. A branch of the Rectified Rite of Strict Observance, this was a well-known lodge established in 1807 by Prince Karl of Hessen-Kassel. In German, its name was given as *Aurora zur aufgehenden Morgenroete,* and sometimes referred to simply as "Aurora." Indeed, almost one hundred years before the publication of Scholem's autobiography, Wynn Westcott, one of the founders of the Hermetic Order of the Golden Dawn in England, would state that his order was merely the English branch of the *Chabrat Zereh Aur Bocher,* which he wrote as ChBRTh ZRCh AVR BQR (as it appeared in the Cypher Manuscripts) or as he later transcribed it, *Chabrath Zerek Aour Bokhr.* There can be no doubting, therefore, that such a lodge existed, that it was Masonic, and that it was also Jewish. What is also important is the location of this lodge in

Frankfurt, Germany, which is precisely where the Cypher Manuscripts located the residence of Fräulein Sprengel, the German contact for the order. While we may doubt the veracity of the account of Westcott or any of the other founders or members of the Golden Dawn, we are hard pressed to discount Scholem's evidence.

If, then, Westcott was correct in identifying the Frankfurt lodge of the "Golden Dawn," then we may ask whether he was also correct in identifying one Rabbi Falk as a member? According to Westcott's history of the Golden Dawn, there had been a London branch as early as 1810 and Falk had been a member.

Hayyim Samuel Jacob Falk (1708?–82) was another Sabbatean who hailed from a village in Podolia, the same province that witnessed the birth of Jacob Frank.[15] According to Scholem:

> It seems certain that he was, at the same time, a kabbalist, a practicing magician, and an alchemist.... As esteemed as the Ba'al Shem of London was in non-Jewish circles, even within the aristocracy, as controversial was his reputation among the Jews. It was tainted not only by the dark aura of magic but by the even darker (presumably not baseless) accusations of being a crypto-Shabbethaian. When he died in 1782, the epitaph on his grave praised him as "an accomplished sage, an adept in Cabbalah."[16]

This was the man the Golden Dawn claimed as a member. The only problem, of course, is with the dating. Falk died in 1782, but the London Golden Dawn lodge in question did not exist until 1810. There has been confusion on this issue, with one source claiming that Falk's son had taken over stewardship of the order, but this has not been proven. The lodge, however, is a matter of public record. Due to anti-Semitism there had been attempts to have this Jewish lodge removed from normative Masonic rolls, but in 1817 it received a warrant by the Duke of Sussex of the Grand Lodge of England and continued in existence at least until 1873 and probably much later.[17]

Thus we have a documented case of the movement of a sect of Kabbalists away from a traditional Jewish environment, through Islamic and Catholic milieus and intellectual and aristocratic circles, toward European Freemasonry and secret societies, bringing with them their secret teachings and most especially their taste for counter-cultural, political activism and revolutionary ideals. The antinomian character of the Frankist sect reached its apotheosis in the underground cells of French radicals dedicated to overthrowing the monarchy, something of which Jacob Frank would have approved and to which he presumably lent his moral support while alive.

The Asiatic Brethren came into existence while Frank was still in Offenbach. Dobruschka had been bruited about as his successor. The close association between these two individuals can therefore be assumed with some degree of comfort; whether or not Frank was aware of the Asiatic Brethren is another issue for which we have no documentation at present. What we do know is that Dobruschka converted to Catholicism and changed his name, and then became a Jacobin and changed his name again. As a Catholic, he was a Viennese nobleman; as a Jacobin, he was a French revolutionary. Like Frank himself, he changed names and affiliations with easy, even cynical, abandon. The Asiatic Brethren would have been an ideal vehicle for the promotion of Frankist ideals, as it combined Masonry — with its three degrees of initiation based on the legends surrounding the building of the Temple of Solomon — with Christian iconography, secret rituals, and esoteric lore, all mixed together in an atmosphere of revolutionary fervor.

We also know that the Sabbatean movement was essentially a Kabbalistic sect, and that the "descent to the Chariot" was a common motif, familiar to the Kabbalistic cognoscenti if not to the average devotee. Nathan of Gaza, Sevi's prophet, practiced the technique and, during Frank's lifetime, so did Rabbi Israel Ba'al Shem Tov, the founder of the modern Hasidic movement. Yet this practice seems to have been unknown among the Christian Kabbalists and remained unknown until the middle of the twentieth century, at the earliest.

Did information concerning the descent to the Chariot manage to work its way into the initiation structure of the Golden Dawn as an "oral teaching" or "secret doctrine"? Mathers and Waite, both Golden Dawn initiates, claimed that such a teaching did, indeed, exist and claimed either not to know what it was or refused to comment on it. If such information did influence the theosophy and practice of the Golden Dawn, the avenue surely had to be the Asiatic Brethren and its Frankist founders, for the Jewish Masonic lodges they created did not die on the guillotine with Dobruschka/von Schoenfeld/Frey, but survived the French Revolution to wind up in Germany and England in the nineteenth century and beyond.

Frater Perdurabo and Twentieth-Century Occultism

One of the "supreme charlatans" identified by Scholem, Frater Perdurabo — or to give him the name by which he is more commonly known, Aleister Crowley — was another initiate of the Golden Dawn and had advanced rapidly through all of its degrees before leaving to form his own society. Like Sevi and Frank before him, Crowley believed that the Abyss could be crossed and that the higher *sephiroth* were attainable by him in his lifetime. An adventurer, mountain-climber, chess-player, poet, and magician, Crowley was born into the strict Plymouth Brethren sect of Christianity against which he rebelled for most of his life. The son of a brewer, he was left with a considerable fortune when he was still quite young but managed to spend it all quite quickly. He developed a serious heroin habit, as well as a reputation for sexual excess that guaranteed him front-page headlines several times throughout his career.

He was a prolific writer on occult themes, and his approach to Kabbalah and initiation had much in common with Jacob Frank. His focus on the Abyss, the sphere of *Da'ath*, was just as pronounced, and his belief in total sexual license was identical to that of Frank. He joined orders, societies, and cults with the same cynical view toward self-promotion and hidden agendas, and railed against organized religion, all the while cultivating his mystique as a Kabbalist and magician. For Crowley, magic was largely a matter of theurgy and ritual although he wrote extensively on Asian forms of meditation and yoga as well. There is no hint in his writings of a direct reference to the works of the Chariot, even though in virtually every other respect he would have found much common cause with the Sabbateans and Frankists.

His most important contribution, in the eyes of many commentators, was his collected writings on Kabbalistic themes, which include *Gematria, Sepher Sephiroth,* and *Liber 777.* Although based in part on work that had already been done by his predecessor in the Golden Dawn MacGregor Mathers, they (and *Liber 777* in particular) are encyclopedic in their ambition to organize all religious and mythological symbol systems into a coherent and internally consistent system based on the Tree of Life, although tainted by Crowley's own "religious" ideas and his obsession with sexuality.

Together with the Golden Dawn, Aleister Crowley is one of the more influential personalities in modern occultism. One of the esoteric societies he ran — the Ordo Templi Orientis, or Order of the Eastern Temple — still exists to this day, and its American version claims about three thousand members worldwide, with other groups (notably in the UK and South America) claiming unknown numbers of members. Crowley's works can be found in every bookstore chain, as can works by other members of the Golden Dawn such as Israel Regardie, A. E. Waite, and MacGregor Mathers. Various Golden Dawn groups have formed all over the world, based on the rituals published in Regardie's huge volume, and one such group has blended Golden Dawn ritual with Crowleyan philosophy.[18]

Yet with all of this publication, there is virtually no mention of the *ma'aseh merkavah:* a Kabbalistic practice that was so influential on a number of groups within normative Judaism as well as those considered heretical. With the close involvement of Frankists in Masonic lodges in Europe and

England one would expect that the descent to the Chariot would have become a topic of study if not actual practice.

Allusions to the seven palaces exist in the Golden Dawn rituals, but no explanation is given. When one examines the lengthy rituals and their associated commentaries, one is struck by the absence of clarification on this issue. Did the Frankist and other Kabbalist influences on these societies feel it was a secret they could not share with their Christian brothers? Then how did it come about that the initiatory structure of the SRIA and the Golden Dawn mimicked the ascent to the *merkavah?*

While the Masonic societies in general utilized initiation rituals and degrees, they were not based on the Kabbalah per se but were heavily influenced by Christian and Egyptian symbolism. Even though the Masons built their *mythos* around the mysteries of the Temple of Solomon, their focus was clearly elsewhere. They were anti-Semitic in origin, and indeed the Jewish Masonic lodge referred to above was under pressure to disband and was saved only at the last moment by the Duke of Sussex, who was himself interested in Kabbalah.

It can safely be said that the Golden Dawn, and to some extent the SRIA, were unique in their concentration on the Kabbalah and the Sephirotic Tree of Life as the template for initiation and study. The Golden Dawn represented a sea change from the usual focus of Masonic societies and considered itself a working magical order with an emphasis on what we would call "practical Kabbalah." The addition of material culled from seventeenth-century manuscripts known as "Enochian" only adds to this atmosphere of Jewish mystical practice.

To take the issue one step further, the previous holders of the title "Golden Dawn" were both Jewish Masonic lodges, created by Kabbalists and Frankists, one in Germany and one in London. The "History Lecture" of the Golden Dawn insists that it derives its lineage from one or both of these. It would not be too extreme to suggest, therefore, that the Hermetic Order of the Golden Dawn — an enormously influential British occult society that numbered many leading intellectual and cultural lights among its members, including the Nobel Prize winner William Butler Yeats — was a crypto-Frankist operation, the last manifestation of the dreams of Jacob Frank and Moses Dobruschka, an encoded form of the *ma'aseh merkavah,* reworked for non-Jewish mystics, Gentile Kabbalists, Christian descenders to the Chariot.

Ironically, as the opening pages of Scholem's *Major Trends in Jewish Mysticism* reveal, Scholem's project was the denial of the claims by Eliphas Levi and Aleister Crowley to be "legitimate" Kabbalists.[19] This aspect of Scholem's work has been largely ignored, even by the modern New Age movement that has grown up around Crowley, Levi, Regardie, et al., but it is a fascinating commentary on the popularity of the works by these "supreme charlatans." Scholem single-handedly rescued the study of Kabbalah from the margins of academic scholarship, placing it front-and-center in the field of religious studies, and he did so motivated by an intense contempt for the writings of Crowley and Levi. This is a fascinating gloss on the history of modern Kabbalism and religious studies, which has yet to find its chronicler.

Conclusions

What men like Samuel Falk and Moses Dobruschka contributed to the western secret society was a sense of legitimacy where Kabbalah was concerned since these were Jewish men — Falk was considered a rabbi whereas Dobruschka had "converted" to Catholicism but still retained the patina of one who had been a follower of Jacob Frank — who it was believed could add to the existing framework of Christian Kabbalah something more, something *genuine*. According to Scholem,[20] they were also practitioners of alchemy, and this combination of Kabbalah and alchemy raised their profile among the esoterically minded Masons, Swedenborgians, and others in western Europe at the end of the eighteenth century. Indeed, it has been suggested that Falk trained Swedenborg in *merkavah* ascent techniques, which then resulted in the latter's complex theories of angelic forces.[21]

Sabbatai Sevi was "recognized" as the Messiah by a learned Kabbalist, Nathan of Gaza, who beheld his name engraved on a *merkavah* during a mystical vision. According to Scholem, in his exhaustive biography of the heretic and apostate, Sabbatai Sevi was said by his followers to have risen "seven rungs on the mystical ladder, corresponding to the seven *sefiroth* from *Malkhuth* to *Gedullah* [*Chesed*]."[22] Thereafter, he was said to rise to the level of *Binah*.[23] Thus, we have a precedent for the initiatory structure of the Golden Dawn and its precursor, the SRIA; the idea that one could "rise up the Tree," *sephira* by *sephira*, as an indicator of spiritual attainment was thus a familiar concept among some Jewish mystics of the late seventeenth century. The only amendment or addition to this idea was that of human intervention: could someone who had already ascended some of these rungs reach down, as it were, and bring someone else up to the same level? That was, of course, the raison d'être of groups like the Golden Dawn, the SRIA, and later, Aleister Crowley's A∴A∴, or *Argentum Astrum* ("Silver Star").

In addition, we learn that Sabbatai Sevi was also engaged in both practical Kabbalah as well as "the Mysteries of the Chariot."[24] The movement of this Kabbalistic Messiah would eventually influence seventeenth-century Jewry throughout Europe and the Middle East and as far west as England. Later developments such as Dobruschka's Asiatic Brethren would enshrine some of Sabbatai Sevi's teachings in a dramatically new form: a nondenominational, syncretistic secret society that accorded to itself the right and the power to offer to its initiates what the "descenders to the Chariot" could achieve only on their own through prayer, meditation, learning, and a serious personal commitment to God. The learning was still an integral part of organizations like the Golden Dawn, but it was far less demanding than, say, a thorough knowledge of the Torah and its commentaries. Instead, the learning spanned disciplines from Kabbalah to alchemy, from magic to Egyptology, from necromancy to the Enochian system of John Dee. It was eclectic, to be sure, but at the same time a comprehensive course in symbol systems.

Although *merkavah* mysticism was practiced only within a relatively isolated group of Jewish mystics in the nineteenth and twentieth centuries — isolated, that is, from non-Jewish academic circles and the general, predominantly Christian, public — its methodology had been incorporated into the initiatory system of an English secret society of the Victorian age whose members were men and women of mostly Christian background who had little or no knowledge of Hebrew or of the Jewish religion beyond what they could read in their King James Bibles. Their knowledge of Kabbalah was restricted to muddled translations of translations of portions of the Zohar and the *Sepher Yetzirah*. Yet there can be no doubt that *merkavah* terminology made its way into their rituals, and that their initiatory system mimicked that of the ascent to the Chariot.

While the prevailing view for years had been that the Cypher Manuscript, on which the Golden Dawn had based its rituals, was a hoax, recent scholarship (as we have seen in the previous chapter) supports its insistence that it was the British branch of a German Masonic society based in Frankfurt; moreover, it was a Jewish society with a name identical to theirs: the Golden Dawn. Since the Golden Dawn was a Jewish society, and since the only Jewish Masonic society in Germany of which there is any record at all was the one created by Moses Dobruschka, we have demonstrated that its structure, initiations, and rituals were informed by Jewish and particularly Frankist teachings. Thus, the practice of *merkavah* mysticism in the Golden Dawn *rituale* owes its survival to a renegade Frankist, an apostate, and political adventurer.

To be sure, the founders of the Golden Dawn added some of their own ideas and data to the basic, skeletal structure they inherited from the Frankists. The importation of the so-called "Enochian" material enabled them to flesh out the *merkavah* system — a basic system with seven palaces and the angels, names, and seals appropriate to each level — with a more ambitious set of correspondences that brought in Roman, Greek, Egyptian, and other ideas and images in a veritable memory theater of religion. If Freud was right, and dreams are "the royal road to the unconscious," then the rituals of the Golden Dawn were intended to enable its practitioners to dream while still awake.

Excursus 2

The Chemical Wedding:
The Alchemical Process
as Celestial Ascent

One of the most famous and simultaneously the most obscure of seventeenth-century alchemical texts is *The Chymical Wedding of Christian Rosenkreutz*. Considered to be the third part of the Rosicrucian canon that began with the publication of the *Fama Fraternitatis* in 1614 and the *Confessio* in 1615, the *Chymical Wedding*, published in 1616, is a fantastic allegory that has defied most attempts at interpretation. Most writers approaching such a task have been either members of theosophical-type societies who see the symbols of the tale through the lens of their own agenda, or members of the psychiatric profession who interpret the story as a matrix of Jungian archetypes or Freudian complexes. There have been virtually no "initiated" interpretations published that are in the slightest bit convincing with the notable exception of that of Adam McLean, who very wisely restricted his analysis to pointing out the more obvious symbol-sets in the story and calling our attention to certain repeating themes. His commentary on the modern translation by Joscelyn Godwin is a valuable contribution to the literature.[1]

We would like to expand on the work done by McLean and, based on the themes already explored in these pages, take another look at this four-hundred-year-old document with a view toward incorporating it into the literature of celestial ascent. Before we can do this, we should lay some groundwork in the field with which the *Chymical Wedding* is most associated: western European alchemy.

The derivation of the word "alchemy" is itself subject to controversy. One of the most detailed examinations of the origins of the word appears in *The Origins of Alchemy in Graeco-Roman Egypt* by Jack Lindsay (a Classics scholar who wrote a series of books on Roman Egypt). He explores the common interpretations of the word as referring either to the process of making chemical alloys or as a reference to the land of Egypt. The prefix *al* indicates a possible Arabic derivation of the term, but *chemia* is more properly Greek. If, however, we interpret *chemia* as *chem*, then we have our Egyptian connection, for *chem* is an Egyptian root meaning "black" and suddenly we have *al-chemia* as "the black art." The origins of the word "alchemy" are lost in obscurity, but the use of the word has demonstrated its flexibility through the ages, including everything from the transmutation of metals, the formulation of herbal elixirs, medicines, and poisons, to an allegory, or a mechanism, for the transformation of the human spirit. The general conceit has been to declare alchemy the superstitious precursor of chemistry, just as astrology would be to astronomy. Both alchemy and astrology share a common approach to reality, however, and that is that the measurement and calculation of the world's phenomena is *meaningful.* With the scientific revolution, particularly as characterized by the work of Thomas Kuhn[2] and others, the relevance of observable phenomena to the spiritual life of the average human being was denied. Science became the province of materialists, and religion was relegated to the backwaters of superstition and ignorance at worst, or ethics and morals at best. We may think of religion as a pre-psychology or a pre-sociology in much the same way as we are taught to think of astrology and alchemy as evidence of the quaint ignorance of our ancestors. To do otherwise, to acknowledge the importance of religion to a healthy human environment, would also entail the excavation of alchemy and astrology from the dungheap of history. Religion is all about meaning; alchemy and astrology are all about imbuing phenomena with meaning. Science may be about data; religion — but most certainly alchemy, astrology, and the other "occult" arts — is about the interpretation of that data. This interpretation, this search for meaning, is an essential part of what it means to be human. Without it, we stumble blindly through life and toward death — in many cases enduring unbelievable hardships, pain, suffering, torture, rape, addiction, and abuse — without context, without hope. Atheism, in this context, then becomes a luxury of the ruling class.

The alchemists saw hope in the observation of the changes that take place in nature. Metals, they believed, underwent a gradual transformation in the earth from the baser elements such as lead to the more refined metals such as gold. They saw that these elements had to endure the same sort of suffering as humans experienced, even including torture, mutilation, and murder, before they could attain the perfect state. The implication was that human suffering was not in vain, that a kind of spiritual gold was its inevitable outcome. On the basis of that premise, the alchemists decided it should be possible to accelerate that process of transformation. If they could do that, if they could change lead into gold, they could also achieve that other goal that would render all humanity's deepest anxieties irrelevant; they could achieve the *elixir vitae*, the elixir of life, and in the process defeat sickness and even death itself.

As we have noted, this was an obsession of the Chinese alchemists as much as those of Europe. The pursuit of remedies both herbal and chemical was undertaken in tandem with spiritual exercises and meditations directed toward the North Star and the immortal lights of the Northern Dipper. By extrapolating from human gestation, birth, life, and death — with all the physical changes that take place within the human organism at the same time as emotional, psychological, and spiritual changes take place — the alchemists of both cultures understood that the entire created universe also underwent change and transformation. In some cases, the transformation was spectacular: the metamorphosis of a caterpillar to a moth or butterfly, for instance, could be examined with hope for a similar human transformation from the ugly mammalian animal struggling for survival on the surface of the earth to something winged, ethereal, colorful, and beautiful.

In order to mimic nature, then, nature had to be observed very closely. Metals were subject to all sorts of tortuous experiments in furnace and athanor; retorts, alembics, and crucibles cluttered the alchemist's laboratory, but they were symbolic of other, more biological, paraphernalia. The Chinese alchemists were blatant in their iconography, showing cauldrons illustrated on anatomical drawings of the human body. Human sexuality was considered a grosser form of something altogether more remarkable and powerful: If two humans could actually create another human being through an act as relatively thoughtless as sexual intercourse, then what other creative potential did human beings have? Did they not possess the Philosopher's Stone, the magical powder of immortality and perfection, within their own bodies?

Was every human body a laboratory for creating immortality?

The implications of this type of research were enormous, and dangerous. Alchemical literature is the most obscure in any language; its art has been the inspiration for a generation of French Surrealists. It is obviously a literature heavily encoded; to be clear about the nature of the experiments was to call down the wrath of the church and the state, for it would have included frank discussions of bodily functions as well as chemical processes, but it could also be understood as a license to manufacture gold, i.e., to compete with the state in generating wealth. As it is, the alchemical texts are full of references to menstruation, semen, and gestation — and to torture, dismemberment, and murder. Alchemy is the most profound, the most beautiful and compelling of all the mystical and occult "arts." It is also, at the same time, the most dangerous if only because we have long ago lost the code for understanding it in all its detail. For that reason, experimentation easily could prove fatal.[3]

Yet it also shares a considerable amount of theory and practice with the technology of celestial ascent. In fact, many of its texts speak quite openly about celestial matters and such images as Jacob's Ladder and the seven planets, various gods and goddesses, angelic forces, etc. Could alchemy give us another key toward understanding celestial ascent?

Lindsay's work, mentioned above, is notable for the link he has made between alchemy and the rites of the Mithra cult. By placing alchemical history squarely within the Greco-Roman world, he has identified the strongest influence of all: the idea of a celestial ascent of the soul upward through seven levels of the heavens. In this case, the concept of celestial ascent being associated with the perfection of metals finds its expression in the cult of Mithra as described by the early church fathers beginning with Origen.

According to Origen in *Contra Celsus*,[4] the seven stages of the Mithraic initiation have planetary — and from there, chemical — analogues and are said to be gates located along a ladder of seven rungs leading to heaven. The first stage, or gate, corresponds to lead and Saturn; the second to tin and Venus; the third to copper and Jupiter; the fourth to iron and Mercury; the fifth to an alloy and Mars; the sixth to silver and the Moon; and finally the seventh to gold and the Sun. That these are not the traditional associations will be obvious to anyone who has read the medieval grimoires, for normally copper refers to Venus, iron to Mars, and tin to Jupiter. Mercury may be an alloy, or may refer to the element mercury itself. The others are consistent with what we know of the "Platonic" elements and their correspondences, but their order as given by Celsus via Origen is also full of inconsistencies if we understand the series of initiations to correspond to the actual planetary orbits themselves for Saturn, the planet furthest from the earth, should be the last in the series. If Origen is correct, however, then we may actually have a genuine insight into the "alchemy" of the Mithra cult, for of course the process of transformation is mirrored in the art of transmutation from the baser materials represented by lead and Saturn to the final goal, the perfect metal represented by the sun. In that case, the association with the planets is a blind (as is most everything else in the alchemical literature). The sun as characterized by the Mithraists is not the visible sun we see every day, but Sol Invictus, the Unconquerable Sun, what Ulansey calls the "hypercosmic" sun. In astronomical terms, as we have seen, this would be the North Star. Thus, the goal of the alchemists more properly corresponds to this star, the "eighth gate" of the Mithraists, with the implication that the seven "planets" are really analogues for the stars of the Northern Dipper.

Since the alchemists are forever warning us in the texts not to take their nomenclature literally, it would be wise perhaps to take this advice to heart. There are, after all, enough clues in their writings and their illustrations to lead us in the right direction. For this, we can start with a discussion of the *Chemical Wedding*.

Hieros gamos, Hieros logos, Hieros ludus

The Chemical Wedding is a strange story — a fable, a fairy tale for adults — that takes place over seven days and involves an ascent up a tower of seven levels. And at the heart of the story is not a wedding, but a massacre.

On the first day, we meet our hero, Christian Rosenkreutz, at home, alone, at meditation on an "evening before Easter." His meditation is interesting, for he says he is preparing "inwardly" an unleavened loaf of bread to "accompany my blessed Paschal Lamb." Thus, he is interiorizing the Jewish and Christian themes of the unleavened bread of Passover and the Paschal Lamb, the sacrificial offering of the Jews and the iconic sacrifice of Jesus. As we know, the crucifixion of Jesus took place during Passover, and the Orthodox churches still observe this fact in calculating the day of Easter.

During this meditation, a terrible wind assaults his cottage, but he does not look up since he is accustomed to this type of phenomenon during his meditations. However, he feels a tug at his clothes and turns around to see a beautiful angel with a golden trumpet in one hand and a sheaf of letters in the other. Her wings are "studded all over with eyes" and thereby references the cherubim seen by Ezekiel in his vision near the river Chebar. Both the wind and the appearance of the angel with the eye-studded wings call to mind this biblical vision and can only be intended to remind the reader of that fact. The golden trumpet is inscribed with a name, which he does not immediately reveal, and the letters are in "all the languages." The angel then leaves one of the letters, and departs with a great blast on the trumpet.

The letter is an invitation to the wedding of a king. He is told that if he is chosen by God and is "clean," he can "ascend the mount whereon three temples stand." Christian is unnerved by this, because it calls to mind a vision he had seven years earlier and the date of which he had calculated using his "planetary tables." Of course, we must pause here for a moment and ask ourselves what this means.

The seven-year period of course is suggestive, especially after everything we have already seen. It is reminiscent of the calculation of the Jubilee year in the ancient Jewish tradition, which is seven times seven years. Christian is also using planetary tables to calculate the date of the wedding, and this is an important clue. This indicates that the alignment of the stars and planets is critical and that Christian, for all his piety and God-fearing nature, is also a kind of astrologer. So immediately in this tale we have themes that bring to mind that theory of celestial ascent we have been studying all along. References to the vision of Ezekiel begin the tale, along with the number seven and astronomical calculations. There is also a mountain to be ascended, and a requirement of spiritual purity. There is also a reference to three temples, which to a Jewish mystic might refer to Solomon's Temple, Herod's Temple, and the Heavenly Temple, or the as-yet unbuilt Third Temple.[5]

He then recounts the dream he had seven years previously. It involved a tower, at the base of which were masses of humanity in chains. A rope was lowered from the top of the tower, and those who could get hold of it would be saved. The rope was lowered seven times. Christian finds himself raised up, and shortly thereafter the dream ends. Then Christian sets out from his "hermitage" for the wedding. He is dressed in a white tunic with a red sash crossed over his shoulders. (This is reminiscent of the manner of wearing a stole by traditional Roman Catholic and Orthodox Christian clergy.)

On the second day, he is on a path through a forest and sees before him three trees. On the trunk of one of them there is a sign, telling him he has four paths to choose from. They all lead to the wedding castle, but some are more dangerous than others. One is "short but perilous"; another is longer and circuitous, but as long as one has a "magnet" one would arrive safely; yet another is the Royal Way, but few have found it; and lastly there is the fourth path, which only the pure and most "incorruptible" may choose, as it is the most dangerous.

Christian does not consciously choose a path, but in chasing a dove and a raven he finds himself on what appears to be the second of the four paths mentioned. He has a compass, however, and manages to reach the castle before nightfall. Now, he must pass through a series of gates, and at each gate he speaks with the porter, or gatekeeper, and must give the porter something he owns. The porter, in turn, gives him a token (usually a gold coin on which some cryptic Latin letters are written). This is, of course, consistent with the *merkavah* system described earlier: passing through a series of gates and exchanging information — a password, a seal or sign — with the gatekeepers. By the time the story has ended, Christian will have given up seven personal items, in very similar fashion to the Sumerian "Descent of Inanna" scripture. The fact of the compass is suggestive as well, for it means he is finding his way using the magnetic north-south axis.

There is a long discussion concerning a feast to which many have been invited. As one of the last to arrive, Christian takes his place at the lowest table and is revolted at the crudeness, noise, arrogance, and vanity of his fellow attendees. Finally, the guests are told that there will be a test the following morning and that those who are pious and have led lives of sanctity and grace will win the contest, whereas those whose conscience bothers them will be in danger of losing. The contest consists of scales on which each guest will be weighed. The weights are seven in number, three large and four smaller.[6] As they are piled on, each guest will strive to stay on the scales as long as possible.

Christian knows his conscience is not pure, so he is quite afraid of what the morning will bring. Instead of repairing to a separate bedchamber to rest peacefully, he remains behind in the dining hall with a few of the others who are similarly worried. These guests are bound and left in darkness, their torment palpable.

On the third day, the guests are all assembled and the contest begins. Emperors, kings, noblemen all fail the test. One by one they are taken away, with very few exceptions. One of these exceptions is Christian, who remains on the scales after the total of seven weights have been laid on and is thus rewarded and invited to the feast.

On the fourth day, the King, the Queen, and five others are murdered.

The beheading of the wedding guests by an executioner with an axe, and his subsequent beheading, is a potent alchemical symbol. We find beheaded figures in many of the alchemical illustrations that accompany the most famous of the texts, and the murder of the King and Queen is a constant theme in the literature. It may have analogues with the shamanic experience of dismemberment and death referenced by Eliade, for instance; but in any event, the bloody sacrifices are a central element of the alchemical process as encoded in the documents. Christian witnesses these murders, but is reassured by a Virgin that the murdered monarchs will be reborn through the efforts of the alchemists themselves.

The tale is full of strange occurrences, odd speeches, and iconic figures (a Virgin, a Bridegroom, a Bride, a King, a Queen, etc.) whose attributes are sketched in briefly even though they occupy important positions during the events that transpire. A full discussion of this story is beyond the scope of this study, as the tale is replete with hundreds of mysterious events and personages, odd calculations, and a narrative that is by turns surreal and matter-of-fact... or surreal in its matter-of-fact account of scenes of horrendous cruelty juxtaposed with those of an ornate beauty. If one were to film the *Chymical Wedding,* one would require the services of a Jodorowsky or a Lynch, perhaps a Fellini and a Soderbergh. Or Quentin Tarantino working with a script written by Jung. Instead, we will abandon a full examination of the story and instead focus on the central theme of the Tower with its seven levels and the means employed for ascending it.

The obsessive references to the number seven in the *Wedding* is reminiscent of the constant, hypnotic refrains of the *Song of the Sabbath Sacrifice* found at Qumran, or of the *merkavah* texts in general. On the fifth day, after the wedding massacre, Christian and his associates are guided by the Virgin up the Tower, called Olympus Tower after the famous abode of the Greek gods. At the bottom of the Tower the group is given one of three methods of ascent: a ladder, a rope, or wings. It is Christian's lot to carry a ladder around with him for the rest of the day. One could speculate on the possible interpretations of these three methods of ascent by assuming that a ladder signifies that one must ascend by one's own deliberate effort, step by step; that a rope signifies that it is lowered from above by a benevolent or at least a helpful agent; and wings, the easiest and swiftest means of all signifying natural flight as a result of one's spiritual preparedness.

There are many more cryptic events that take place on this day, but we are drawn to the sixth level of the Tower for an important clue. It is here that Christian is made to believe that he has not fulfilled the necessary requirements for further ascent; that in his laziness he has forfeited the right to reach the seventh level. It is a trick, an illusion perpetrated by the Virgin and her colleagues, and happily Christian is brought to the seventh level of the Tower, where he is made a Knight of the Golden Stone.

This idea that the sixth level is the dangerous one, the level where all may be lost, is consistent with the *merkavah* texts that usually identify the sixth level as the place of danger. That there is a trick at this level is also interesting, for we are told in the famous tale of the *Four Who Entered the Pardes* that there is an illusion in the area right before the Throne: that one must not say "water, water" when confronting the sea of marble. Whoever mistakes the marble for water is cast out of the Palace and doomed.

The punishment depicted in the *Wedding* is not quite so dire. Those who think they have passed the tests have actually not: they will find themselves working the alchemical bellows and furnaces, believing that they have attained the ultimate knowledge and illumination, while Christian, who believed he had failed, had actually succeeded to full understanding and revelation. The King and Queen will be reanimated as their newly purified souls descend from above; the alchemists laboring over their retorts will believe that they had caused the rebirth themselves, through their efforts, but they will be in error. No matter: the seventh level of the Tower is the level of rebirth, regeneration, and immortality. The Chymical Wedding thus becomes a *merkavah* text, at least in general details and much expanded. And what happens to Christian? He winds up as the gatekeeper himself before the text mysteriously comes to an abrupt end with two pages missing.

Christian Rosenkreutz is a central figure in the history of modern Hermetica. It is the legend of the discovery of his tomb that becomes the rite around which the Hermetic Order of the Golden Dawn is based. As such, then, it is the tomb of the gatekeeper: the guardian of the entrance to the celestial ascent and to spiritual regeneration. As one attains this exalted degree of enlightenment, one is charged with showing the way to others who may follow. It is, in a sense, part of the process. The celestial ascent is not complete until one has been found to take one's place among the living: i.e., the uninitiated, the seekers. This replacing of oneself may represent a kind of social validation. Until one has initiated another, one cannot be certain that one's own initiation is complete.

The seven levels of the Wedding refer to seven operations in the art of alchemy. These operations refer to stages in the extraction of the "soul" of the metal and its purification. A brief acquaintance with the subject matter will reveal that there are two important components to the alchemical goal: the first may be described as the Philosopher's Stone, made famous in our time by the Harry Potter books. The Philosopher's Stone, or the Golden Stone, of which Christian Rosenkreutz has become a Knight, is the key chemical component for transformation and transmutation. The Stone is that which, when added to a base metal, transforms that metal into gold. By creating gold, by creating wealth, the alchemist becomes independent of the state. He or she is no longer in servitude to a landowner or a shopkeeper; the need for mindless toil has been eliminated.

The second component is the Elixir Vitae, the elixir of life itself. It is a universal medicine, a panacea. It grants a kind of immortality and immunity from disease. Thus, the alchemist has now been liberated from concerns about health as well as wealth. It is not for nothing that the Philosopher's Stone is referred to as the "Stone of the Wise." All of the attentions of the alchemist may now be focused on other concerns.

What are they?

This we are rarely told. In the Rosicrucian manifestos of the seventeenth century we are advised that the Rosicrucians are to become involved with society in general for one purpose only: to heal the sick. They may use their expertise only to alleviate pain and suffering. They are not to abuse their knowledge and wisdom in any other way, nor are they to identify themselves as Rosicrucians. Otherwise, we have no idea what purpose the life of a Rosicrucian — i.e., of one who has discovered the Stone of the Wise — serves. And that may be the point.

If suddenly any one of us were to find ourselves with no financial worries whatsoever and in perfect health, what would we do? We can observe from the lives of celebrities that untold wealth and coddling leads in many cases to scenes of excess, of mental and emotional breakdown, of serial monogamy (at best), of lavish displays of money and power: all of the factors that have moved others to revolution, the espousal of communism or radical political ideologies, or the cloister.

However, there was one case in particular that might be instructional in terms of what a genuine alchemist or Rosicrucian could do, and that is the legend of Nicholas Flamel (c. 1330–1417).

Also made famous in our time by a reference in one of the Harry Potter books and the movie, *Harry Potter and the Philosopher's Stone,* Flamel seems to have been a genuine alchemist of a sort, although that has been debated in recent years. There is a street in Paris named after him, however, and he has been praised as a true benefactor of society, a philanthropist of incredibly humble origins who claimed to have discovered the secret of the Philosopher's Stone and used the wealth he generated to finance a broad program of public works in Paris.

How Flamel came into such a fortune is the subject of controversy. What is known about him is that he was a scrivener and a bookseller and restorer in fourteenth-century Paris. His wife, Pernelle, was a widow of some means, which enabled Flamel to open his own bookstore near the church of St. Jacques de Boucherie. According to legend, Flamel had come into possession of a mysterious book of twenty-one leaves. The book was written in strange characters and with odd illustrations (which would have been typical of a book on alchemy). After searching for the meaning of the encoded text for more than twenty years, Flamel eventually was able to use it to make the Philosopher's Stone. It is said — again, according to legend, for there is very little reliable documentation of this story — that he managed to obtain the key for translating the book from a Jewish Kabbalist (which, of course, brings us back full circle to the environment in which we first discovered the *merkavah* texts).

What is beyond doubt is that this humble bookseller was able to commission construction and repair projects in the city, and there is at least one building still standing in Paris that was built by Flamel some six hundred years ago. Critics have suggested that he earned his income from traditional means, or that he was simply a shrewd investor, etc., but that is to ignore the fact that there are no other examples of persons in Flamel's circumstances who were able to command the attention and the praise of their neighbors for the abundant largesse that Flamel was able to rain upon them. Further, he had caused to have engraved on his tombstone many figures of an obviously alchemical nature. If his discovery of the Philosopher's Stone was a hoax, it certainly was an elaborate one.

The Seven Stages

> He who has ears to hear shall hear what the spirit of wisdom tells the son about the doctrine of the seven stars through which the holy work is fulfilled.... After you have distributed those seven (metals) through the seven stars, and attributed them to the seven stars, and cleansed them nine times till they look like pearls, that is the state of whiteness.
> — *Aurora Consurgens,* Chapter VI, the First Parable[7]

The alchemical process generally consists of seven distinct phases, each of which refers to the physical state of the alchemical material and is suggestive of the means to be employed in making it. There are hundreds if not thousands of alchemical texts that describe this process, and few are in total agreement as far as can be deduced. It is important to realize that these texts are all, virtually without exception, encoded. Heavy allegorical language is employed as a means of explaining what may very well be inexplicable. Pious allusions abound, intermixed freely with sexual, chemical, and biological references, and all encased in a mythological context replete with eagles, dragons, Greek and Roman gods, murder, bloodshed, and heavenly hosts. The Swiss psychiatrist and father of depth psychology, Carl Gustav Jung, expended prodigious amounts of time and effort in an attempt to understand these texts and to expose them as representative of psychological states and the process of what he called individuation: an inner healing and centering of the mind that could take place only when the various warring elements that make up the human psyche are brought into harmonious relation.[8] Jung understood that dreams play a large role in offering evidence of the kind of psychic turmoil and unconscious processes that take place in the human mind; the alchemical texts are like dream journals, with many odd and seemingly unrelated events taking place in wild abandon. While Jung's researches and his analyses are fascinating, it is doubtful that he was able to truly understand what the alchemists were driving at. To insist that they were only speaking of a spiritual process may reveal more of the analyst's frame of mind than the alchemist's.

The seven steps alluded to in many of the alchemical texts are sometimes identified as: Calcination, Dissolution, Separation, Conjunction, Fermentation, Distillation, and Coagulation (in no particular order; the order of these seven steps is a matter of some controversy, for it is believed that to reveal the correct order is to give away too much information about the preparation of the Philosopher's Stone). In addition, there are generally believed to be three stages in the process, referred to as the Nigredo, the Albedo, and the Rubedo (the Blackness, the Whiteness, and the Redness). The Black Stage is the stage of putrefaction, of the breaking down of something into its component parts; the White stage begins at the deepest level of the Nigredo when putrefaction is complete and the grosser elements have been purified, reduced to a single adamantine substance. The Rubedo, or the Red stage, is the final act and the most obscure and difficult to explain. It represents the creation of new life from the germ of the old; it is often shown as a *hieros gamos* or divine wedding between a Red King and a White Queen. The seven steps are often assigned to the three stages in different combinations, the steps themselves resulting in one or other of the process stages. For instance, Dissolution and Fermentation may fall under the heading of the Nigredo, and Conjunction under the heading of the Rubedo, etc.

A set of frescoes designed by Nicholas Flamel is revealing of these seven steps. Reproduced in many books on alchemy, it shows the seven steps arrayed across the top of the diagram and represented by the usual cryptic illustrations. You will see, for instance, a mountain with seven caves surrounded by seven serpents; in another panel, a king has ordered the massacre of seven children. These are called, by Flamel, the figures of "Abraham the Jew," and represent the Massacre of the Innocents by King Herod. (Abraham the Jew is an enigmatic figure believed to have been the author of a grimoire, or magician's workbook, known as *The Book of the Sacred Magic of Abramelin the Mage*.) Again, as in the Chymical Wedding, we have scenes of carnage mixed with mythological motifs and the recurrence of the number seven.

It may seem obvious that the seven alchemical stages represent an approach to spirituality that is quite different from that found in the *merkavah* texts. The latter are directed solely toward a direct experience of the Divine, and the seven stages in the process are merely placeholders, with very little individual significance beyond the names of the angels and the chariots or palaces assigned to each level. The entire emphasis is on the final stage or level: finding oneself before the Throne.

However, there has always been a magical element to the texts and to the process of celestial ascent. The names of the angels were often used to make talismans or amulets to protect against disease or to vanquish one's enemies. A practical side to the *merkavah* practice was recognized, if not always embraced, and this side emphasized health, wealth, and protection. The successful ascenders to the Chariot were believed to be possessed of occult powers: their proximity to the Throne implied an ability to share in some of the divine attributes in order to heal illness, for example. The goal of the alchemists was the purification of metals and the creation of the elixir of life. While the two systems may at first seem unrelated, at the heart of each was a mission that was quite similar if not identical: improving life on earth and attaining immortality; in short, transcending human weakness and infirmity.

Eventually, such an esteemed Kabbalistic scholar as Gershom Scholem would recognize that there was a kind of parallel between alchemical practice and Kabbalistic practice; that, in fact, several important, if controversial, Kabbalists were also alchemists.[9] The origin of this idea may be found in an odd document that was included in a collection of the first translations of Kabbalistic texts into a modern European language, the *Aesch Mezareph*, or Purifying Fire.

More than any other single text, the *Aesch Mezareph* forges a strong link between the language of the Kabbalah and the language of alchemy. Assigning the various metals to the ten *sephiroth*, in particular the seven metals of the alchemists to the seven "inferior" *sephiroth,* and stressing not only chemical processes but also mathematical structures found in the *kameas* or magic number squares that are so familiar to students of ceremonial magic and the rituals of the Golden Dawn, the *Aesch Mezareph* is a rather neglected work due to the extreme difficulty of interpreting its coded references, which are replete with biblical proof texts and Kabbalistic citations.

In the very first chapter, however, we read the cryptic admonition:

> Learn, therefore, to purify Naaman, coming from the north, out of Syria, and acknowledge the power of Jordan: which is, as it were, Jar-Din, that is the river of judgment flowing out of the north.
>
> And remember that which is said in Baba Bathra, fol. 25, col. 2. He that will become wise, let him live in the South: and he that will grow rich, let him turn himself toward the North.

Naaman was a Syrian king, and his story is mentioned in the Book of Kings, chapter 5. He was afflicted with leprosy and was cured when he bathed seven times in the River Jordan. (The Baba Bathra that is mentioned above is a section of the Babylonian Talmud.) Thus, we have a river flowing from the north, and a king who bathed seven times in the river to be healed of leprosy, i.e., to be purified. The north is also identified as the place from which riches flow and, later in the text, is the place associated with gold. The Philosopher's Stone, therefore, is identified with this cardinal direction. In fact, only north and south are indicated here, thus emphasizing the poles rather than the east-west axis, which is concerned with the rising and setting of the planets along the ecliptic. The north, you will remember, is the locus of Ezekiel's vision as well as the site of the Pole Star, and indeed in chapter 6 there are direct references to Ezekiel's vision.

In chapter 7, the section dealing with Mercury, seemingly both the planet and the element, we find some very cryptic references to Kokab. Kokab is one of the ancient Hebrew words for the planet Mercury, so it would come as no surprise to find it mentioned here except that it is referenced a second time with the warning:

> This is that which, not without a Mystery, is called Kokab, a Star: because according to the natural Kabbalah, Numbers c. 24 v. 17[10] out of (the Metal) Jacob comes a Star; or in plain language the shapes of Rods, and Branches, arise; and from this Star flows this influence, of which we speak.

What is important about this verse is that it tends to separate Kokab from the usual planetary correspondence, which may offer us a clue, for Kokab was also the name of Beta Ursae Minoris, a star in the Little Dipper, which was formerly the Pole Star itself circa 1000 BCE. In fact, for a time

Kokab shared this dignity with another star in the Little Dipper — Pherkad (Gamma Ursae Minoris) — when they were called the Guardians of the Pole. Kokab could be considered the closest candidate for a Pole Star for more than a thousand years, including the time of the Babylonian Captivity, the period when the Hebrew Bible was being written, up to the life of Jesus and to the time the first *merkavah* texts were being composed (and thus to about 500 CE at the latest).

These examples are used to inform a treatise on the Kabbalah and alchemy, a treatise that, moreover, includes biological references as well. In the opening chapter we read that the two *sephiroth* of Netzach and Hod are described as "the two median places of the body, and the seminal receptacles, and refer to the hermaphroditic brass." The strong sexual component that we find in the Zohar is alluded to here, and it is difficult not to see alchemy, the Zohar, and Tantra as diverse manifestations of a similar if not identical impulse. There is a common desire in all of these sources to consider, or reconsider, what many might feel are the grossest aspects of human experience: sexuality, blood, semen, murder, dismemberment and decapitation, cannibalism, putrefaction of corpses, excrement, etc. Might this impulse find its modern equivalent in an undirected fascination with true crime, serial murder, and pornography?

Sexuality and the interpretation of it from a spiritual or at least a theological point of view was a distraction for the rabbis as well as for the church fathers who struggled with the Song of Solomon and its blatant sexual overtones. St. Bernard of Clairvaux, spiritual father of the infamous Order of the Knights Templar, wrote an entire sermon cycle based on it; and it is this same biblical text that gave rise to the controversial *Aurora Consurgens,* believed by some to have been written by St. Thomas Aquinas in the last months of his life.

The Jungian philosopher and analyst Marie-Louise von Franz has devoted a great deal of work to an interpretation of this text and its putative authorship by Aquinas, which she believed she may have proven. Jung himself was said to have discovered the text and found that it aroused his intense interest during the period when he was devoting a great deal of attention to alchemical literature as evidence of psychological processes. What concerns us here is the conflation of elements of the Song of Solomon with citations from the Book of Revelation (Apocalypse) and the Gospels, all within an alchemical context with its references to the Art and the four elements, etc. In fact, *Aurora Consurgens* reads like a Christian (or Christianized) version of the *Aesch Mezareph.*

As in virtually every text we have examined thus far, the number seven recurs several times in the *Aurora,* including the quotation that begins this section. It is associated with seven stars, and resonates with the multiplicity of sevens that we find in the Apocalypse. This association of the number seven with stars and with the alchemical process can almost be seen as an exegesis on the *merkavah* texts which are themselves, as we have attempted to suggest, an exegesis on the more ancient scriptures of the Egyptians and the Babylonians. All point to spiritual transformation, and all use the symbol of the seven stars as a marker in their texts for the process of transformation itself, a process that is inextricably linked to ideas concerning divinity and immortality.

Bernard of Clairvaux wrote his sermons on the Song of Solomon in the eleventh century CE; Aquinas wrote his alchemical treatise in the fourteenth century CE. By the time of the fifteenth century, and the rise of the Florentine Academy, we had a more insistent approach to this material that reached its apotheosis in the publication of the *Chymical Wedding of Christian Rosenkreutz* in the seventeenth century and the beginning of the modern era of occult investigation into these same themes, an investigation that will bear strange fruit indeed.

The Seven Stages of Paracelsus

> It is very necessary also to know the degrees to Transmutation, and how many they be. And they are no more than seven. For although many do reckon more, yet there are no more but seven which are principal and the rest may be reckoned betwixt the degrees, being comprehended under those seven; and they are these: Calcination, Sublimation, Solution, Putrefaction, Distillation, Coagulation, Tincture. If anyone will climb that Ladder, he shall come into a most wonderful place.   — Paracelsus, *Of the Nature of Things*, Book VII

The seven stages of the alchemical process are relevant to this discussion because they represent an intellectual refinement of the very basic seven steps of transformation and immortality we have found described in the Egyptian, Babylonian, and Chinese systems. In these systems the seven stars/stages are individually rather anonymous. There is an emphasis on the sixth step/palace/chariot in the *merkavah* texts; but the other chariots or palaces are little more than placeholders. In the Chinese system, we have individual names for each of the stars that seem to indicate discrete qualities or functions, but these are rarely found in any expanded form in the Daoist scriptures. The seven levels of the Mithraic initiation sequence are likewise mysterious to us. If we were to assign planetary values to them, as previous commentators have done, we would approximate a kind of qualitative nature to each of them, but I feel that such a mechanical and somewhat cavalier approach to what was a closely guarded secret initiation system would be ill-advised.

In western European alchemy, however, we have a fully articulated, if equally cryptic, exposition of the nature of each of the seven levels. The problem resides in (*a*) knowing the precise order of the levels or stages and (*b*) understanding what is meant at each stage of the process. The texts either disagree with each other or contain information that is inconsistent, even as to the number of levels and their relative importance. Thus, it is impossible to know with any certainty what each level truly represents. However, it is possible to characterize each of the levels on the basis of their names and a general level of agreement to what the names mean, if not the actual processes — chemical, psychological, or spiritual — that they represent. There are also three or sometimes four stages that are characterized by their color: black, red, white, and sometimes yellow. These are not operative stages in the physical process but represent developments that take place concerning the material being transformed: in other words, they describe the results of the actions taken during the seven stages.

Thus the level known as the Nigredo, or the blackness, is generally equated with the process of putrefaction and sometimes with calcination. What putrefies? It is the *prima materia*, the first matter of the alchemists which, it is claimed, is everywhere on the planet, on every street and in every forest, and even in the air itself. This matter must be identified (no easy task) and then "buried" in some sort of alchemical vessel for a certain period of time so that the essential nature of the matter may be released. Various other things happen to this material, including dismemberment (which is reminiscent of Eliade's shamans), before it is refined to the point that it becomes the Philosopher's Stone. There is the stage of *conjunctio*, which may be cognate with *coagulation*, and which seems to refer to a kind of divine marriage, or *hieros gamos*, after which the bride and groom — the King and Queen in most depictions — are murdered, and from that death the next incarnation of metal is obtained. This may refer to the phase known as the Rubedo, or the redness.

The seven stages seem to refer more specifically to what you might encounter in an old chemical text, which are referred to in the citation from Paracelsus (1493–1541) above: calcination, distillation, etc. The overall process seems to entail identifying the *prima materia*, extracting from it the quintessence or "fifth element," and then refining it to the point that it acquires the supernatural properties associated with it by the alchemists: the ability to transform base metals into gold and to provide the elixir of life. The fifth element is something beyond or within the four Platonic elements of fire, earth, air, and water: an element that represents the unity of the four and of which Jung made much in his various commentaries on alchemy and in his work on mandalas.

It is easy to see that the burial process represented by the Nigredo stage is analogous to the trance state invoked by the *merkavah* mystics and the Chinese alchemists. The *prima materia* is sought within the consciousness of the mystic; a state of absolute stillness is attained, permitting the essential nature of the mystic — something not ordinarily experienced during the course of everyday life — to blossom forth. It is this quantum that begins the celestial ascent and goes through the remaining levels. It is, in a sense, analogous to being buried alive, and in many of the alchemical drawings we find the figure of a bearded man asleep or dead, either buried beneath the earth, or in a cave, or in an alchemical retort or otherwise enclosed. In one such alchemical illustration from the seventeenth century, the bearded man is in a cave in what appears to be a trance, the cherubim of Ezekiel arrayed around him and the seven stars clearly seen in the sky above (see p. 41).

The danger here is in interpreting the alchemical texts solely in terms of psychological, or even spiritual states, popularly understood. The chemical practices, it seems to this observer, are essential parts of the alchemical process. They represent in the material world the transformation taking place in the interior, psychological, or spiritual world. They also provide validation in terms of the physical changes taking place before the eyes of the alchemist. It is a mutually reinforcing system of inner transformation and outer chemical process. In a sense, the physical practices of the alchemist are analogous to the rituals of the magicians: it is necessary to extend into the material world the ideas and psychological states experienced in the mind, as well as it is necessary to enact in the material world those states and experiences one wishes to have in the mind. It is a technology that seeks to erase the Cartesian fallacy by uniting mind and body in such a way that the boundaries between them disappear.

Of course, in an unguided and unprepared individual this would lead either to madness or to an implication of madness. The solitude necessary for these practices, whether alchemical or mystical or magical, serves to keep the practitioner safe from the ridicule or concern of society. It can also contribute to the social isolation of the practitioner, which itself can lead to unhealthy mental states. Thus, the Jewish injunction that anyone desiring to study Kabbalah must be over forty and married, as well as male and possessing a keen knowledge of the Torah. It is believed that the engagement of such a person with the mundane realities of marriage and livelihood would preserve him from psychological obsessions and total derangement, and that a knowledge of the Torah would give him an intellectual context within which to interpret his experiences (a very important tool). While Rimbaud exhorted us to achieve a total derangement of the senses, this was for the purpose of becoming an artist and a "seer." Unfortunately, modern western society does not provide the type of environmental support that Eliade's Siberian shamans, for instance, could enjoy when they returned from their vision quest in the forest. Likewise, Jewish mystics lived and worked in a very social situation that frowned on the type of self-imposed exile so necessary for the extremes of spiritual vision and transformation spoken of by Eliade and Rimbaud. The Jewish mystic was expected to remain a valuable member of society; his spiritual experiences had to be interpreted within the context of orthodox Judaism and used as inspirational material for the community. Such a mystic may have also developed healing abilities or other paranormal powers. Similarly, the alchemists would have been able to make gold and to heal the sick, abilities that would presumably be of service to society, while the alchemist himself or herself would continue to undergo spiritual training and transformation.

What Scholem did for the Kabbalah and for Jewish mysticism generally, Jung tried to do for alchemy. As learned as Jung was in the Greco-Roman, neo-Platonist milieu of western alchemy, however, it is doubtful that he can be considered to have contributed to the discussion of alchemy the same level of academic acceptability that Scholem offered for the Kabbalah. Jung's project was made more difficult by the fact that it was not as ethnically or culturally contextual as Kabbalah. In order to truly study alchemy one has to draw on a wide variety of sources in a large number of languages both ancient and modern; one also has to rely on an educated interpretation of the images. The Kabbalists seemed to have been at pains to explain their field of study and to constantly support it with proof texts and other references to known source material; the later Kabbalists, e.g., Isaac Luria and Abraham Abulafia, described cosmological and procedural systems and methods with even greater detail and precision. The alchemists strove in the opposite direction: to make their study as obscure and incomprehensible as possible, with codes and secret language and misdirection, mixing biblical references with those from Greek and Roman and sometimes Egyptian mythology, as well as chemistry, biology, and astronomy. It is only by reducing their philosophy to this handful of basic ideas and concepts that we can even begin to understand what they were writing about so feverishly and insistently.

Chapter 12

The Hermetic Brotherhood of Light

The progenitor of many occult orders, the Hermetic Brotherhood of Light is believed to have exerted considerable influence over the ideas of groups as disparate as the Hermetic Order of the Golden Dawn, the Ordo Templi Orientis, and even the Theosophical Society. Its traces can be found in the cult around Max Theon as well as in that of Sri Aurobindo. Its belief system is permeated by ideas concerning sacred astronomy, and its very logo reveals an understanding of Dipper mysticism and celestial ascent.

It would do well, therefore, to pay some attention to this organization and its founders and leaders in an effort to determine what they knew and how they may have transmitted this knowledge to the groups that came after them.

The H.B. of L.

The Hermetic Brotherhood of Light (H.B. of L.) has been the subject of several research projects in the last ten years[1] as it has become gradually evident that its ideas have been influential in the ideologies of modern esoteric movements. The history of this order and its associates is too byzantine and convoluted to bear describing here in any great detail. Instead, we will focus not on the individuals, several of whom seemed to have had criminal records, but on the documents they generated. In all fairness, the careers of such men as Thomas H. Burgoyne (a.k.a. "Zanoni") could be favorably compared to those of Jacob Frank or Moses Dobruschka (or Aleister Crowley). We are confronted with men who had multiple aliases, pretended to fantastic titles and degrees of spiritual illumination, were accused of all sorts of sexual license, frequently ran afoul of the law in various countries, and were often on the run from the authorities.

In "Zanoni," an Englishman born Thomas Henry Dalton (1855?–95?), who changed his name to Thomas H. Burgoyne, we have such a case. What we know of him, and of most of the leading lights of the H.B. of L., is scant and contradictory, often confused with other identities and other agendas. The H.B. of L. itself is as shrouded in mystery as most of the groups we have been discussing. It made its first public appearance in 1884, through

209

newspaper advertisements offering training in the occult sciences, although it has been suggested that they were in operation at least as early as 1870. The H.B. of L. claimed to represent a more secret organization with hidden masters, much the same way the Theosophical Society and the Golden Dawn spoke of "secret chiefs." In fact, it was a Hermetic Brotherhood of Luxor (either a forerunner of the Hermetic Brotherhood of Light, or identical with it), based in Egypt, that was connected to Madame Blavatsky years before the creation of the Theosophical Society. In her travels around the world before she became the celebrated occultist and author of *Isis Unveiled* and *The Secret Doctrine,* she became acquainted with an occult teacher and Coptic magician named Paulos Metamon of the Hermetic Brotherhood of Luxor. Metamon was the teacher of one Louis Maximilian Bimstein (a.k.a. Max Theon), who in turn had so much influence over the group around the famous Indian teacher Sri Aurobindo and "the Mother." The Mother, whose birth name was Mirra Alfassa, had been a disciple of Theon at the latter's villa in Algeria.

Theon (1850?–1927) was promoting something called the Mouvement Cosmique and was publishing the *Revue Cosmique,* which dealt with occult and spiritual matters. In the end, though, it was Theon who would act as a channel for the sexual teachings of the American occultist P. B. Randolph (1825–75). Randolph was another major influence, not only on the H.B. of L. but also on the occult methods of the Ordo Templi Orientis and on other western occult societies that claimed to have the key to "sexual mysteries."

While men like Jacob Frank proposed arcane and scandalous sexual practices, it was theoretically within the context of the Zohar and other Kabbalistic ideas that had Tantric elements. Randolph, on the other hand, was believed to have received his teachings from Asian or Middle Eastern masters, although he insisted that the ideas were original with him. This was also the story put out by the O.T.O. in Germany: that they were the repository of sexual secrets transmitted to them from Sufi or other Asian adepts, even though there is evidence to show that they were quite familiar with the H.B. of L. and even, to this day, claim to represent a survival of that order. While Blavatsky and her Theosophical Society were aggressively Asian in their outlook, they were notoriously prudish when it came to sexuality. Societies like the O.T.O. and the H.B. of L. provided an alternative to this Victorian perspective, with advice that ran the gamut from using sexual energy to charge talismans to channeling sexual energy toward spiritual goals. This was also the mainstay of biologically oriented Chinese alchemy as well as Tantric Hinduism. Sexual energy was believed to be something that could be "cultivated" and redirected. Specific techniques were recommended (especially for the male). These involved avoiding seminal emission under any circumstances, even during the act of intercourse. Seminal emission was considered tantamount to a waste of spiritual energy, energy that was better employed within the athanor and retorts of the human body. As in Indian Kundalini yoga, this energy was conserved and made to travel up the *sushumna nadi*, the analogue to the spinal column, through all seven chakras until it blossomed in the thousand-and-one-petaled chakra above the head. Thus, sexual energy was the vehicle and the occult channels within the body composed the map.

In the western esoteric tradition, much of the same imagery and many of the same concepts were adapted within a strongly Hermetic and Kabbalistic context. Thus, we have the template of the Sephirotic Tree of Life — representing a human figure, Adam Kadmon — and the energy visualized as traveling up the *sephiroth*, path by path and *sephira* by *sephira*, in an alchemical process of purification and transformation. All of this, meanwhile, was represented in rituals and knowledge lectures that would have seemed quite alien at first glance to an Indian adept or a Chinese alchemist, although, once stripped of its peculiarly western terminology, the technology would be recognized at once. The writings of Kenneth Grant, a claimant to the O.T.O. throne, are representative of this theme. For instance, he goes into great detail in describing the *kalas* — the essences of female exudation during the entire course of her menstrual cycle — from both an Indian perspective as well as a western, esoteric point of view.[2] As such, the writings of Grant represent a modern refinement of this nineteenth-century concept.

What is interesting about the H.B. of L. in terms of its rituals, however, is the solitary nature of the initiations. In this order the ritual furniture and lengthy speeches were minimized or omitted in favor of a more meditative approach. Partly, of course, this is due to the very nature of an order that initiates "through the mail"; however, the instructions given in the documents as published by Burgoyne and others are concise and coherent, designed for the solitary practitioner. This has more in common with the practice of descending to the Chariot than it does with the more elaborate Masonic rituals that serve as the order's spiritual pedigree. If a member was accepted into the order — a process that involved providing the order with one's horoscope chart (a practice reminiscent of that used by the Qumran group two thousand years earlier) — then one would be given a personal mentor. This mentor would probably be the only person the initiand would see in the normal course of events, thus ruling out the complicated initiation ceremonies familiar to the Masons and the Golden Dawn. Oddly enough, people *were* rejected for membership (which is odd only if one considers the order nothing more than a scheme to bilk innocent persons out of the monthly fees).

Further, the number seven is emphasized in the order's structure of only seven degrees, and in various references to Seven Guardians, Seven Archangels, etc. If we peer through the purple prose of *The Light of Egypt* and other order publications, we can discern the bare outlines of a *merkavah* practice that has acquired some of the heavy ornamentation of a Masonic-inspired Brotherhood.

Running through the rituals and the published writings of these sects, however, we come across blatant admission of the importance of the Dipper as the core of the entire belief system. Oddly, this has so far gone unremarked by most commentators and in the writings of the initiates of their respective orders.

For instance, the two volumes of Thomas H. Burgoyne's collection of instructions for the H.B. of L., *The Light of Egypt,* boast the following citation on the title page of each volume:

> "Write the things which thou hast seen, and the things which are, and the things which shall be hereafter; THE MYSTERY OF THE SEVEN STARS, which thou sawest in my right hand." Revelations, Chap. I, 19 and 20.[3] [emphasis in the original]

The phrase "mystery of the seven stars" is provided in full capitalization, in an obvious attempt to get our attention. Chapter 5 of volume 1 is an examination of sacred astronomy, the precession of the equinoxes, and an explanation of the importance of the Pole. In volume 2, chapter 5, the chapter entitled "Astro-Mythology," we see the importance assigned by the cult to the Pole Star once again, as it is identified it with Mount Olympus and Mount Zion.[4]

More than this, however, is the sign and seal of the H.B. of L. On the cover of the two volumes of *The Light of Egypt* we find seven stars arrayed in a circle around an arrow, and a serpent. The full seal of the H.B. of L., as it appears in their publications, is even more blatant in its iconography, for here we have the same array of seven stars, arrow and serpent but within a six-pointed star, a "Star of David." On the left and right side of the star, respectively, we find a moon and a sun: once again, subtly reminding us that the seven stars in the diagram are not the seven planets. Above and below the hexagram, in the angles formed by its points, can be seen the four cherubic images of the lion, the ox, the man, and the eagle: references once again to the vision of Ezekiel. The whole is enclosed within an ouroborous, a serpent biting its tail (see page 133 above).

The serpent in the center of the image, stabbed with an arrow, may represent the constellation Draco, and the arrow through it may represent the *axis mundi* or the Pole itself. On the cover of *The Light of Egypt,* however, there is a symbol at either end of the serpent. This symbol represents the *Cauda Draconis* and the *Caput Draconis:* the Tail and Head of the Dragon, respectively. These are the imaginary points on the ecliptic — the descending node and the ascending node, respectively — which are used to calculate eclipses (the Dragon "swallows" the moon, for instance). Thus we may admit the possibility that the serpent design represents the ecliptic and not the constellation Draco, except for the fact that the serpent is depicted in an S-shape, which does not bring to mind the zodiacal belt but rather the constellation Draco itself.

In a thought-provoking translation by the late Aryeh Kaplan, a Kabbalah scholar who was also (it is claimed) a practitioner, the *Sepher Yetzirah* may contain a clue as to the meaning of this symbol and thus provide another piece of evidence supporting the idea that there was genuine Kabbalistic knowledge behind some of these more outlandish or controversial occult orders.

As mentioned previously, the *Sepher Yetzirah* is one of the oldest Kabbalistic texts in existence. It is quite short, but obscure. It introduces the concept of the *sephiroth*, although there is no mention of a Sephirotic Tree. It also introduces the idea of the twenty-two paths and their association with the twenty-two letters of the Hebrew alphabet. Wynn Westcott, one of the founders of the British Golden Dawn, published his own translation of it, and there were also translations by Dr. Gerard Encausse (the French magician and author known as "Papus") and many others.

Chapter 6 of this document contains the enigmatic phrase: "He set them in the Teli, the Cycle, and the Heart."[5] Kaplan devotes more than seven pages to a discussion of the term "Teli," admitting that it "is one of the most mysterious words in the Sefer Yetzirah. The term occurs neither in the Bible nor in the Talmud."[6] Yet according to the Kabbalist authors consulted by Kaplan, "the Teli mentioned here in Sefer Yetzirah is the imaginary axis around which the heavens rotate."[7] Further, he cites other authorities who identify the *Teli* with the "Pole Serpent," i.e., with Draco, noting that a star in Draco's tail, Thuban, was the Pole Star forty-five hundred years ago. He further cites other Kabbalists, e.g., as Abraham Abulafia, who claims that the *Teli* represents "love and mystical union,"[8] again introducing the concept of divine (or spiritualized) sexuality into our discussion of celestial ascent. It represents the link between the physical world and the spiritual world, the "knots" that serve as tangent points in the winding Serpent where heaven and earth meet. Kaplan actually goes so far as to state that the word *Teli* comes from a Hebrew word meaning "hanging" or "to hang," and relates that concept to the hairs of the divine beard. "The Zohar," Kaplan writes, "relates this to the word *Talpiot,* which, as the Talmud teaches, is the 'hill (*tell*) to which all mouths (*piot*) turn.' This 'hill' is the mount upon which the Temple was built, which Jacob called the 'gate of heaven' (Genesis 28:17)."[9]

If we are to accept Kaplan's exegesis we find ourselves with a consistent argument in favor of a reconsideration of the importance of the *actual* heavens in any discussion of heavenly ascent. The Pole Star is once again introduced into the equation in a set of interlocking correspondences that bring together the Pole, the Temple, and the Gate of Heaven.

The design of the H.B. of L. seal is a copy of the seal of Count Cagliostro, the founder of the Egyptian form of Freemasonry. Cagliostro was another one of these relentlessly unusual characters, accused of all the same things as Frank, Crowley, and the rest, a mysterious individual who was at once involved in political intrigue as well as occult initiations and Masonic lodges. His form of Freemasonry, supposedly based on Egyptian teachings and known as the Egyptian Rite, was introduced to the world in London in 1786 and later on the Continent. After establishing another such lodge in Rome, he was arrested by the Inquisition and sentenced to death, but he died in prison. A few years after his death, other Egyptian Rite lodges began to appear, most notably the Rite of Memphis and the Rite of Mizraim, which eventually were combined. The Ordo Templi Orientis (the O.T.O.) would be organized by German adepts who were also members of the Rites of Memphis and Mizraim. Thus, we have two separate channels (at least) flowing into the O.T.O.: the first from the H.B. of L. and the teachings of Randolph, Burgoyne, and others, and the second directly from the Egyptian Rite mysteries of Cagliostro. Remembering that the H.B. of L. purported to be Egyptian and was probably the same as the Hermetic Brotherhood of Luxor familiar to Blavatsky and Max Theon, we have come full circle. From the Pyramid Texts and Coffin Texts of ancient Egypt in the third millennium BCE to the English drawing rooms of the late nineteenth century CE, ideas of immortality, celestial ascent, and the seven stars of the Northern Dipper provide a continuum of belief and practice for generations of spiritual seekers as disparate as Egyptian priests, Babylonian kings, Hindu tantrickas, Haitian vodouisants, Siberian and Dogon shamans, Sufi mystics, Yezidis, Chinese alchemists, and, perhaps most of all, Jewish Kabbalists in the *merkavah* tradition.

All looked up.

All were interested in coming before the divine presence. All understood that this could not be obtained by the spiritually impure. The body and the soul had to be refined, as if in an alchemist's furnace. Spiritual transformation was necessary if divine immortality was to be assured. Through trance, meditation, visualization, ritual, drugs, fasting, even weeping and sex, the derangement of the senses was sought as a means for cutting through materialism and everyday thinking in order to obtain a brief glimpse of the Divine.

The rest was hard work, concentration, prayer, and sacrifice. But the goal was always before them, every night, in the heavens they yearned to reach: the Pole Star. It floated eternally above their heads in that stately, cosmic dance performed by the seven stars of the Northern Dipper: the seven steps on the stairway of heaven and spiritual transformation.

Conclusions

There is a mechanism for celestial ascent whose basic technology can be discerned from the examples given here. In the first place, the astronomical component cannot be ignored. The constant references to the "heavens" should be taken as a literal reference, at least in the preliminary stages of exploring this theme. The "heavens" did not denote a vague or ambiguous location to the ancients; it is clear that they had a comprehensive view of the stars and planets and various schemas for categorizing them and organizing information about them. In some cases, their ideas seem capricious to us today; in others, they demonstrate a very real, very earnest fixation on the stars as tools for divination, for the orientation of temples, and for navigation.

This is particularly true, as we have shown, in the case of the Pole Star and true north. All of the religions and mystical practices we have examined show that ideas about an *axis mundi* are related to the heavens and specifically to the Pole Star; and ideas about the *axis mundi* are fundamental to many ancient cosmological systems. Ideas about a Pole, a World Tree, a Ladder, or a Stairway to the heavens can be found in many of the world's major religions; in the religions of the ancients, such ideas were fundamental to their ideas of macrocosm and microcosm. The Pole was situated in the north, but also in the human body. If the Pole in the human body could be aligned with the Pole in the northern sky, then celestial ascent was possible.

In the earliest scriptural references we can find, those of ancient Egypt, celestial ascent was the prerogative of the pharaoh. The pharaoh, as a divine being, could be expected to return to the stars after death. The Pole Star represented constancy, stability, unchangeability, and thus immortality. One did not simply leap from the earth to the Pole Star, however; the voyage was gradual, and the seven gates and their respective guardians had to be passed before access could be enjoyed at the Throne of the Gods.

As this type of access became available to the common man and woman, however — as celestial ascent became "democratized" — it took on various new meanings. It is no longer the pharaoh alone who partakes of the divine essence, but all human beings. This led, perhaps, to the idea of an immortal soul as the birthright of everyone. If everyone had an immortal soul, then everyone could, theoretically, ascend to the heavens.

If so, then what was the difference between a commoner and a king? How could both attain the audience before the Throne so easily? The answer, of course, was that they could not. What the commoner lacked in royal blood had to be made up for in other ways. A king is always tested, and a king's success or failure as a monarch is obvious to everyone in the kingdom. He constantly undergoes a kind of spiritual struggle, an *agon,* by the very virtue of his position. As the leader of a nation, he can be judged only by God or the Gods. Thus, the common man or woman, the independent mystic, must now prove spiritual competence by undergoing severe ordeals and trials in imitation of those undergone by the monarch. Fasting, abstention from sex, concentration, prayer — all of these and more will be demanded of the soul that desires to come before the Throne because these ordeals will test the soul in ways that mimic the tests given to the king. The stress on the psyche and on the body will "derange the senses" and lead to altered states of consciousness. The individual will, for a time, no longer be a commoner but will be jerked out of his or her normal life — the normal, everyday perception of self and others — and will have experience of palaces, *hekhalot,* chariots, *merkavot,* and wander through the same halls, the same chambers, as members of the court.

The life of a pharaoh or king could not be compared to that of a commoner. Reality was different for the ruling class. They had the power of life and death over their subjects. They lived lives of exceptional ease and luxury, even licentiousness. Their senses were massaged regularly by perfumes, sweet music, rare foods and wines, and beautiful courtesans. They had the experience of heaven on earth, an experience that was denied to the commoners. When the infamous leader of the cult of the Assassins in eleventh-century Persia promised his followers virgins and delicious wine in Paradise, every sort of luxury and sensory wonder if they died for him, he did not mention that such was the life of monarchs everywhere, every day. What he was promising, then, was what Marx would promise eight hundred years later: a Workers' Paradise. Except, in the case of the Assassins, this Paradise could be approached only after death.

In the case of the descenders to the Chariot, however, we have the example of individuals outside the religious mainstream who, if they performed the practices correctly, could have direct experience of the heavenly realms while alive. Indeed, the case of the Descenders was almost unique. They had lost their kingdom, the kingdom of Israel, and the Temple. They could not walk in the palace or stand before the throne, neither the throne of kingship, nor the Throne of God. The only experience they could have of this type of monarchy, both mundane and heavenly, material and spiritual, would be the method of celestial ascent. The only palace they could call their own, the only one open to them after the Diaspora, was the "virtual" palace, the palace in heaven. In order to go there, in order to rise out of servitude in the physical world, every one of an average human being's basic impulses and appetites had to be controlled and redirected. One had to break the servitude of the soul to the body in order to liberate the spirit. The body, as the Sufis have written, belongs to the Prophet Adam. In order to free Adam and bring him back to Paradise, one has to control the body and the urges of the body for food, drink, sleep, sex, and diversion. One has to make of the body a vehicle, a chariot, for rising up to the seven heavens.

The obsessive preoccupation with purity that characterizes the Qumran sect, for example, is indicative of a general attitude among mystical groups in various cultures toward the domination of the body and its impulses for a "higher" purpose. Among the Qumranites, it would appear that they felt purity was a necessity in order to belong to the company of angels that would serve in the heavenly Temple. Food, drink, sex, even defecation and other bodily functions were the subject of stringent control. Each Qumranite, therefore, was, if not a mystic, then a mystic in training.

Adam was cast out of Paradise due to the sin of disobedience. In order to reenter Paradise, or the *pardes,* one had to remove the stain of this sin. That was the first step in the Sufi ascent motif, and it remains so for other groups around the world. The body is the vehicle, the Chariot.

And the heavens are the map. The only reason for the near-monotonous emphasis on the number seven in cultures as diverse as that of Egypt, Babylon, Israel, India, and China, the only reason that can be determined with any degree of confidence, is the asterism that we in the United States know as the Dipper and that other cultures knew as the Chariot, or the Wagon. It is a constant for all cultures in the northern latitudes that have visual access to the Pole Star; it is a fact of life that unites these diverse peoples, living in different physical environments, speaking different languages, professing different religious faiths. It is as constant and familiar a figure as the sun and moon. The Pole Star represents the axis of the world, of the entire cosmos. It is where we can find the Throne of God, accessible only after passing through the seven chambers before it.

By interiorizing the seven chambers in the human body, we meld the vehicle and the map. The seven stars, sparkling in their austere and singular beauty in the cold northern night, are either brought down into the body or the body travels in its "astral" — starry — form to the stars. In either case, an identification is made between the human body and the celestial court. To travel to the stars, to make the celestial ascent, is to leave the world behind, to experience life from another point of view entirely, perhaps to see the world as it really is, from the vantage point of the heavens looking down.

In modern esoteric orders, the celestial ascent motif is preserved in rituals. The ascent from one star to another is the purpose of a graduated degree system of initiation. The solitary mystic is now part of a group of Descenders who, ideally, assist each other to rise to the Throne. It represents a kind of demonstration of the possibility that celestial ascent and all that it implies, from immortality to spiritual liberation, can be attained by society at large and is no longer the province of a handful of solitary Kabbalists, emaciated yogis, or intense Chinese alchemists in their mountain retreats. The democratization of immortality — begun when the first commoner was buried according to Egyptian custom, with the Opening of the Mouth ceremony — has thus extended, in modern times, to the ready availability of rack-sized paperbacks on the occult, on yoga, Tantra, alchemy, and the like, and to the proliferation of Internet websites devoted to these themes.

There is much that is incorrect, inane, or even dangerous in these ready-made offerings of spiritual liberation, of course; but that is the price of democracy in this case. Individuals take responsibility for their own immortality, their own vision of the Throne, their own celestial ascent. Liberation has never been won without a fight. In this case, the fight is purely internal, the aggressor one's own nature. Modern-day mystics like Gurdjieff and Ouspensky wrote about the need to "wake up" from our everyday lives, our everyday consciousness; the idea is that we have become robotized to a certain extent, believing that what we experience every day is the only possible reality. That is the definition of spiritual servitude, in the terms of the yogis, the alchemists, the Kabbalists. One needs to wake up.

And in order to wake up, one must learn to look up.

Notes

Introduction

1. Most especially Graetz (1846) and Odeberg (1928).
2. For instance in Arbel (2003).
3. For instance in Davis (1977).
4. Ulansey (1989).
5. De Santillana and von Dechend (1977).

1. Ascent Myth and Ritual in Ancient Egypt

1. Utterance 267, Section 365, Mercer Translation.
2. A well-presented argument for the etymology of Poimandres, the putative author of the *Corpus Hermeticum,* can be found in Kingsley (1993), 1–24.
3. Published in various editions, originally in French and with various dates. One in the author's possession has a date of 1652, which must be spurious. A. E. Waite (1999, orig. 1911; p. 115) makes the case that internal evidence shows it to have been written at or after the time of Napoleon's invasion of Egypt.
4. This is subject to some controversy, depending on how we define "scripture." With the late-nineteenth-century discovery of the cuneiform texts of the Sumerian civilization (to be discussed in the following chapter) the historical and archaeological timelines have had to be revisited more than once. It is safe to say, however, that both the Egyptian and the Sumerian religions have given us the oldest written scriptures in the world.
5. Budge (1895), 20.
6. As Steven M. Wasserstrom (1999) has pointed out, the trend of these extremely influential thinkers has been to elevate the mystical experience at the expense of the importance of ethics and morals in their study of religion; yet the candidate for mystical experience, like the soul of the deceased king — has to demonstrate ritual purity, i.e., adherence to the Law. The two are inseparable from a purely technical point of view; this has led some occultists and Kabbalists to propose that a complete violation of purity laws would also be appropriate in the quest for mystical experience, as absolute purity stimulates a mental state equally as extreme as that of absolute impurity, an argument that tends to support the importance of ethical and moral studies in any examination of mysticism and occult practices.
7. This theme has been explored in detail by Ann Macy Roth in a series of articles published in the *Journal of Egyptian Archaeology,* "The pss-kf and the 'Opening of the Mouth' Ceremony: A Ritual of Birth and Rebirth" 78 (1992): 113–47, and "Fingers, Stars, and the 'Opening of the Mouth': The Nature and Function of the ntrwj-Blades" 79 (1993): 57–79. In the latter article she explores some of the celestial correspondences to which we refer in this chapter.

8. Budge, *The Book of the Dead* (1895), 246.

9. The "Talisman of Set" even makes an appearance in a Dennis Wheatley novel, *The Devil Rides Out*. It should be pointed out that Wheatley was personally acquainted with Aleister Crowley and with James Bond creator Ian Fleming as well. The story of their relationship is referenced in my *Unholy Alliance*.

10. Budge (1895), 268.

11. Ibid., 269.

12. Ibid.

13. Ariel (1988), 19.

14. Scholem (1972), 50–51.

15. Arbel (2003), 92–95.

16. Davis (1977), 161–79.

17. Faulkner (1966), 153–61.

18. Wainright (1932), 3–15.

19. Ibid., 6.

20. Ibid., 8.

2. *Ascent Myth and Ritual in Ancient Babylon*

1. Some Sumerologists insist on a sixth–fifth millennium BCE date for the establishment of the first Sumerian or proto-Sumerian civilization, the Ubaid culture, in the region. However, writing was not developed until circa 3500 BCE, about the time of what is known as the Late Uruk period (named after the town of Uruk, north of Ur, where many important Sumerian monuments were discovered). The bulk of the Sumerian scriptural texts, however, begin to appear about the time of the Early Dynastic period, or 3100–2390 BCE. This is roughly the same period in which the Pyramid Texts of Egypt were composed. The tomb of Unas was built circa 2345 BCE; the Pyramid Texts are generally agreed to be older than that.

2. Kramer (1981).

3. Oppenheimer (1977).

4. Woolley (1965).

5. Jacobsen (1978).

6. Herodotus, *Histories,* Book 1, Paragraph 181–82.

7. For instance Kramer (1969), chapters 3–5.

8. See Hoyrup (1993), 281–86, where it is admitted "that 7 did, in fact, acquire a much more widely recognized special status within Babylonian and related cultures." This is well known in a larger discussion of the Babylonian algebraic texts in which manipulations of certain numbers such as 7, 11, 13, 17, and 19 are examined and the peculiar status of 7 is remarked.

9. See Reiner (1995), 56–58.

10. See, for instance, Regardie (2005), 272–77.

11. Taken from J. A. Black et al., *The Electronic Text Corpus of Sumerian Literature* (http://www-etcsl.orient.ox.ac.uk/), Oxford 1998–.

12. Ibid.

13. Ibid.

14. For instance De Santillana (1977), Ulansey (1989), Bauval and Gilbert (1997), Hancock (1998), etc.

15. The earliest references to personal, as opposed to state, horoscopes do not appear until about 400 BCE.

16. Reiner (1995), 57.

17. Walker and Dick (2001), 78, line 18 (BM 45749, obverse, section E).

18. Roth (1993).

19. Boden (1998).

20. Berlejung (1998).

21. The example of the juggernaut in India comes readily to mind; but one could add many other examples of the transport of statues of the gods or saints through city streets, either carried on litters or wheeled on carriages and floats. In the case of ancient Israel, the Ark of the Covenant was transported with ceremonial solemnity; the fact that the Jewish god was invisible, i.e., had no statues depicting him, did not stop the priests from carrying an emblem of divinity in procession. Once the Temple was erected, however, the Ark maintained a permanent residence in the Holy of Holies, became fixed in space, and did not appear outside the sanctuary until the sack of Jerusalem by the Babylonians in 585 BCE, when the Ark disappeared. In a sense, the invisibility of the Jewish god was thus maintained: from the sacred precincts of the Holy of Holies in the Temple of Solomon to the disappearance of the Ark in 585 BCE. From that moment on, the idea of the Temple and the Ark became even more idealized until the vision of Ezekiel — and the whole corpus of Temple liturgics and mysticism from Qumran to the *merkavah* texts — placed the Temple itself in sacred time and sacred space, removed from the three-dimensionality of the world. The Temple became etherealized: a virtual Temple, invisible except to the initiated mystics in thralls of ecstatic contemplation.

22. This description is much abridged from the translation provided in Walker and Dick (2001), 77–82.

23. Reiner (1995), 24, 56, and 70–72.

24. Ibid., 71.

25. Tzvi Abusch, in Collins and Fishbane (1995).

26. Ibid., 20–24.

27. Ibid., 23.

28. Ibid., 21.

29. Ibid.

3. The Vision of Ezekiel

1. The insistence on "likeness" could be a deliberate attempt by Ezekiel, or later interpolators, to escape any accusation of idolatry. To say that Ezekiel had seen God Himself, when even Moses was denied that possibility, would have been blasphemy. It could also, however, refer to statues, which are "likenesses"; it could also be a clever play on words, since man was made in "the image and likeness" of God. Further, this could demonstrate an intent to show that what was happening was a vision and not taking place in normal waking consciousness. The actual intention of the writer of Ezekiel is so far unknown, however.

2. This influential text of the Freemasons demonstrates an obsession with the Temple that is almost as reverent and as extreme as that of the Qumranites. The

various Masonic degrees, such as the Royal Arch of Solomon, the Prince of Jerusalem, Chief of the Tabernacle, Prince of the Tabernacle, etc., relate in some way to the Temple service. Pike in several places compares the design of the Masonic temple with that of the descriptions of Solomon's Temple in, for instance, Clement of Alexandria and Josephus. That Freemasonry and allied esoteric societies of eighteenth- and nineteenth-century Europe were repositories of a form of *hekhalot* mysticism is a theme the author will explore later in this work.

3. For instance, the Temple Scroll, the Halakkhic Letter, the Zadokite Fragments, etc.

4. A Hebrew term, *halakah,* that can be translated as "religious precepts."

5. Scholem (1972, originally 1947).

6. Scholem (1972), 46–47, suggests a date of the sixth century CE for the change from "employment of the glory" to "descenders to the chariot" as the categorization of this genre in Jewish literature.

7. Ibid., 42.

8. Newsom (1985).

9. See for instance Frances Yates (1966), who explores the idea that in the Hellenistic period the art of memory was known to readers of Aristotle, Cicero, and, later, Augustine. Further, the idea of the "spiritualization" of the Temple was known in seventeenth-century religious circles, seemingly without reference to either the *hekhalot* literature (which was virtually unknown outside Kabbalistic groups) and certainly with no knowledge of the Dead Sea Scrolls. John Bunyan's *Solomon's Temple Spiritualized* (London, 1688), is such an example, with its opening citation of Ezekiel 43:10–11 and much Masonic ritual symbolism as well, which is based on the building of an allegorical Temple.

10. Elior, *The Three Temples,* 2005, Oxford, 15.

11. For instance in Newsom (1985).

12. Ibid., 193.

13. Ibid., 306.

14. Schiffman (1995), 359.

15. Scholem (1972), 60.

16. Lesses (1998).

17. Ibid., 117–60.

18. Ibid., 159.

19. Janowitz (1989), 89.

20. Schiffman (1995), 358.

4. Ezekiel and the Apocalypse

1. Note the similarity between this image and the practice of the Yezidi sect that employs a standard (a brass pole representing God) and seven lamps surrounding it, in their liturgies. See Excursus 1.

2. For instance, *The Omen* (1976, remade in 2006), *The End of Days* (1999), and others.

3. Krupp (1983), 184–89.

4. Turner (1969).

5. See chapter 10 for a discussion of some of these topics.

5. Ezekiel's Vision as Template for Mystical Ascent

1. Dan (1993), 13.
2. See Excursus 1 for a discussion of the *mir'aj.*
3. Dan (1993), 21.
4. As quoted in its entirety in Jacobs (1996), 35–44.
5. See the works of Samuel Noah Kramer, such as *The Sumerians* and *History Begins at Sumer,* for discussions of these and other relevant myths. There is, however, a section of the Zohar that discusses these seven "hells" as well (the section known as *Pekudei,* 2:244b–62b).
6. Jacobs (1996), 38.
7. For instance in the medieval *Grimorium Verum,* where the directions for making this mirror are quite explicit and include engraving the name of Metatron on the mirror's frame. See Waite (1999), 318–19, and also the *Leyden Papyrus,* col. 3, Griffith and Thompson (1904), for a much earlier source dating to the first century CE.
8. A photograph of this stone — courtesy of the British Museum, where it is held — can be found in various popular publications, including the Time-Life series *Mysteries of the Unknown,* where it is found in the volume entitled *Magical Arts* (no author, no date) on page 57.
9. See chapter 10 for a more detailed explanation.
10. Kraushar, 229, and sayings #500, 516, 1517, 1294, etc.
11. Janowitz (1989).
12. Pritchard (1969), 575.
13. Bidmead (2002), 32–33.

Excursus 1: Celestial Ascent in Middle Eastern Mysticism

1. Surah 17, "The Israelites," with another reference in Surah 53, "The Star."
2. Book One, Number 0313, of *Al-Jami' al-Musnad al-Sahih* (Bukhari's Hadith).
3. Surah 17, "The Israelites," first section.
4. Maulana (2002), 17, note 29b.
5. Joseph (1919), 37.
6. Ibid., 36–38.
7. Joseph (1919), 75–76.
8. Zaehner (1969), 93–134.
9. This schema is from Bakhtiar (1976), 12–24, 97.
10. The late Israel Regardie, a famous apologist for the Golden Dawn (to be discussed in part 4), often insisted that persons desiring to become involved in occult practice undergo at least one hundred hours of psychotherapy beforehand. Regardie (1985), 30–36.
11. From *il-Qasd ila Allah,* cited in Smith (1976), 240–41.
12. Zaehner (1969), 124–25.

6. Ecstatic Flight in Shamanism

1. See Couliano (1991), 44.
2. Eliade (1999).
3. Couliano (1991).

4. See chapter 8.
5. Zohar, 1:149b, in Matt's translation, vol. 2, 333.
6. Wolfson (1997), especially his concluding remarks on 396.
7. See for instance Eliade (1972), 274–79, for an overview of the literature.
8. Ibid., 274.
9. Ibid., 275.
10. Ibid.
11. Ibid.
12. Wolfson (1997), 326ff.
13. Eliade (1972), 275.
14. Ladders, ropes, and wings will appear as ascent vehicles in the seventeenth-century Rosicrucian allegory described in Excursus 2.
15. Eliade (1972), 195.
16. Ibid., 196.
17. Ibid., 278–79.
18. Ibid., 279.
19. Idel (2005), 25.
20. Ibid., 56.

7. Celestial Ascent in Afro-Caribbean and African Religion

1. For instance, Desmangles (1992) and Brandon (1997).
2. Desmangles (1992), 108.
3. Ibid.
4. Ibid., 109.
5. Ibid.
6. Ibid., 68.
7. Ibid., 87.
8. For instance, the way in which the Zohar describes the Sephirotic Ladder of Lights and principally the first "rung" on the tree, *Shekhinah*, and the phallic nature of *Yesod*.
9. Crowley (1988; orig. 1914), 14.
10. See chapter 8.
11. Griaule and Deterlen (1986), 83–84.
12. Details of this system can be found in Abimbola (1997), Fatunmbi (1992), Karade (1994), Peek (1991), and Bascom (1969).
13. Griaule and Deterlen (1986), 186.
14. Ibid., 90–91.
15. Ibid., 193.
16. See chapter 8.
17. Griaule and Deterlen (1986), 140–41.
18. Ibid., 196.
19. Ibid., 499.
20. Ibid., 345.
21. Temple (1976), 199.

8. Celestial Ascent in Asian Ritual and Alchemy

1. Kloetzli (1987), 18–19.
2. *Artharva Veda,* XIX, 53.
3. Danielou (1985), 45.
4. Ibid., 316.
5. Ibid., 317.
6. Ibid.
7. Ibid., 172.
8. See Scholem (1978), 138–39, for a summary of this idea.
9. Ibid., 105–6.
10. Idel (1988), 75–88.
11. Woodroffe (1974), 1–2.
12. Ibid., 22–24.
13. In fact, during a typical Hindu marriage ceremony the bride takes seven steps to the north to face Ursa Major and the Polar region, addressing the star as the pillar of the universe. In other variations, the couple walk around the central altar (an *axis mundi*) seven times, clockwise. Thus, the idea of a sacred marriage linked with the number seven and the northern heavens is consistent in both native Indian religious practice as well as hints found in the Zohar and other Kabbalistic literature.
14. Snodgrass (1994), 1:146–47.
15. In a lecture before Florida International University students and guests, Miami, February 2006.
16. Robinet (1989), 159–91.
17. *Zhuangzi,* Book VI, Part I, Section VI. See the Legge translation in *Sacred Books of the East,* vol. 39.
18. Tsai (2003).
19. *Baopuzi,* 17.5A.
20. Tsai (2003), 36.
21. Robinet (1989), 165.
22. Williams (1976), 371.
23. Ibid., 104–5.
24. Robinet (1989), 172.
25. Ibid., 176.
26. Ibid.
27. Strickman (1979), 177.
28. Robinet (1989), 172.
29. Lissner (1957), 205–7.

9. Origins of a Western Tradition

1. Cumont (1956), 120.
2. Ulansey (1989).
3. Ibid., 105.
4. See for instance the illustrations in Black and Green (2000), 100, 142, etc.
5. Cumont (1956), 107.
6. Ibid., 105.
7. Ibid., 53.

8. For instance, the mithraeum at Riegel, Baden-Wurtemberg shows an orientation to the northwest.

9. Allen (1963), 434.

10. Ibid., 445.

11. Ulansey (1991).

12. Betz (1986), PGM IV.475–829, 48.

13. Ibid., 50.

14. Ibid., 50–51.

15. Ibid., 52.

16. Stratton (2000), 309.

10. Christian Kabbalah and the Esoteric Orders

1. Burgoyne (1963), 2:45.

2. Levi was probably the most influential occultist of nineteenth-century Europe. His works have been translated into many languages, and he has been referenced as the inspiration for a variety of esoteric orders and personalities including the Martinists, several Rosicrucian societies, and the above-mentioned Papus and Crowley (the latter considered himself the reincarnation of Levi!). In English translation are Levi's *The History of Magic, Transcendental Magic, The Mysteries of the Qabalah,* and *The Key of the Mysteries* (the last translated from French into English by Crowley).

3. Papus's works have also been translated into at least a dozen languages, and he was considered by many to be a kind of successor to Levi. His *Tarot of the Bohemians* was inspired by Levi's "discovery" of the relationship between the Kabbalah and the Tarot, which Scholem criticizes in the above citation.

4. Of all the twentieth-century occultists, Aleister Crowley has probably had the most influence on a generation of seekers. His books have been widely distributed in the decades after his death, and several esoteric orders devoted to his writings, teachings, and example are still in existence, such as the Ordo Templi Orientis (O.T.O.) active in the UK, the United States, Australia, Serbia, and several other countries, and the Argentum Astrum (A∴A∴). Crowley's photo appeared on the cover of The Beatles' *Sergeant Pepper's Lonely Hearts Club Band* (1967) album as one of the "people we like"; Jimmy Page, the lead singer of the original heavy metal band Led Zeppelin, bought Crowley's old estate in Scotland, Boleskine, in order to practice occult rituals there.

5. Scholem (1978), 203; the date of Crowley's death is actually 1947.

6. Aside from the instance quoted above, there is virtually nothing else in Scholem that addresses nineteenth- and twentieth-century Christian Kabbalah, a field that he clearly feels was nothing more than a playground for charlatans and poseurs. In *Major Trends* (1941) he declares his mission is "to reclaim this derelict area [from Eliphas Levi and the 'highly colored humbug of Aleister Crowley and his followers'] and to apply to it the strict standards of historical research" (p. 2). So we see that in the very first pages of his revolutionary study of the Kabbalah, Scholem identifies the nineteenth- and twentieth-century Christian Kabbalists as the enemy to be defeated and admits that this attack is his raison d'être. At the time Scholem published this work in 1941, Aleister Crowley was still alive and still at least nominally in control

of two of the secret societies with which he has been identified, the Ordo Templi Orientis (O.T.O.) and the Argentum Astrum (A.˙.A.˙.), both of which still exist today. Crowley enjoyed a scandalous reputation in England and on the Continent during his lifetime, a reputation of which Scholem was presumably aware. A footnote to his statement concerning Crowley and Levi, on page 353 of *Major Trends,* shows that Scholem was aware of Crowley's *Equinox,* an erratically published magazine on esoteric subjects that is much-prized among Crowley's followers. As early as 1927, the footnote indicates, Scholem had compiled a Bibliographia Kabbalistica that included the works of Eliphas Levi. As Scholem was a member of the influential Eranos circle, which included Carl Jung and Mircea Eliade, one wonders if Aleister Crowley and Eliphas Levi ever came up in conversation, and in what context. Joseph Dan, while sympathetic toward the Christian Kabbalah of the Florentine Academy, has little time for its later manifestations. The work of Janowitz (1989, 2002) concentrates on the literary aspect of the *merkavah* literature and of Greco-Roman magic; Himmelfarb (1993) develops themes of ascent introduced by Scholem, and Wolfson (1994) has focused on medieval Jewish mysticism. Idel (1988) speaks of Jewish scholarship in the nineteenth century but ignores the Christian Kabbalists of the same period.

7. Mathers (1887; reissued in 1926).

8. See, for instance, Dan (1993), 15, which claims that dating this literature to the second century–fifth century CE is "universally accepted by scholars." This dating is repeated in Dan (1986), 38, n. 4. See also Arbel (2003), 8.

9. This would be defined for the purpose of this study as groups and individuals identified as Kabbalists and studied by Scholem, Idel, and others such as the Ashkenazic Hasidim, the groups that developed from the example and teaching of the Baal Shem Tov, the '*Iyyun* Circle, etc.

10. Scholem (1972), 43–44.

11. Pico della Mirandola had access to portions of the Zohar, as did Johannes Reuchlin and Cornelius Agrippa, and their works were based on these — often incomplete and misunderstood — versions.

12. See for instance the many books on the subject by Francis Israel Regardie, the Golden Dawn's most prolific apologist. Other authors who were Golden Dawn initiates include MacGregor Mathers, A. E. Waite, Aleister Crowley, Dion Fortune, Wynn Westcott, and the Irish poet William Butler Yeats.

13. Specifically Godwin, Chanel, and Deveney (1995) and Greenfield (1997). There are also references to the Brotherhood in histories of the Theosophical Society.

14. *The Secret Rituals of the O.T.O.,* edited by Francis King (1974). This book was pulled from distribution and from bookstores and rare book dealers by the O.T.O. itself soon after publication. However, other documents pertaining to the order's rituals, beliefs, and organization have been published in other media and are widely available on the order's own websites on the Internet. See the work by Kenneth Grant, the idiosyncratic head of a British version of the O.T.O., listed in the Bibliography.

15. Tractate *Hagigah* 2:1; a theme repeated in *Hagigah* 14a.

16. Dan (1993), 13; besides that of Scholem, the other authors referenced by Dan are Heinrich Graetz (*Gnosticismus und Judenthum,* 1846) and Hugo Odeberg (*Third Book of Enoch,* 1928). Odeberg classed the *Sepher Hekhalot* with the Apocryphal

literature. He believed it to be a continuation of the Book of Enoch. This was, of course, problematic since it placed an important *merkavah* text outside the Jewish mainstream and, by implication, all the *merkavah* literature became viewed as post-biblical apocrypha. Odeberg's interest in the *Sepher Hekhalot* was from his position as a priest, which might have influenced his point of view. In any event, this work did not appear until 1928, long after the formation of the Golden Dawn in 1888. As for Graetz's possible influence on the Golden Dawn, it is certainly possible since Waite mentions Graetz in his work on the Kabbalah, although dismissing him as hostile to mysticism. His interest in Graetz only seems to go so far as to try to date the Sepher Yetzirah and the Zohar, but he categorically denies any influence on his thought from Graetz, saying "The German school of Dr. Graetz, whose English exponent was Ginsburg, has passed utterly away" (1990), 572. Graetz, of course, is hostile to the whole field of Jewish mysticism, seeing it as the result of corrupting Islamic influences during the Geonic period. Of course, he might have been used purely as a source of data and his opinions ignored, but Graetz's insistence that the *merkavah* tradition was late, alien, and corrupt was not a point of view put forward by the GD, who saw it as a mysterious, ancient, and oral tradition. The insistence of the GD — of Waite and Mathers specifically — that *merkavah* was a purely oral tradition means that they did not see in Graetz a source for their ideology or rituals.

17. For instance, A. E. Waite (1990), 37, where he specifically states that the *ma'aseh merkavah* was never written down. Also, Israel Regardie, an initiate, like Waite, of the Golden Dawn, has written concerning Golden Dawn co-founder MacGregor Mathers, "Speaking of the question as to whether he himself knew anything of the so-called unwritten Qabalah, Mathers publicly refused to admit either that he did or did not" (Regardie [1971], 34); and Mathers himself in his *Kabbalah Unveiled* states, "The term 'Unwritten Qabalah' is applied to certain knowledge which is never entrusted to writing, but communicated orally. I may say no more on this point, not even whether I myself have or have not received it. Of course, until the time of Rabbi Schimeon Ben Jochai none of the Qabalah was ever written" (13–14). Except for the reference by Waite, it is difficult to determine from these cryptic utterances if the *ma'aseh merkavah* is the unwritten doctrine that is being described; the rabbi to whom Mathers refers is credited with having written the *Sepher ha-Zohar* and appears as the central figure in that work. Mathers is thus dating the existence of the Kabbalah either to the time the Zohar first appeared (the thirteenth century CE) or to the lifetime of Rabbi Simeon ben Yohai himself (second century CE); it is not clear which. In any event, it is clear that these Golden Dawn initiates insisted that there was an unwritten Kabbalah; and Waite identifies it with the *ma'aseh merkavah*.

18. See his sermon cycle entitled *Cantica Canticorum,* in translation by Killian Walsh, O.C.S.O., in four volumes, by Cistercian Publications, 2005. Bernard of Clairvaux was also the primary supporter and apologist for the Knights Templar, an order of knighthood that has come under intense scrutiny in discussions concerning the Holy Grail, the Cathars, and of course the Freemasons and other secret societies.

19. See, for instance, Newsom (1985), 12, and her commentary on 4Q405 20–21–22 which analyzes the Songs from the point of view of the many and pointed references to Ezekiel 1. The Songs of the Sabbath Sacrifice are liturgical hymns

that reiterate the importance of the number seven in terms of the Temple, multiple *merkavot,* cherubim, etc., prefiguring much of what would later appear in the *merkavah* texts. This theme is expanded in Rachel Elior (2005).

20. These circles would include the Ashkenazic Hasidim of the eleventh and twelfth centuries CE and would also include the ʿIyyun Circle. See Dan (1986), 26, and 43–56.

21. There were degree systems in the cults associated with Mithras and possibly in the Pythagorean academies. However, there is no evidence to show a continuum of ritual practice from Mithraic cults to Renaissance or premodern societies. Although the number and nomenclature of the Mithraic degrees seems to be known to us from classical authors (such as Porphyry in *De antro nympharum;* Origen in *Contra Celsum,* etc.), the nature of these degrees and the ritual methods for bestowing them are not recorded. The possibility that stories pertaining to the Mithraic degree system may be at least partially the result of romantic imagination or Christian polemic cannot be discounted. See, for instance, Roger Beck (2000) for a concise summary of what is known today of the Mithraic cult, remembering that much of this information was not available at the time the Masonic societies were being formed and only became popularly known at the time of publications by Franz Cumont (1956). For a compelling counter-argument to those contemporary Mithra studies that emphasize astrological or astronomical themes, see N. M. Swerdlow (1991), 48–63. Classical and modern authorities seem to agree, however, that there were seven degrees in the Mithraic initiation system, a fact that may be relevant to the present discussion. The Golden Dawn membership did not demonstrate any cognizance of Mithraism and did not incorporate Mithraic concepts within their initiatory structure, however, and there is no evidence that they were familiar with the works of the church fathers, such as St. Jerome or Tertullian, and therefore were not conversant with their (possibly biased) reproductions of Mithraic ideas and concepts. Further, the emphasis in the Golden Dawn was always on Kabbalah, albeit with Egyptian trappings since they understood Kabbalah to be something that Moses learned in Egypt (much in line with Masonic theories that were current at the time). They were definitely trying to avoid as much blatant "paganism" as possible and saw themselves instead as neo-Rosicrucians.

22. Regardie (1936), 58.

23. As admitted by Scholem himself in his *Major Trends in Jewish Mysticism,* when he wrote, "Both historically and metaphysically [Kabbalah] is a masculine doctrine, made for men and by men. The long history of Jewish mysticism shows no trace of feminine influence.... [It] therefore, lacks the element of feminine emotion which has played so large a part in the development of non-Jewish mysticism, but it also remained comparatively free from the dangers entailed by the tendency toward hysterical extravagance which followed in the wake of this influence" (1972, 37).

24. Dan (1986).

25. This concept of the "wonder working word" is represented by Johannes Reuchlin (1455–1522) in his *De verbo mirifico* (1494) and based on access to the texts of the Lurianic and post-Lurianic Kabbalists, such as Abraham Abulafia (1240–91). It is a far cry from understanding the word as a human-created "sign" that has

only the meaning assigned to it by humans to Reuchlin's idea of words, and specifically Hebrew words, that have innate supernatural power and represent cosmological or divine forces. In his later work, *De arte cabalistica* (1517), Reuchlin would expand his discussion of how the manipulation of words and letters would enable the Kabbalist to summon angels and attain a level of knowledge and wisdom normally beyond the reach of human beings.

26. Regardie (1971), 43–44.

27. Ibid., 44.

28. This might be seen as relevant to what Maurice Bloch (1992) has proposed concerning the concept of "rebounding violence" in initiation rituals. What is interesting is that Bloch also understands that the three phases of Turner's initiation schema do not quite apply here, either: that reintegration or reaggregation into society is not the primary goal of the initiation systems he discusses but rather a more transcendental transformation of the initiand's psyche.

29. As an addendum to his magnum opus, *Kabbalah Denudata*, von Rosenroth included a curious Kabbalistic/alchemical text, *Aesch Mezareph*, or "The Purifying Fire," showing the confluence of these two mystical trends in one Kabbalistic text.

30. Pike (1871), 520.

31. Eliade (1958), x.

32. Ibid., xii–xiii.

33. Ibid., 132–34.

34. See, for instance, the work of Michael Taussig in this regard, especially *The Nervous System* (1992) and *Shamanism, Colonialism, and the Wild Man* (1987).

35. The case of shamanism and *merkavah* mysticism has been raised by Moshe Idel (2005), who sees similarities between Eliade's study of shamanism and many elements of *merkavah*. He uses the example of the Baal Shem Tov's "descent to the Chariot" as evidence of a "conjugation between the shamanic element and the eschatological one" which is "quite an exceptional mixture if judged from the perspective of an Eliadean description of the archaic-universal structure of religion" (145). He explores the writing and the life of the Besht in terms of Carpathian shamanism and declares that one of the Besht's writings, *The Epistle of the Ascent of the Soul*, "may be described as an encounter between two different traditions: the ancient Jewish traditions and shamanic elements lingering in the Carpathians" (160). It should be noted that this work of Idel represents his Ioan P. Couliano lectures, and that Eliade was Couliano's mentor at the University of Chicago.

36. See for instance Kwame Gyeke (1994), 32–54, where this tension between written and unwritten texts is reflected as tension between European concepts of knowledge and African concepts, which is itself considered in a colonialist context. Also useful is Jahn (1961), in which he observes, "Since it could not be accommodated to European systems of thought, the African way of thinking was considered non-logical" (97).

37. Regardie (1988), 160.

38. Joscelyn Godwin is a professor of musicology at Colgate University who has written on Christian Kabbalah, modern esoteric societies, and Hermeticism. See, for instance, his *Robert Fludd* (1979), *Athanasius Kircher* (1979), and, with Christian

Chanel and John P. Deveney, *The Hermetic Brotherhood of Luxor: Initiatic and Historical Documents of an Order of Practical Occultism* (1995).

39. Although biased, his *Magicians of the Golden Dawn: A Documentary History of a Magical Order 1887–1923* (1972) is perhaps the definitive history of this organization.

40. D. Michael Quinn's *Early Mormonism and the Magic World View* (1998) gives the most comprehensive and compelling evidence for Smith's occult practices and beliefs.

41. Data on Theosophical Society president Annie Besant's intimate connection with the Indian Nationalist Movement is well-documented in many sources, for instance, Nicholas Goodrick-Clarke's *Helena Blavatsky* (2004), Joscelyn Godwin's *The Theosophical Enlightenment* (1994), Sylvia P. Cranston's *HPB: The Extraordinary Life and Influence of Helena Blavatsky, Founder of the Theosophical Movement* (1993), and an official history published by the Theosophical Society, *The Theosophical Movement 1875–1950* (1951).

42. Research begun during a summer semester at Gadjah Mada University in Yogyakarta, Indonesia, by the author. See, for instance, Laurie J. Sears, *Shadows of Empire: Colonial Discourse and Javanese Tales* (1996), 140–42.

43. See, for instance, Francis King's alarmingly entitled *Sexuality, Magic and Perversion* (1974) for a full discussion of C. W. Leadbeater and the "discovery" of Krishnamurti.

44. Information on Hubbard's involvement with Crowley's O.T.O. in California at the end of World War II is a matter of the public record, including court documents. Relevant sources may be consulted in George Pendle, *Strange Angel: The Otherworldly Life of Rocket Scientist John Whiteside Parsons* (2005), 252–74; the pseudonymous John Carter's *Sex and Rockets: The Occult World of Jack Parsons* (1999), 101–7; and Peter Levenda, *Sinister Forces: A Grimoire of American Political Witchcraft* (2005), vol. 1, 145–61. Jack Parsons was an influential member of the O.T.O. and a rocket scientist who was one of the founders of the Jet Propulsion Laboratory.

45. Reference could be had to Moshe Idel's prescription for "methodological eclecticism" — "applying many methodologies to the same phenomenon, given its multidimensional complexity" — in his *Ascensions on High in Jewish Mysticism: Pillars, Lines, Ladders* (2005), 9, as an appropriate strategy to take when confronting this data.

46. "Sapere Aude" in Kuntz (1996), 46–51.

47. Coincidentally, Frankfurt is also the site of the fictional conversation that takes place between the three sages in Reuchlin's *De arte cabalistica*.

48. Ron Heisler, "Precursors of the Golden Dawn," in Kuntz (1996), 115–22.

49. See, for instance, David Stevenson (2000).

50. Lecture to Florida International University students and guests, Miami, February 2006.

51. The founders in question were Dr. W. Wynn Westcott, S. L. MacGregor Mathers, and Dr. W. R. Woodman.

52. "The Beginnings of the Christian Kabbalah" in Dan (1997).

53. Scholem, "The Beginnings of the Christian Kabbalah," 24, in Dan (1997).

54. "The Kabbalah of Johannes Reuchlin," in Dan (1997), 57.

55. Ibid., 56–57.

56. See, for instance, the bibliography of Encausse's *The Qabalah* (1892), which lists more than three hundred volumes.

57. Yates (1966), 368–89.

58. Couliano (1992), 42.

59. That Moses carried with him out of Egypt knowledge of the practices of Egyptian magicians has been the subject of much recent research in the field. Note, for instance, Noegel (1996).

60. Waite (1990), 37.

61. Scholem (1978), 203.

62. In this, then, the leaders of the Golden Dawn would be in disagreement with one of the "Cabalistic Conclusions" of Pico della Mirandola which suggest that such an ascent up all the *sephiroth* is possible. See Yates (1985), 21.

63. Regardie (2005), 272.

64. The ritual specifically refers to the "seven palaces" without, as mentioned, specifying what they are. Ibid., 223.

65. Scholem (1971), 78–141.

66. Mathers (1887), 20.

67. In Dan (1997), 22.

68. See Yates (1985) for a detailed discussion of the role of Jews and Jewish thinking in the Elizabethan Age.

69. Forty-Eighth Cabalist Conclusion, *Opera omnia,* p. iii; see Yates (1985), 21.

70. Waite (1990), 445–52.

71. See the volume of his collected writings as presented by A. E. Waite entitled *The Works of Thomas Vaughan: Mystic and Alchemist* (1968), which is a reproduction of the original volume published in 1919 by the Theosophical Society. His essay "Magia Adamica" is a Kabbalistic approach to alchemy or an alchemical approach to Kabbalah, replete with references to the *Sephiroth,* and contains such statements as "Now, that the learning of the Jews — I mean their Kabalah — was chemical and ended in true physical performances cannot be better proved" (171).

72. See Godwin (1979).

73. Scholem (2006), 90–91.

74. For a fuller discussion of this problem, see Segal (1977).

75. Yates (1985), 79–108.

76. See below.

77. "The first Temple founded in England in 1887–88 under the governance of the Hermetic Order of the Golden Dawn was named very appropriately Isis-Urania. Isis-Urania is Venus, and she is the occult planet which represents the Genius of this Order — Venus, the Evening and the Morning Star, presaging the rising of the Sun of ineffable Light. Venus is also, as Isis, a symbol of the Qabalistic *Shekhinah,* the Glory of the Presence Divine, the Holy Spirit." Regardie (2005), 272, in the essay entitled "The Secret Chiefs." One notices the equation of Kabbalistic ideas such as the *Shekhinah* with Egyptian religion.

78. Regardie (1988), 137.

79. Regardie (2005), 413–22.

80. Ibid., 423–29.
81. Ibid., 402–12.
82. Ibid., 524–94.
83. Ibid., 624–83.
84. Ibid., 21.
85. As quoted in its entirety in Jacobs (1996), 35–44.
86. See the works of Samuel Noah Kramer, e.g., *The Sumerians* and *History Begins at Sumer,* for discussions of these and other relevant myths. There is, however, a section of the Zohar that discusses these seven "hells" as well (the section known as *Pekudei,* 2:244b–62b), but this section was not translated by Mathers so it is not known if it was known to him or to other members of the Golden Dawn or its parent lodge(s) in Europe.
87. In Baigent (1994), 154–55.
88. For instance, Rabbi Israel Baal Shem Tov, the founder of the Hasidic movement in the eighteenth century CE, has written of this practice himself in letters to his brother-in-law as reprinted in Idel (1988), 94, and elsewhere. He admitted that he himself descended to the Chariot on *Rosh ha-Shonah* on several occasions.
89. In Dan (1993), 98–102; Cohn-Sherbok (1998), 81.
90. For instance, in Crowley (1976), 233, "Every active Member of the Order has destroyed all that He is and all that He has on crossing the Abyss." Among the Hasidim this is known as *bittul ha-yesh.*
91. Scholem (2006), 82–83.
92. Scholem (1980), 133–34, as cited in Kuntz (1996), 159.
93. For instance, Scholem (2006), 81–83.
94. And sometimes over all ten *sephiroth,* as in the drawing on page 82 of Regardie (2005) showing the "seven palaces."
95. Regardie (2005), 159–60.
96. Ibid., 223. This has some resonance with the characteristics of the number seven to be found in the fourth chapter of the *Sepher Yetzirah,* yet the latter does not equate this number with the seven lower sephiroth since the structure of the Tree of Life was not described in the *Sepher Yetzirah,* and there is no mention of seven Palaces, although the word *hekhal* is mentioned once, as the palace "in the center" of the six directions. See Aryeh Kaplan's translation of the *Sepher Yetzirah* (1995), 159–93.
97. Mathers (1887), 104.
98. Ibid., 23.
99. In Scholem (1972), 47–52, we read of the existence of a "school of mystics who are not prepared to reveal their secret knowledge, their 'Gnosis,' to the public" and the "establishment of certain conditions of admission into the circle of the Merkabah mystics." These include passing certain tests of a chiromantic and physiognomic character, as well as moral attributes, tests that are reminiscent of those required for entry into the Qumran community. Scholem actually uses the word "initiation" in this context, but that is the only instance in which this word is used. It does not seem to be a ritual initiation, but only regulations for admission into a society that studied Merkabah mysticism. The word "initiation" does not appear in the

indices of any of the other books by Scholem or Idel mentioned in the bibliography to this work, or in any other works by these authorities consulted.

11. Frankist Influences on Western Esotericism

1. Scholem (1973), 206.
2. Ibid., 836–37, discusses briefly the possibility that Sabbatai Sevi (and eventually the Doenmeh) had contact with the Bektashi and considers it likely though he does not explore the issue.
3. Scholem (1978), 287.
4. Ibid., 289.
5. Ibid., 292.
6. Kraushar (2001) and Lenowitz (2004).
7. Lenowitz, dicta 300.
8. Ibid., dicta 746.
9. Ibid., dicta 1303.
10. Scholem (1978), 107.
11. Scholem (2006), 83.
12. This is a relatively new and unexplored area of research, and forbidding due to the number of pseudonyms, membership mottoes, secrecy, multiplicity of orders, pseudepigrapha, and the like. There were dozens, if not hundreds, of Rosicrucian and Masonic-type orders in Europe in the eighteenth and nineteenth centuries. Add to this the extreme complexity of European noble houses and their individual histories and biographies — including titles, genealogies, etc. — and then add to this the alarming phenomenon of the *episcopi vagantes* (irregular bishops and their equally irregular churches) and you have pandemonium. Some relatively recent research in the field has been accomplished by Polish heraldry and genealogy expert Dr. Rafal T. Pinke (1985), 5–14.
13. MacKenzie (1877).
14. Scholem (1980), 133.
15. Scholem (1978), 282.
16. Scholem (2006), 81–82.
17. Kuntz (1996), 25–26.
18. The Thelemic Temple and Order of the Golden Dawn based, of course, in Los Angeles.
19. "From the brilliant misunderstandings and misrepresentations of Alphonse Louis Constant, who has won fame under the pseudonym of Eliphas Levi, to the highly coloured humbug of Aleister Crowley and his followers, the most eccentric and fantastic statements have been produced purporting to be legitimate interpretations of Kabbalism. The time has come to reclaim this derelict area and to apply to it the strict standards of historical research. It is this task which I have set myself." Scholem (1941; 1972), 2–3.
20. Scholem (2006), 80–83.
21. Schuchard (2000), 45–93.
22. Scholem (1973), 146.
23. Ibid., 147.
24. Ibid., 149.

Excursus 2: The Chemical Wedding

1. McLean (1991).
2. Kuhn (1962).
3. The danger of alchemical experimentation was due not only to the explosions that sometimes took place in the laboratories of the alchemists and the "puffers" (inexperienced or greedy amateurs who imitated the experiments of the alchemists in order to get rich quickly) but also in other ways, as can be discerned from a careful reading of the letters of one Welsh alchemist, Thomas Vaughan. The letters are usually considered to be a record of sexual practices, alchemically encoded, of course. A twentieth-century edition of Vaughan's collected works contains a perceptive foreword by Kenneth Rexroth, which emphasizes the danger of "unguided autonomic nervous system experiments." Waite (1968), 10.
4. *Contra Celsus*, 6.22.
5. For an exploration of this theme, see Elior (2005).
6. This calls to mind the three stars of the Dipper's handle and the four stars of the Dipper's scoop.
7. As cited in von Franz (1980), 220.
8. See in particular Jung (1967).
9. Scholem (2006).
10. This is a reference to Balaam's famous fourth oracle, which reads "I see him, but not now; I behold him, but not near. A star will come out of Jacob; a scepter will rise out of Israel." The "rods and branches" could be construed as referring to the scepter in this verse.

12. The Hermetic Brotherhood of Light

1. Godwin, Chanel, and Deveney (1995); Greenfield (1997).
2. Grant (1972), 125–29, and many other places.
3. Burgoyne (1889; 1963), title page.
4. Burgoyne (1963), 2:45.
5. Kaplan (1995), 231.
6. Ibid.
7. Ibid.
8. Ibid., 237.
9. Ibid., 239.

Bibliography

Abimbola, Wande. *Ifa: An Exposition of Ifa Literary Corpus*. New York: Athelia Henrietta Press, 1997.

Abusch, Tzvi. "Ascent to the Stars in a Mesopotamian Ritual: Social Metaphor and Religious Experience." In *Death, Ecstasy and Other Worldly Journeys*, ed. Collins and Fishbane. Albany: State University of New York Press, 1995.

Agrippa, Cornelius. *De occulta philosophia*. London: Moule, 1651.

Allen, Paul M., ed. *A Christian Rosenkreutz Anthology*. Blauvelt: Rudolf Steiner, 1974.

Allen, Richard Hinckley. *Star Names: Their Lore and Meaning*. New York: Dover, 1963.

Arbel, Vita Daphna. *Beholders of Divine Secrets*. Albany: State University of New York Press, 2003.

Ariel, David S. *The Mystic Quest: An Introduction to Jewish Mysticism*. Northvale, N.J.: Jason Aronson, 1988.

Baigent, Michael. *From the Omens of Babylon: Astrology and Ancient Mesopotamia*. London: Arkana, 1994.

Bakhtiar, Laleh. *Sufi: Expressions of the Mystic Quest*. New York: Thames & Hudson, 1976.

Bauval, Robert, and Adrian Gilbert. *The Orion Mystery*. London: Mandarin, 1994.

Beck, Roger. "Ritual, Myth, Doctrine and Initiation in the Mysteries of Mithra." *Journal of Roman Studies* 90 (2000): 145–80.

Berlejung, Angelika. *Die Theologie der Bilder: Herstellung und Einweihung von Kultbildern in Mesopotamien und die altestamentliche Bilderpolemik*. Freiburg: University of Göttingen, 1998.

Betz, Hans Dieter. *The Greek Magical Papyri in Translation*. Chicago: University of Chicago Press, 1986.

Bidmead, Julye. *The Akitu Festival: Religious Continuity and Royal Legitimation in Mesopotamia*. Piscataway N.J.: Gorgias Press, 2002.

Black, J. A., et al. *The Electronic Text Corpus of Sumerian Literature*. Oxford, 1998.

Black, Jeremy, and Anthony Green. *Gods, Demons and Symbols of Ancient Mesopotamia*. Austin: University of Texas Press, 2000.

Bloch, Maurice. *Prey into Hunter: The Politics of Religious Experience*. Cambridge: Cambridge University Press, 1992.

Boden, Peggy Jean. "The Mesopotamian Washing of the Mouth *(mis pi)* Ritual." Ph.D. dissertation, Johns Hopkins University, 1998.

Brandon, George. *Santeria from Africa to the New World*. Bloomington: Indiana University Press, 1997.

Brown, David. *Mesopotamian Planetary Astronomy-Astrology*. Groningen: Styx, 2000.

Budge, E. A. Wallis. *The Book of the Dead.* New York: Gramercy Books, 1960 (reprint of the 1895 edition).

———. *The Book of the Dead.* London: Kegan Paul, Trench, Trubner, 1899.

Burgoyne, Thomas H. *The Light of Egypt, Or, the Science of the Soul and the Stars.* 2 vols. Denver: H. O. Wagner, 1963.

Carter, John. *Sex and Rockets: The Occult World of Jack Parsons.* Venice, Calif.: Feral House, 1999.

Casaubon, Meric. *A True and Faithful Relation of What Passed for Many Years between Dr. John Dee and Some Spirits.* London: Garthwait, 1659.

Churton, Tobias. *The Magus of Freemasonry.* Rochester, Vt.: Inner Traditions, 2004.

Cohen, Mark E. *The Cultic Calendars of the Ancient Near East.* Bethesda, Md.: CDL Press, 1993.

Cohn-Sherbok, Dan, ed. *Jewish Mysticism: An Anthology.* Oxford: Oneworld, 1998.

Colquhoun, Ithell. *Sword of Wisdom: MacGregor Mathers and the Golden Dawn.* New York: Putnam, 1975.

Couliano, Ioan P. *Out of This World: Otherworldly Journeys from Gilgamesh to Albert Einstein.* Boston: Shambhala, 1991.

———. *The Tree of Gnosis.* San Francisco: HarperSanFrancisco, 1992.

Cranston, Sylvia P. *HPB: The Extraordinary Life and Influence of Helena Blavatsky, Founder of the Theosophical Movement.* New York: Putnam, 1993.

Crowley, Aleister. *777 and Other Qabalistic Writings of Aleister Crowley.* York Beach, Me.: Samuel Weiser, 1973.

———. *Magick in Theory and Practice.* New York: Dover, 1976.

———. *De Arte Magica.* Edmonds, Wash.: Sure Fire Press, 1988.

Cumont, Franz. *The Mysteries of Mithra.* New York: Dover, 1956.

———. *Textes et monuments figures relatifs aux mystères de Mithra.* Brussels: H. Lambertin, 1896 and 1899.

Dan, Joseph. *Three Types of Ancient Jewish Mysticism.* Cincinnati: University of Cincinnati Press, 1984.

———. *The Early Kabbalah.* New York: Paulist Press, 1986.

———. *The Ancient Jewish Mysticism.* Tel-Aviv: MOD, 1993.

———. *The Christian Kabbalah: Jewish Mystical Books and Their Christian Interpreters.* Cambridge: Harvard College Library, 1994.

Danielou, Alan. *Hindu Polytheism.* New York: Inner Traditions, 1985.

Davis, Whitney M. "The Ascension-Myth in the Pyramid Texts." *Journal of Near Eastern Studies* 36, no. 3 (July 1977).

Day, John, ed. *In Search of Pre-Exilic Israel.* New York: Continuum, 2004.

De Santillana, Giorgio, and Hertha von Dechend. *Hamlet's Mill.* Boston: David R. Godine, 1977.

Desmangles, Leslie G. *The Faces of the Gods: Vodou and Roman Catholicism in Haiti.* Chapel Hill: University of North Carolina Press, 1992.

Eliade, Mircea. *Rites and Symbols of Initiation.* New York: Harper Torchbooks, 1958.

———. *Shamanism: Archaic Techniques of Ecstasy.* New York: Arkana, 1972.

Elior, Rachel. *The Three Temples: On the Emergence of Jewish Mysticism.* Portland, Ore.: Littman Library, 2005.

Encausse, Gerard ("Papus"). *The Tarot of the Bohemians*. London: Chapman & Hall, 1892.

———. *The Qabalah*. York Beach, Me.: Weiser Books, 2000.

Fatunmbi, Awo Fa'Lokun. *Awo: Ifa and the Theology of Orisha Divination*. Bronx, N.Y.: Original Publications, 1992.

Faulkner, R. O. "The King and the Star Religion in the Pyramid Texts." *Journal of Near Eastern Studies* 25, no. 3 (July 1966).

Fine, Lawrence, ed. *Essential Papers on Kabbalah*. New York: New York University Press, 1995.

French, Peter J. *John Dee: The World of the Elizabethan Magus*. London: Routledge & Kegan Paul, 1972.

Godwin, Joscelyn. *Athanasius Kircher*. London: Thames and Hudson, 1979.

———. *Robert Fludd*. Boulder, Colo.: Shambhala, 1979.

———. *Arktos: The Polar Myth in Science, Symbolism, and Nazi Survival*. Grand Rapids: Phanes Press, 1993.

———. *The Theosophical Enlightenment*. Albany: State University of New York Press, 1994.

Godwin, Joscelyn, Christian Chanel, and John P. Deveney. *The Hermetic Brotherhood of Luxor: Initiatic and Historical Documents of an Order of Practical Occultism*. York Beach, Me.: Samuel Weiser, 1995.

Goodrick-Clarke, Nicholas. *Helena Blavatsky*. Berkeley, Calif.: North Atlantic Books, 2004.

Graetz, Heinrich. *Gnosticismus und Judenthum*. Krotoschin: 1846.

Grant, Kenneth. *The Magical Revival*. London: Frederick Muller, 1972.

———. *Outside the Circles of Time*. London: Frederick Muller, 1980.

———. *Outer Gateways*. London: SKOOB, 1994.

Greenfield, T. Allen. *The Story of the Hermetic Brotherhood of Light*. Beverly Hills, Calif.: Looking Glass Press, 1997.

Greenia, Conrad. *Bernard of Clairvaux: In Praise of the New Knighthood*. Kalamazoo, Mich.: Cistercian Publications, 2000.

Griffith, F. Ll., and Herbert Thompson. *The Leyden Papyrus: An Egyptian Magical Book*. London: Grevel & Co., 1904.

Gyeke, Kwame. *An Essay on African Philosophical Thought: The Akan Conceptual Scheme*. Philadelphia: Temple University, 1994.

Hancock, Graham. *The Mars Mystery*. Toronto: Seal Books, 1998.

Heisler, Ron. "Precursors of the Golden Dawn." In *The Golden Dawn Source Book*, ed. Darcy Kuntz. Edmonds, Wash.: Holmes Publishing, 1996.

Himmelfarb, Martha. *Ascent to Heaven in Jewish and Christian Apocalypses*. Oxford: Oxford University Press, 1993.

Howe, Ellic. *The Magicians of the Golden Dawn: A Documentary History of a Magical Order 1887–1923*. New York: Samuel Weiser, 1978.

Hoyrup, Jens. "Remarkable Numbers in Old Babylonian Mathematical Texts: A Note on the Psychology of Numbers." *Journal of Near Eastern Studies* 52, no. 4 (October 1993).

Idel, Moshe. *Kabbalah: New Perspectives*. New Haven: Yale University Press, 1988.

———. *Ascensions on High in Jewish Mysticism: Pillars, Lines, Ladders*. Budapest: Central European, 2005.

Jacobs, Louis. *The Schocken Book of Jewish Mystical Testimonies.* New York: Schocken Books, 1996.

Jacobsen, Thorkild. *Treasures of Darkness: A History of Mesopotamian Religion.* New Haven: Yale University Press, 1978.

Jahn, Janheinz. *Muntu: The New African Culture.* New York: Grove Press, 1961.

Janowitz, Naomi. *The Poetics of Ascent.* New York: State University of New York Press, 1989.

———. *Icons of Power: Ritual Practices in Late Antiquity.* University Park: Pennsylvania State University Press, 2002.

Johnson, K. Paul. *The Masters Revealed: Madame Blavatsky and the Myth of the Great White Lodge.* Albany: State University of New York Press, 1994.

Joseph, Isya. *Devil Worship: The Sacred Books and Traditions of the Yezidiz.* Boston: Richard G. Badger, 1919.

Jung, C. G. *Alchemical Studies.* Princeton, N.J.: Princeton University Press, 1967.

Kalisch, Isidor. *Sepher Yezirah.* New York: L. H. Frank & Co., 1877.

Kaplan, Aryeh. *Sepher Yetzirah.* Northvale, N.J.: Jason Aronson, 1995.

Karade, Baba Ifa. *The Handbook of Yoruba Religious Concepts.* York Beach, Me.: Samuel Weiser, 1994.

King, Francis. *The Secret Rituals of the O.T.O.* New York: Citadel, 1974.

———. *Sexuality, Magic and Perversion.* New York: Citadel, 1974.

Kingsley, Peter. "Poimandres: the Etymology of the Name and the Origin of the Hermetica." *Journal of the Warburg and Courtauld Institutes* 56 (1993).

Kloetzli, W. Randolph. *Buddhist Cosmology.* Delhi: Motilal Banarsidass, 1987.

Knorr Von Rosenroth, Christian. *Kabbala denudata seu doctrina Hebraeorum transcendentalis et metaphysica.* Sulzbach: Abraham Lichtenthaler, 1677.

———. *Kabbalae denudatae tomus secundus. Id est Liber Sohar restitutus.* Frankfurt: Johann David Zunner, 1684.

Kramer, Samuel Noah. *The Sacred Marriage Rite.* Bloomington: University of Indiana Press, 1969.

———. *The Sumerians: Their History, Culture, and Character.* Chicago: University of Chicago Press, 1971.

———. *History Begins at Sumer.* Philadelphia: University of Pennsylvania, 1981.

Kraushar, Alexandr. *Jacob Frank: The End to the Sabbataian Heresy.* Lanham, Md.: University Press of America, 2001.

Krupp, E. C. *Echoes of the Ancient Skies.* New York: New American Library, 1983.

Kuhn, Thomas. *The Structure of Scientific Revolutions.* Chicago: University of Chicago Press, 1962.

Kuntz, Darcy, ed. *The Golden Dawn Source Book.* Edmonds, Wash.: Holmes Publishing Group, 1996.

Lenowitz, Harris. *The Collection of the Words of the Lord [Jacob Frank] from the Polish Manuscripts.* Salt Lake City: University of Utah Press, 2004.

Lesses, Rebecca. *Ritual Practices to Gain Power.* Harrisburg, Pa.: Trinity Press, 1998.

Levenda, Peter. *Sinister Forces: A Grimoire of American Political Witchcraft.* Walterville, Ore.: Trine Day, 2005.

Levi, Eliphas. *Transcendental Magic.* New York: Weiser, 1968.

———. *The Key of the Mysteries.* London: Rider, 1984.

———. *The History of Magic.* York Beach, Me.: Weiser, 1999.

————. *The Mysteries of the Qabalah, or Occult Agreement of the Two Testaments.* York Beach, Me.: Samuel Weiser, 2000.

Lindsay, Jack. *The Origins of Alchemy in Graeco-Roman Egypt.* New York: Barnes and Noble, 1970.

Lissner, Ivar. *The Living Past.* New York: Putnam, 1957.

Mackenzie, Kenneth. *The Royal Masonic Cyclopaedia.* 1877.

Mathers, S. L. MacGregor. *The Kabbalah Unveiled.* New York: Gordon Press, 1887, 1926, and 1974.

Matt, Daniel C. *The Essential Kabbalah.* San Francisco: HarperSanFrancisco, 1996.

————. *The Zohar.* Pritzker Edition. Vol. 2. Stanford, Calif.: Stanford University Press, 2004.

Maulana, Muhammad Ali. *The Holy Qur'an.* Dublin, Ohio: Ahamdiyya Anjuman Isha'at Islam Lahore, 2002.

McLean, Adam, ed. *The Chemical Wedding of Christian Rosenkreutz.* Grand Rapids: Phanes Press, 1991.

Newsom, Carol. *Songs of the Sabbath Sacrifice: A Critical Edition.* Atlanta: Scholars Press, 1985.

Northup, Lesley A., ed. *Women and Religious Ritual.* Washington, D.C.: Pastoral Press, 1993.

Odeberg, Hugo. *Third Book of Enoch.* New York: Ktav, 1928.

Oppenheimer, A. Leo. *Ancient Mesopotamia: Portrait of a Dead Civilization.* Chicago: University of Chicago Press, 1977.

Origen. *Contra Celsum.* Trans. Henry Chadwick. Cambridge: Cambridge University Press, 1980.

Peek, Philip M., ed. *African Divination Systems.* Bloomington: Indiana University Press, 1991.

Pendle, George. *Strange Angel: The Otherworldly Life of Rocket Scientist John Whiteside Parsons.* New York: Harcourt, 2006.

Pico Della Mirandola, Giovanni. *Opera Omnia.* Bologna: Benedictus Hectoris, 1496.

Pike, Albert. *Morals and Dogma of the Ancient and Accepted Scottish Rite of Freemasonry.* Richmond, Va.: L. H. Jenkins, 1947.

Pinke, Rafal T. "Lampado Trado: From the Fama Fraternitatis to the Golden Dawn." *Hermetic Journal* 30 (1985): 5–14.

Porphyry. *De antro nympharum.* Trans. Thomas Taylor. London: Watkins, 1917.

Pritchard, James, ed. *Ancient Near Eastern Texts.* Princeton, N.J.: Princeton University Press, 1969.

Quinn, D. Michael. *Early Mormonism and the Magic World View.* Salt Lake City: Signature Books, 1998.

Regardie, Israel. *My Rosicrucian Adventure.* St. Paul, Minn.: Llewellyn, 1971.

————. *An Interview with Israel Regardie.* Phoenix: Falcon Press, 1985.

————. *A Garden of Pomegranates.* St. Paul, Minn.: Llewellyn, 1988.

————. *What You Should Know about the Golden Dawn.* Phoenix: Falcon, 1993.

————. *The Golden Dawn.* St. Paul, Minn.: Llewellyn, 2005.

Reiner, Erica. "Astral Magic in Babylonia." *Transactions of the American Philosophical Society* 85, part 4 (1995).

Reuchlin, Johannes. *De verbo mirifico.* 1494.

————. *De arte cabalistica.* Hagenau: Thomas Anshelm, 1517.

Rigaud, Milo. *Secrets of Voodoo.* San Francisco: City Lights, 1985.

Robinet, Isabelle. "Visualization and Ecstatic Flight in Shangqing Taoism." In *Taoist Meditation and Longevity Techniques,* ed. Livia Kohn. Ann Arbor: Center for Chinese Studies, University of Michigan, 1989.

Roth, Ann Macy. "The pss-kf and the 'Opening of the Mouth' Ceremony: A Ritual of Birth and Rebirth." *Journal of Egyptian Archaeology* 78 (1992).

———. "Fingers, Stars, and the 'Opening of the Mouth': The Nature and Function of the ntrwj-Blades." *Journal of Egyptian Archaeology* 79 (1993).

Schafer, Edward H. *Pacing the Void: T'ang Approaches to the Stars.* Warren, Conn.: Floating World Editions, 2005.

Schiffman, Lawrence H. *Reclaiming the Dead Sea Scrolls.* New York: Doubleday, 1995.

Scholem, Gershom. *The Messianic Idea in Judaism.* New York: Schocken Books, 1971.

———. *Major Trends in Jewish Mysticism.* New York: Schocken Books, 1972.

———. *Sabbatai Sevi: The Mystical Messiah.* Bollingen Series 93. Princeton, N.J.: Princeton University Press, 1973.

———. *Kabbalah.* New York: Meridian, 1978.

———. *Origins of the Kabbalah.* Princeton, N.J.: Princeton University Press, 1987.

———. *On the Mystical Shape of the Godhead.* New York: Schocken Books, 1991.

———. *Alchemy and Kabbalah.* Putnam, Vt.: Spring Publications, 2006.

Schuchard, Marsha Keith. "Why Mrs. Blake Cried: Swedenborg, Blake, and the Sexual Basis of Spiritual Vision." *Esoterica: The Journal of Esoteric Studies* 2 (2000): 45–93.

Sears, Laurie J. *Shadows of Empire.* Durham, N.C.: Duke University Press, 1996.

Segal, Alan F. *Two Powers in Heaven: Early Rabbinic Reports about Christianity and Gnosticism.* Boston: Brill, 2002.

Sharon, Diane M. "A Biblical Parallel to a Sumerian Temple Hymn? Ezekiel 40–48 and Gudea." *Journal of the Ancient Near Eastern Society* 24 (1996).

Smith, Margaret. *The Way of the Mystics.* London: Sheldon Press, 1976.

Smith, William Robertson. *Lectures on the Religion of the Semites.* London: A & C Black, 1927.

———. *A Dictionary of the Bible.* Boston (undated).

Snodgrass, Adrian. *Architecture, Time and Eternity.* 2 vols. New Delhi: Aditya Prakashan, 1994.

Stevenson, David. *The Origins of Freemasonry: Scotland's Century 1590–1710.* Cambridge: Cambridge University Press, 2000.

Stratton, Kimberly B. "The Mithras Liturgy and *Sepher Ha-Razim.*" In *Religions of Late Antiquity in Practice,* ed. Richard Vantasis. Princeton, N.J.: Princeton University Press, 2000.

Strickman, Michael. "On the Alchemy of T'ao Hung-Ching." *Facets of Taoism,* ed. Holmes Welch and Anna Seidel. New Haven: Yale University Press, 1979.

Swerdlow, N. M. Review of David Ulansey, *The Origins of the Mithraic Mysteries. Classical Philology* 86, no. 1 (1991): 18–63.

Taussig, Michael. *Shamanism, Colonialism, and the Wild Man.* Chicago: University of Chicago Press, 1987.

———. *The Nervous System.* New York: Routledge, Chapman and Hall, 1992.

Temple, Robert K. G. *The Sirius Mystery.* New York: St. Martin's Press, 1976.

Theosophical Society. *The Theosophical Movement 1875–1950.* New York: Cunningham Press, 1951.

Time-Life. *Magical Arts.* New York: Time-Life Press, n.d.

Tsai, Julius N. "The Transformation of Myths Concerning Yu the Great into Daoist Narrative and Ritual." *Annual Meeting of the Association for Asian Studies.* 2003.

Turner, Victor. *The Ritual Process: Structure and Anti-Structure.* Chicago: Aldine, 1969.

Ulansey, David. *The Origins of the Mithraic Mysteries: Cosmology and Salvation in the Ancient World.* New York: Oxford University Press, 1991.

Van Gennep, Arnold. *The Rites of Passage.* Chicago: University of Chicago Press, 1960.

Von Franz, Marie-Louise. *Alchemy: An Introduction to the Symbolism and the Psychology.* Toronto: Inner City Books, 1980.

Wainright, G. A. "Iron in Egypt." *Journal of Egyptian Archaeology* 18, no. 1/2 (May 1932).

Waite, A. E. *The Holy Kabbalah.* New York: Carol Publishing, 1990.

———. *The Book of Ceremonial Magic.* New York: Barnes & Noble, 1999.

Waite, A. E., ed. *The Works of Thomas Vaughan: Mystic and Alchemist.* New York: University Books, 1968.

Walker, Christopher, and Michael Dick. *The Induction of the Cult Image in Ancient Mesopotamia.* Helsinki: University of Helsinki, 2001.

Walsh, Killian, trans. *Cantica Canticorum.* Kalamazoo, Mich.: Cistercian Publications, 2005.

Wang Ming, ed. *Baopu zi neipian jiaoshi.* Beijing: Zhonghua Shuju, 1980.

Wasserstrom, Steven M. *Religion after Religion: Gershom Scholem, Mircea Eliade, and Henry Corbin at Eranos.* Princeton, N.J.: Princeton University Press, 1999.

Williams, C. A. S. *Outlines of Chinese Symbolism and Art Motives.* New York: Dover, 1976.

Wolfson, Elliot R. *Through a Speculum That Shines.* Princeton, N.J.: Princeton University Press, 1997.

Woodroffe, Sir John. *The Serpent Power.* New York: Dover, 1974.

Woolley, Sir Leonard. *The Sumerians.* New York: W. W. Norton, 1965.

———. *Digging Up the Past.* Baltimore: Penguin, 1967.

Yates, Frances A. *The Art of Memory.* Chicago: University of Chicago Press, 1966.

———. *The Occult Philosophy in the Elizabethan Age.* Boston: Ark, 1985.

Zaehner, R. C. *Hindu and Muslim Mysticism.* New York: Schocken Books, 1969.

Zalewski, Patrick J. *Secret Inner Order Rituals of the Golden Dawn.* Phoenix: Falcon Press, 1988.

Index

Numbers in **bold face** indicate artwork.